BOOK **1**

Joseph C. Gainsburg

*Formerly Principal of William Cowper Junior High School and Chairman
of the Reading Curriculum Committee, New York City Schools*

Skills
in
Reading

MACMILLAN PUBLISHING CO., INC.
New York

COLLIER MACMILLAN PUBLISHERS
London

ACKNOWLEDGMENTS

For permission to use copyright material in this book, grateful acknowledgment is made to:

Irving Shepard, for Chapter V from *White Fang,* by Jack London.

The John C. Winston Company, for "The Sound Stage," from *Moving Ahead,* by Gertrude Hildreth, Allie Lou Felton, Alice Meighen, Mary Meighen, Marjorie Pratt. The John C. Winston Company, Copyright 1957.

Illustrated by Denman Hampson

MACMILLAN PUBLISHING CO., INC.
866 Third Avenue
New York, N.Y. 10022
Collier Macmillan Canada, Ltd.

PRINTED IN THE UNITED STATES OF AMERICA

2 - R

Pupil Edition: ISBN 0-02-153450-0
Teacher's Edition: ISBN 0-02-153460-8

Contents

v

INTRODUCTION

THE PURPOSE OF THIS BOOK

Your life is filled with reading. As you go about from day to day, you read everything from street signs to encyclopedias. Some things you can read quickly and with little thought—for example, a calendar. Other things, such as your books in school, you must read carefully. There are many different kinds of reading, and many different ways to read.

This book will give you tools, or reading skills, for different kinds of reading. It will help you sharpen the kit of tools, or reading skills, that you already own. In other words, this book will help you improve your reading. As you gain the skills you need, your enjoyment of reading will be greatly increased. Even more important— you will be able to read more easily and more efficiently.

What Is Meant by Reading Skills?

You may wonder what is meant by "reading skills." Perhaps you think of them only as the skills used to recognize words or to pronounce them. Perhaps you feel that efficient reading is only a matter of knowing more and more words and of selecting facts from a printed page.

Reading words and facts is really only a small part of what people do when they read. Other important skills must be used if you are to obtain the full meaning from your reading. For example, one of these skills lets you see that facts are brought together in a paragraph to express just one important idea. This skill, when fully developed, shows you how these facts help to explain the larger idea. Your reading ability improves greatly when you can recognize the main idea quickly.

Another skill is that of recognizing which ideas are important enough to remember and which are not. A related skill tells you what should be read with care and what may be hurried over. If, in addition, you have the skill to recognize the author's plan in what he has written, the whole meaning of several pages together will suddenly become clear to you. When you can see how facts and ideas are related, you will be reading with complete understanding. This understanding, resulting from the use of various skills, will make you an efficient reader indeed.

How This Book Will Help You

We have mentioned just a few of the important reading skills that you will meet in this book. Keep in mind that *this book has been planned to help you develop and practice skills*. It has a larger purpose than simply to provide you with material to read. It aims to help you improve your reading.

In the beginning, the study and practice of skills may not be easy for you. Beginning anything new is not easy, but you should never feel discouraged. The material in this book introduces each skill step by step and allows you to feel confident that you are really learning and improving with each lesson. This feeling of confidence will give you a great deal of satisfaction, and there will be much more pleasure for you when you recognize that you are making real progress toward becoming an efficient reader.

READING
THE
PARAGRAPH

There is more to reading than getting the meaning of one sentence alone, then of another. In a paragraph, sentences must be read together. You must follow the thought from one sentence to the next *all through the paragraph.* In this way you get the meaning of the whole paragraph.

Try reading the following sentences. How much meaning can you get from them?

They may be grouped by color, such as red or yellow or green.

They may be classified according to the part of the plant they represent, such as the root, the stem, or the leaf.

They may be grouped according to the season of the year during which they're planted.

They may be classified according to the way they react to temperature—that is, their reaction to heat and cold.

1. GETTING MEANING FROM SENTENCES

Each sentence you have just read is easy to understand by itself. But each sentence gives you a separate idea and sends you off in a different direction. Those sentences do not seem to have anything in common, yet it is possible to bind them together so that one sentence will lead naturally to the next. Try reading the paragraph below:

> **There are many ways that vegetables may be classified or grouped together.** They may be grouped by color, such as red or yellow or green. They may be classified according to the part of the plant they represent, such as the root, the stem, or the leaf. They may be grouped according to the season of the year during which they're planted. They may be classified according to the way they react to temperature—that is, their reaction to heat and cold.

Now the paragraph is no longer puzzling because you can understand what it is all about. The first sentence gives you the **paragraph meaning** or **main thought**. It tells you that vegetables can be arranged or grouped together in many different ways. All the other sentences help to explain this main thought, even though each one is different from the others.

The sentence that gives you the main thought is often called the **key sentence.** It unlocks the meaning of the paragraph for the reader.

To get the meaning of a paragraph, you must see how its sentences are related and what they have in common. When you can do this quickly and easily, you are really reading. You are

4

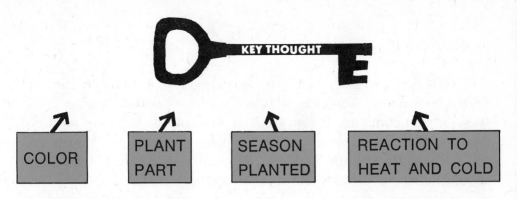

reading with understanding. If you read by paragraph meanings or by main thoughts, instead of just by sentences, many of the important facts will be remembered, and the selection will continue to make sense to you as you read on.

2. HOW TO FIND THE MAIN THOUGHT OF A PARAGRAPH

In reading, it is important to know how to find the meaning of each paragraph or its main thought. This section will help you find it. We shall begin with words instead of sentences.

Read carefully the list of animals in each column.

lions		horses	
elephants		cows	
cows		dogs	
kangaroos		cats	Wild animals?
horses	Animals	donkeys	Animals?
dogs		pigs	Domestic animals?
tigers		goats	
pigs		sheep	
cats		mules	

For the first list above, *Animals* is a good enough heading. It is not good enough for the second list because it is not exact enough.

In the first list many different kinds of animals are mentioned. They are alike only in being animals. But in the second list the animals are alike in another way. Are they all circus animals? Are they all wild animals? Perhaps by now you have the answer: they are all *domestic* animals. The title "Domestic Animals" would be a good one. It is better than "Animals" because it is more exact. Because it is more exact, it tells more.

5

Looking for the Main Thought

Your first problem in reading a paragraph is to see what the sentences have in common. It is important to notice *exactly* what they have in common. Below are two paragraphs. Both are entitled "A Lion Cub." But these two paragraphs are different from each other. Read them both, and decide whether the title of each one should be changed to something more definite.

I. A Lion Cub

Young lion cubs can be as affectionate as kittens. If you hold one of them on your lap it will relax comfortably in your arms, almost as if it were a baby. Pat it on the head or stroke its fur, and you will hear it purr and wait for you to do it again. If mamma lioness is near, she will be growling softly to warn you to be careful with her affectionate baby. But the cub will pay no attention. It just wants you to go on petting it.

What is this paragraph about? A lion cub? That is not accurate enough. A troublesome lion cub? No. Not a single sentence says that it is troublesome. An affectionate lion cub? Yes, because every sentence tells you that the cub can be affectionate. For instance, "it will purr and wait for you to pet it again." Isn't that a way of saying that cubs are affectionate? All the other sentences, too, help to convince you that a lion cub can be affectionate.

II. A· Lion Cub

Despite its playfulness, a lion cub can sometimes suddenly become an armful of trouble. It may be because you have rubbed its whiskers the wrong way or because you touched a tender spot when you thought you were tickling it. Immediately its sharp claws snap out and its mouth opens in an angry snarl. Perhaps it does not intend to scratch you or to hurt you with its teeth. Yet its momentary flash of anger can leave you with a painful scratch that you do not quickly forget. All in all, it would be better to leave lion cubs to the care of their mother.

What is this paragraph about? A lion cub? An affectionate cub? A snarling cub? A troublesome cub?

Your teacher may want you to discuss your answers in class and give a reason for the answer you select.

Now turn back again to the first paragraph about a lion cub. Notice the first sentence, "Young lion cubs can be as affectionate as kittens." Can you see that the author has given you the main thought in that sentence? He did not want you to worry about the meaning of the paragraph, so he started by telling it to you immediately.

In the second paragraph the author did the same thing. He gave you the main thought in the first sentence. Look again and notice in that sentence, "a lion cub can sometimes suddenly become an armful of trouble." Read the other sentences. Each one, in some way, tells you that a lion cub can be very troublesome.

To Find the Main Thought:

1. Read the whole paragraph carefully.
2. As you read, try to see what the sentences have in common.
3. Try to state to yourself what that common meaning is.
4. Look for a sentence that states this meaning, the main thought of the paragraph.
5. Look for clues by which the author has helped you to find the main thought of the paragraph.

EXERCISE 1

Directions: There are five paragraphs in this exercise. Following each paragraph three topics are listed. Decide which of the three (**a**, **b**, or **c**) tells best what the paragraph is about. On your paper write the letter that stands before your choice. Then find the sentence that states the main thought in the paragraph. Write it on your paper.

1. Three types of ants, each with a different task to perform, live in an ant colony. There is usually only one queen ant. She lays the eggs. The male ants fertilize the queen's eggs. Female workers do such things as gather food, defend the colony from enemies, and care for the young ants.

The paragraph is about
    a. kinds of ants in a colony.
    b. workers defending
       the colony.
    c. the queen ant.

7

2. Those flowering plants called herbs have several interesting uses. The leaves, seeds, and even the underground roots can be used as spices when cooking. Fragrances for perfume and soap often come from herbs. One of the most interesting, and perhaps the oldest, use of these plants is for making medicines. Ancient people believed that herbs had the power to heal sickness.

The paragraph is about
a. medicine made from herbs.
b. the uses of herbs.
c. fragrances that come from herbs.

3. Our country's interest in bicycling is growing. Bicycle racing, both indoors and outdoors, is a fast-growing sport. Some people join clubs that have racing teams. Others join clubs that plan tours. These tours may be as short as neighborhood circuits or as long as cross-country trips. More and more people of all ages are taking these bike tours.

The paragraph is about
a. taking a cross-country bike tour.
b. reasons for joining a bike club.
c. the growing popularity of bicycling.

4. Most people are familiar with the cactus, a thick-stemmed, spiked desert plant which often has flowers of beautiful colors. Did you ever wonder how the cactus survives in such a dry place as a desert? The plant is specially built for its desert life. Its roots branch out right under the surface of the soil so they are able to catch rain. The rainwater is then stored in the plant's thick stem. Because the cactus has spines instead of leaves, it doesn't lose any of its water. This ability to catch and hold water allows the cactus to stay alive in the desert.

The paragraph is about
a. how the cactus stores water.
b. how the cactus has adapted to the desert.
c. the root system of the cactus.

5. King crabs are fascinating creatures. In addition to their large size and long life, the crabs are known for the unusual things they do to protect themselves. Young crabs will stand on each other's backs to form large groups for defense. To protect the female when she sheds her old shell, males and females grab each other's claws, as if to shake hands. Because enemies may attack the unprotected body, the crabs keep holding onto each other's claws until a new shell covers the female.

The paragraph is about
- **a.** why young king crabs stay in groups.
- **b.** how king crabs protect themselves.
- **c.** how a female crab sheds her shell.

3. GETTING THE EXACT MEANING OF A PARAGRAPH

You have learned that only a vague, general idea of what a paragraph is about is usually not good enough. For real understanding, you need an exact idea of paragraph meaning.

For all of your reading you need the kind of exact statement that newspaper headlines give you. Read carefully these headlines and the news story that follows them.

1.
BLUES LOSE
ANOTHER GAME

2.
GAME LOST BY
WILD THROW

3.
FIELDER THROWS
WILD BALL

August 5th.—When a fielder made a wild throw to second base at the ball game yesterday, three men reached home plate and the game was practically over for the Blue team. After that the Blues were so discouraged and upset that they made two more costly errors. The game ended with a 6 to 1 victory for the visiting team.

When you read the paragraph above, you probably found that it tells not only about a baseball game, or losing a ball game, or throwing a wild pitch. It tells rather about the loss of the game on account of a wild throw.

Which headline gives you that idea? Not the first, because it says only that the team lost the game, but not why. Not the third, because it mentions only the wild pitch but does not say that it caused the loss of the game.

The second headline tells you the whole thought even though only five words are used.

Now see if you can choose the best headlines for the paragraphs in the following exercise.

EXERCISE 2

Directions: After each paragraph there are three possible headlines. Select the headline that tells the meaning of the paragraph most exactly. Write the headline, with its letter, on your paper.

Paragraph 1

> GREECE, June 22.—A scientist has reported the discovery of a 750,000-year-old skull in a cave in northern Greece. It is the oldest skull ever found in Europe. This major discovery may lead to new ideas about the origin of people. The oldest skull previously found in Europe was about 500,000 years old. Because skulls unearthed in Africa were much older, it was thought that people migrated to Europe from Africa over one million years ago. It now seems possible that people originated in both Europe and Africa.

Headlines

   a. Old Skull Found in Europe
   b. Scientist Reports Major Discovery
   c. Scientist Finds New Clue to Origin of People

Paragraph 2

> SCOTLAND, Aug. 25.—Two people have reported a sighting of the legendary Loch Ness monster last night. During the past week, the couple has used a boat equipped with sonar and underwater cameras in an attempt to locate the monster. They claim that late last night the monster briefly emerged. Reports of sightings date from the Middle Ages, and many myths and stories have grown up around the monster. Some people who claim to have seen the monster say it resembles a serpent. Others believe it is the descendant of an extinct prehistoric beast.

Headlines

    a. Loch Ness Monster Emerges
    b. Monster Sighted
    c. Couple Claims to Have Sighted Loch Ness Monster

Paragraph 3

    SPRINGDALE, April 10.—An unusual event took place on a local chicken farm last night. The farm owner recently succeeded in breeding a new strain of huge chickens weighing 25 pounds apiece. Last night, a fox sneaked into the chicken coop. Upon hearing a tremendous uproar, the owner ran out, expecting the worst. She was astounded to find a very frightened fox hemmed into a corner of the coop by a mob of cackling chickens almost as large as the fox itself. The farmer quickly removed the helpless fox.

Headlines

    a. Fox Enters Chicken Coop
    b. Giant Chickens Frighten Cooped-up Fox
    c. Farmer Raises Large Chickens

4. FINDING THE MAIN THOUGHTS IN A LONG SELECTION

Both in and out of school, you will be reading long selections composed of many paragraphs. If the paragraphs contain a great many details, you must find some way of remembering them and keeping them sorted out. Perhaps you will find it helpful to write down the main thought of each paragraph as you finish reading it. When you have finished the selection, read down the list of main thoughts. You will be surprised to see how often the meaning of the whole selection is thus made clear to you.

You might also find it helpful to write down a title that summarizes each paragraph. Because the title is shorter, it may contain words different from those in the main thought. Even though the words differ, the idea is the same in both the title and the main thought.

The skill of "finding the main thoughts in a long selection" will be very helpful to you in studying history and other school subjects. Try it after you have done the next exercise.

EXERCISE 3

Match the main thought in each paragraph of the following selection with the list of titles at the end of the selection, on page 13.

Directions: Read each paragraph carefully. Decide on the sentence that states the main thought, and write it on your paper. Look at the titles at the end of the exercise. Choose the title that is closest to the main idea of the paragraph and write it on your paper under the main thought. The first paragraph has been worked out for you as a model.

BLUEGRASS MUSIC

1. "Bluegrass" is one kind of country music. The instruments used are the guitar, the banjo, the string bass, the mandolin, the fiddle (violin), and sometimes the dobro (an unamplified steel guitar). Drums are not considered part of the bluegrass band. The instruments are almost always played acoustically—that is, without electrical hook-ups attached to them. As many performers in the band as possible join in singing. The person who has a high range (tenor) is a very valued member of the band. Harmony is important and the listener can expect to hear duos, trios, and sometimes quartets, just as much as solo singing.

Main thought: "Bluegrass is one kind of country music."

Title: One kind of country music

Now continue with the remaining four paragraphs, giving the main thought and the title of each.

2. Bluegrass music is different in several important ways from the earlier "old-time" country music and the contemporary "Nashville-sound." Bluegrass and old-time country music bands have the same instruments, but they are played differently. In bluegrass, the banjo, mandolin, and fiddle players often take solo breaks. The bass player and guitarist keep the rhythm for the group. By contrast, the old-time bands play mostly in an ensemble manner—that is, they all perform together. The difference between bluegrass and Nashville-sound music is even easier to recognize. In Nashville-sound, there is no banjo, and many of the instruments are electrified (for example, the electric bass and steel guitar). The instruments basically serve as the rhythmic background for the singing.

3. The name *bluegrass* comes from the name of a band. The group was called "The Bluegrass Boys." Band leader, Bill Monroe, named his group after the nickname of his home state, Kentucky ("The Bluegrass State"). The sound of the band was so different from other country music that people kept asking country groups to "play music like the Bluegrass Boys." After a while, people simply requested "Bluegrass" music.

4. Bluegrass music can be heard just about everywhere in our country today. There are, for example, over 400 festivals each summer. Bluegrass is very popular in radio and television commercials, especially when music with a fast tempo is needed to back up what is happening in the commercial. Two popular movies, "Deliverance" and "Bonnie and Clyde," used bluegrass music in their soundtracks.

5. People of every age can be found in bluegrass bands today. It isn't at all unusual to see teenagers playing bluegrass music alongside adults. Some of the best known bluegrass performers started playing professionally when they were teenagers. The well-known banjo player, Don Reno, was twelve when he started. When he was only fourteen, Mark O'Connor won the Grand Masters Fiddle Contest in Nashville, playing better than fifty-four other fiddlers—all much older than himself.

From the following list, choose the title that fits each paragraph.

    a. The popularity of bluegrass
    b. Three different music styles
    c. One kind of country music
    d. Musicians of all ages
    e. How "bluegrass" got its name

5. DETAILS ARE IMPORTANT, TOO

Suppose you found this sentence at the beginning of a paragraph: *A blind man's best friend is a dog.* Would you skip the rest of the paragraph? Would that be enough to satisfy you? Or would you want to know more about such a dog? Surely you would want to find out why he is such a good friend, what he does that makes him so important to a blind man, and how he is different from other dogs. The paragraph details provide this information.

The sentence about the blind man's best friend may be the key sentence. It may tell you what the whole paragraph is about. But it does not tell enough. You would also like to know the details that explain this sentence.

Here is the whole paragraph:

> A blind man's best friend is a dog; not any kind of dog, but a Seeing-Eye Dog. Such an animal is more loyal to his master than most human beings could possibly be. His entire life is devoted to thinking and working for his master's safety and comfort. Wherever the man wishes to go, the dog goes with him, at any hour of the day or night. He patiently carries out the man's wishes, stopping when he stops, going on again when the man is ready. The dog is constantly alert to keep the man from the slightest danger. If there is a hole or any obstacle in the path, he leads the man around it. If the traffic light is red, he waits at the curb until it turns green. The animal is so intelligent in his service that he will even disobey his master's command if he sees that it will lead to danger.

There are nine sentences in this long paragraph, but every one of the last eight tells *why* and *how* a dog is a blind man's best friend. Each sentence adds a new and interesting detail. The job of the details is to explain the key sentence, making it clear and convincing.

The job of the key sentence is to tie the details together, making them sensible to you. The key sentence is important for another reason also. It helps you remember most of the details.

6. HOW THE MAIN THOUGHT HELPS YOU REMEMBER DETAILS

Here is a short experiment to show you how main thoughts can help you to remember. Study the list for five minutes. Then turn your book face down and see how many items in the list you can write on your paper.

suit		sugar		football
butter	shirt		socks	button
hockey		hat		ping-pong
cloth	tennis		salt	thread
cereal		thimble		bread
baseball	needle		shoes	

How many of the twenty items did you remember? It is difficult for most people to memorize details that are not clearly tied to each other in some way.

Tying Details Together

The same twenty items are listed below under four headings which show how the items in each list are alike. Spend three minutes studying these lists. Turn your book face down and write as many of the items as you can remember.

GROCERIES	SPORTS	CLOTHING	SEWING
bread	baseball	hat	needle
butter	football	shoes	thread
sugar	tennis	suit	thimble
salt	ping-pong	shirt	button
cereal	hockey	socks	cloth

How many did you remember this time? Did you notice how much simpler it suddenly became? The headings gave you a great deal of help, didn't they? Now you can understand why the main thought or key sentence is important in helping you remember the details of a paragraph. Use this help in doing the next exercise.

EXERCISE 4

Directions: **A.** Read each of the five paragraphs carefully and follow these steps for each one:
   a. Decide on the main thought. In stating this thought to yourself, you need not repeat the entire key sentence, just the main thought.
   b. Determine how each detail carries out the main thought.
   c. Close your book and see how many details you can remember. Do not write them down.

B. Now reread the paragraph to see if you missed any of the details. Close your book. Write down the main thought and the details in the form shown after paragraph **1.**

> 1. Keeping a small aquarium at home can be a rewarding hobby. First, not only is an aquarium an enjoyable sight, but it can also be used to study fish. Second, anyone can learn how to set one up and care for it. Third, for those who like to be creative, there are many ways to decorate an aquarium.

Main thought: Keeping a small aquarium at home can be a rewarding hobby.

Details: **A.** An aquarium is an enjoyable sight and can be used to study fish.

　　　　 B. Anyone can learn how to set one up and care for it.

　　　　 C. There are many ways to decorate an aquarium.

> 2. Setting up a simple aquarium requires only a few steps. To begin, the inside and outside of the tank should be washed carefully with soap and water. After the soap has been rinsed away, the bottom should be covered with a few inches of coarse gravel to hold plants in place. It's important not to add too much gravel. Food may get caught in the gravel and pollute the water. The tank should then be filled with room-temperature water. Finally, fish and plants are added.

Read paragraph **2** a second time, before trying to list details.

Main thought:

Details: **A.** The inside and outside of the tank should be washed carefully with soap and water.

　　　　 B.

　　　　 C.

　　　　 Etc.

3. Other equipment can be added to an aquarium. If there are a lot of fish in the tank, an air pump should be used. Without the pump, there may not be enough oxygen in the tank. When the fish can't get enough oxygen, they will keep surfacing for air. A filter helps keep the aquarium clean. Water enters the filter through one pipe, is purified, and leaves through another pipe. Finally, if the fish tank is located in a cold room, it is wise to add a heater.

(Give paragraph 3 no more than two slow readings before you write your answers.)

4. There are many ways to decorate an aquarium. Fish of various sizes and colors may be chosen. Many stores carry a wide range of exotic and multi-colored fish. Snails add variety to a tank and are useful in eating algae which collect on the sides of the tank. A beautiful setting can be created using plants and rocks. By moving them around, or adding new ones, the scenery can be completely changed. Colorful pieces of broken shells, which may be found at the seashore, add a nice finishing touch.

(Try to decide on your answers to Paragraph 4 without looking back.)

5. Several rules should be followed in caring for an aquarium. It's important to clean the filter at least once a week to prevent the water from becoming dirty. The entire tank should be emptied regularly, even if it has a filter. While the tank is being cleaned, the fish can be placed in pots of room-temperature water. Before the tank is refilled with clean water, it should be scrubbed. It is also important to make sure the tank gets enough light, without putting it in direct sunlight. Finally, before any rocks or plants are added to the tank, they should be washed.

6. There is a proper way to feed fish. They should be fed only twice a day, and the food should be gently sprinkled, a little at a time, on the top of the water. If anything other than prepared fish food is used, it should be broken into tiny pieces so the fish don't choke. Fish should not be over-fed, since what they do not eat falls to the bottom of the tank. The water becomes very dirty when uneaten food collects in the tank. The uneaten food should be removed with a net.

7. WHICH IS THE KEY SENTENCE?

You have already seen that an author usually tries to give you one main thought in a paragraph. Up to now the paragraphs in your exercises have been made easy for you because the main thought or key sentence was always the first sentence in the paragraph. In all such paragraphs the author is practically saying to you, "Dear reader, I will tell you what this paragraph is about so that you will know what to expect when you read it."

But paragraphs are not always written that way. In fact, the key sentence might occur almost anywhere in the paragraph, even in the middle. Therefore, it may take careful thinking to decide just where the key sentence is located. It is necessary to know this in order to understand what the paragraph is saying to you.

Here is a paragraph that will make you think:

> You are watching a movie and the scene shows an empty room. Nothing is happening, yet you suddenly feel that some danger is present. The music that goes with the movie has just struck some strange, heavy chords. You have not actually been listening to the music, but a cold chill creeps up your spine. Then the scene changes, and you see some riders racing their horses furiously. Now you feel hopeful and excited, but you do not realize that the change in music, with its quick runs, adds greatly to your excitement. <u>Few of us recognize how important the movie music is in creating within us the feelings that fit all the changes in the movie story.</u>

The last sentence in the paragraph sums it up. It tells you that, even though you may not realize it, the music that we hardly noticed is doing its share in creating the excitement. Therefore the key sentence is the *last* one. All the other thoughts in the paragraph are examples to explain the main thought.

EXERCISE 5

In some of the following paragraphs, the key sentence may be the last one. In others it may be the first. You must read the whole paragraph and try to find the one thing that *all* the sentences are saying before you decide which is the key sentence. Try to find the key sentence in one reading.

Directions: Decide on the key sentence. Write it on your paper. Then write the details that explain the idea in that sentence. Use this form:

Key sentence:
Its location: (first or last?)
Details:

     A.
     B.
     Etc.

CRYPTOLOGY

1. Cryptology is the art of writing secret messages using either a code or a cipher. Most people use the word *code* to refer to secret writing, but *ciphers* were actually used first. Following some pattern, a cipher changes every letter in the original message. A code is a little different. It uses groups of letters or numbers, each group standing for a word or phrase, not just a single letter. Ciphers can be memorized, but codes must be written down.

2. Cryptology has probably existed since the time when human beings began writing. People have always sent secret messages, especially in times of war. The discovery 4,000 years ago of ancient documents at the top of the Pyramid of Giza proved that the ancient Egyptians used ciphers. The Greeks and Romans also used simple ciphers. The first codes were used in Italy during the fifteenth century.

3. The simplest method of secret writing is to replace each letter of the message with a different symbol. In early times, the symbols came from old and forgotten alphabets. It is very common today to replace the letters of the message with letters of the same alphabet, or with numbers. If the message is long, the order of the words may be changed so that the message no longer makes sense. Finally, the writer may select a code which uses special symbols for whole words. There are many methods of cryptology from which to choose.

19

4. When deciphering a secret message, the decoder hunts for clues. One clue is the number of times each letter (or number) is used. In English the symbol which appears most often stands for the letter *e.* The decoder also searches for double letters (or numbers) and letter (or number) combinations which occur often. If neither of these clues provides the key to the cipher, the message might be compared with other messages from the same source. Sometimes it takes so long to break a code that the message is no longer useful. However, with much study, experience, and just plain luck, a secret message can usually be deciphered.

5. Throughout history, secret-message writing has played an important role. Some historians believe that Napoleon's army was defeated in Russia because his cipher officers were caught. During the American Civil War, the Federalists broke most of the codes used by the Confederates. Because the British broke the German code soon after the beginning of World War II, they were able to intercept messages between German officers throughout the war. Cryptology has been just as important in peacetime. It is used by governments to communicate with diplomats who are sent to other countries.

8. MAKING SURE YOU HAVE THE RIGHT MAIN THOUGHT

As you know, the main thought gives the meaning of a paragraph in one sentence. All the other sentences or details help to prove it or to support it in some way. Just suppose, however, that you had selected the *wrong* sentence for your main thought. How could you tell that you were wrong?

A Test to Apply

There is a simple test that you can make for yourself when you read the next paragraph.

Several millions of years ago the early ancestors of horses looked altogether different from the horses of today. In size they were no larger than a small fox terrier. Instead of hoofs they had toes on their feet. Their existence became known by the discovery of many of their fossil remains. Scientists gave this animal the name *eohippus* (pronounced EE oh HIP pus), from the Greek word *hippus,* which means "horse." They tell us that it took over a million years before these horses gradually developed into their present size. At the same time they also developed hard and bony hoofs.

If you select the first sentence you will be correct, because every other sentence supports that thought. "No larger than a small fox terrier" helps to prove that the early horses looked different. "They had toes instead of hoofs" also proves that those horses looked different. We learned about them from "their fossil remains" tells how we know that they looked different. "They were named *eohippus*" also shows they must have looked different; otherwise they would have been named *hippus.* The other sentences help in the same way.

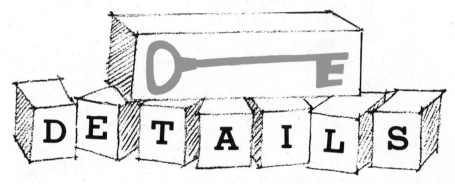

Suppose, however, you had selected some other sentence—for example the last one, the one about developing hoofs. It would now be easy for you to see that "they were no larger than fox terriers" does not prove they developed hoofs. "They had toes instead of hoofs" does not prove they developed hoofs. No other sentence proves or supports the statement that they developed hoofs.

Therefore that sentence could not be the key sentence or main thought. It took long to explain this, but your common sense would recognize such an error very quickly.

EXERCISE 6

Directions: In this exercise each paragraph will be followed by several choices for the main thought. Select the correct one and copy it on your paper or in your notebook. In addition, however, take time to think about why the other choices are wrong. Then be ready to report, during class discussion, your reasons for choosing the right one and for not choosing the others.

THE THEATER AT EPIDAUROS

1. The Theater at Epidauros in Greece is the best naturally-acoustic theater in the world. It is built into the foothills of Mount Kynortion, with the stage at the base of the site. A visitor sitting at the top of the theater can hear a coin dropped, a word whispered, or fingers snapped, just as clearly as if she or he were in the first row. On a very quiet day, the flick of a match lit by someone standing on the stage can be heard by a person sitting in the top row.

a. Someone sitting in the top row can hear the striking of a match from the stage area.
b. The acoustics in the theater at Epidauros are the best in the world.
c. The theater is built into the foothills of Mount Kynortion.

2. The natural surroundings of the site where the theater at Epidauros was built contribute to its acoustical perfection. There is a valley directly below the theater. Trees circle the valley; and beyond the trees, across from the theater itself, are numerous small hills. The valley, the sloping hills, and the dense vegetation help create the acoustics.

a. A valley lies below the theater.
b. There are numerous small hills across from the theater.
c. The theater's site contributes to its acoustical perfection.

3. The theater was built to seat a large number of people and was later expanded to seat even more. During the first phase of the theater's construction, the tiers of seats had a capacity for 6,200 spectators. Later, in the first half of the 2nd century B.C., the upper tier containing twenty rows of seats was added. This addition increased the theater's capacity to about 14,300 spectators and gave the theater its final and present-day appearance.

a. The theater seats over 14,000 people.
b. The seating capacity of the theater has increased since the theater was first built.
c. Twenty rows were added in the 2nd century.

4. Mime-plays and pantomimes were presented at Epidauros. These forms of dramatic art were usually performed without words. Ideas and emotions were conveyed by facial expressions, body movements, and gestures. Greek tragedies and comedies were also performed at the theater. The Theater of Epidauros was the setting for many kinds of dramatic art.

a. The theater was the setting for many kinds of dramatic art.
b. Greek tragedies and comedies were performed.
c. Mime-plays were usually performed without words.

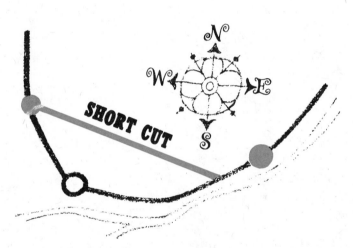

9. A SHORT WAY TO EXPRESS A LONG THOUGHT

The Beginning of Outlining

When we write down the key sentence and list the paragraph details under it, we can recognize which facts ought to be remembered.

But it is difficult to remember all the words in complete sentences. It is much easier to understand the thought and to remember details if we use a **short form** or **outline form.** In this form all the sentences are turned, as far as possible, into phrases that keep practically every important meaning. We can do this by selecting only those few words needed to give us the general idea. This is illustrated with the following sentences.

a. The word *butterfly comes from* → "Butterfly" comes from "flutter
the two-word phrase *flutter by*.   by"

b. It's amazing *how much time* has → Much time passed since launch-
passed since the *launching* of   ing Apollo I
Apollo I.

c. *Nations* realize that *trade* can be → Trade helps nations
of *help to them*.

The phrase that we use in place of the key sentence can be
called the **key phrase.** In changing the sentence to a phrase, some
changes in wording may be necessary. If the paragraph is an explanation of something, the key phrase should begin with *how;* if
the paragraph gives reasons for something, the key phrase should
begin with *why*.

a. It is *healthy* for people of all → Why exercise is healthy
ages to *exercise* often.

b. There are certain *rules* to *follow* → How to pot a plant
for *potting a plant*.

c. *Deaf people read lips* and use → How deaf people communicate
sign language to *communicate*.

If the key sentence is a question, your phrase for it should
turn it back into a direct statement.

a. What is the right way to put a → How to put a bicycle together
bicycle together?

b. What are some of the charac- → Characteristics of dolphins
teristics of dolphins?

c. What are the directions one → How to make a kite
should follow in making a kite?

EXERCISE 7

The sentences in this exercise are key sentences taken out of
their paragraphs. You are going to change the key sentences into
key phrases. Some slight changes may be necessary. Since several
right answers are possible, your classmates may have a different
wording. Be ready to explain in class why you think your phrase is
a good one.

Directions: Copy each sentence on your paper. Underline the words that can be used in making your phrase. Write the phrase below the sentence.

1. To succeed, a mountain climber needs a lot of courage, stamina, and strict training.

Which is your choice?
   a. Mountain climber needs courage, stamina, and strict training
   b. Lots of courage, stamina, and training needed by mountain climber to succeed
   c. How a mountain climber succeeds

2. Mountain climbers using special equipment can scale a vertical wall without falling.
3. Careful climbers pitch their tents when the sun goes down.
4. When they get close to the top of the mountain, climbers put on warm clothing.
5. Mountain climbing is an exciting hobby, but sometimes it can be very dangerous.

10. REDUCING SENTENCES TO PHRASES

If the key sentence can be shortened into a phrase, then the detail sentences can also be shortened. When this is done, an entire paragraph can be turned into an **outline.** The outline makes it easy to understand and to remember the paragraph.

However, do not make the mistake of thinking that books should be written that way. The outline does not really make good sense to you unless you read the material in its original form, and then—by yourself or with help—turn it into the short outline form. Here is an example of how this can be done. Note that the key phrase is called the **topic** of the paragraph.

Key Sentence:
The first railroad train was a very simple and crude construction.

Topic:
First railroad train crude

Details:
Each car was built very much like the old-fashioned stagecoach.

Details:
Each car like a stagecoach

It was very short, and it could seat only eight people.

The wheels were very large, with long spokes, and they were made of wood.

The tracks were very narrow, just the width of an ordinary carriage.

Short; seated only eight

Wheels large, wooden, with long spokes

Tracks narrow like width of carriage

The short form leaves out some minor details, but it will help you recall a great deal of the meaning of the original paragraph. You can see that an outline helps you figure out the meaning of a paragraph and remember its details.

11. THE KEY SENTENCE MAY BE ANYWHERE

You have learned that the main thought of a paragraph may appear in either the first sentence or the last. Now you will meet key sentences that appear in the middle of paragraphs. You will see, in fact, that the main thought may be stated anywhere in the paragraph. This means that you must look carefully in any paragraph for the thought that is supported by all the other sentences. Where is the main thought in the following paragraph?

Everybody knows that tomatoes are grown for food, yet there was a time when they were grown only to be admired as beautiful plants in a garden. They had a variety of colors— yellow, pink, and red. They looked bright and so pretty that they were known as "love apples." They were thought of as decorations in the garden, just like flowers.

You can surely recognize that this paragraph is about the tomato as a beautiful plant. That thought is in the first sentence. Yet the first part of the sentence tells of the tomato as food, not as something to be admired. Therefore the *whole* of the first sentence is not the real key sentence. We must be careful, then, to select only that part of the sentence which gives us the main thought. That part is:

. . . yet there was a time when they were grown only to be admired as beautiful plants in a garden.

You have just seen that the main thought sometimes consists of only one part of a sentence rather than the whole sentence. In the paragraph above it was the second part of a sentence. In some other paragraph it might be the first part.

Now let us look at another way of presenting the main thought.

The word "curfew" has gone through a complete change in meaning since it was first used about 1000 years ago. Originally it came from two French words that meant "cover the fire." A bell was rung soon after nightfall to warn people to *cover their fires* or *put them out* before they fell asleep. After several hundred years the bell was rung for other purposes, such as informing people of the exact time at nine o'clock. Much later it was used to warn boys and girls that they must be off the street at the sound of the bell. **The present meaning of the word is certainly different from the original meaning.**

First, Last, or Middle?

The main thought of the paragraph above is in the first sentence, of course, since the paragraph told about the changes in the meaning of "curfew." But what about the last sentence? Did you notice that it expressed practically the same thought in different words? In this kind of paragraph the main thought is found in *both* sentences, the first and the last. There are actually two key sentences here.

Such paragraphs are a great service to the reader. The first sentence says to you, "This is what the paragraph will be about." The last one says, "In case you forget, I am reminding you about the thought of this paragraph." Do not expect to find many such paragraphs in your reading. Authors are not always so kind to their readers.

The following paragraph is the kind that requires the most careful kind of reading.

> Every morning cowboys begin their work of the day by riding out to look for lost cattle. They are in the saddle practically all day to keep cattle from straying too far. At roundup time they have to ride furiously back and forth to keep the whole herd moving in the right direction. **Cowboys have many kinds of duties.** They take part in branding the cattle. They go on long trips when the herd is taken to a distant market. They keep the cattle from hurting each other. Even late at night they may still be in the saddle for some emergency tasks.

Notice that the main thought occurs in the middle of this paragraph, and that all the other sentences describe various things the cowboys do. The key sentence ties them all together by saying that they are cowboys' duties. If that sentence had been printed in the same type as the other sentences, you might have missed it. Now you will be able to find a buried key sentence in other paragraphs.

Where to Look for the Main Thought

The main thought may be
1. in part of a sentence.
2. at both the beginning and end of a paragraph.
3. in the middle of a paragraph.
4. in the first sentence.
5. in the last sentence.

EXERCISE 8

In this exercise you will have to read with care before you can be sure how to word your key phrases.

Directions: Read the paragraph. Locate the key sentence. Decide on the key phrase. Write it on your paper, using the form shown at the top of page 29. Note that you will use the word *Topic* instead of "key phrase." Under the Topic, write the details, using the short form. Pay particular attention to the underlined portions of the paragraphs. They will give you help where you may need it most. Do not write in this book.

Topic:

_____

Details:
  A. _____
  B. _____

PRIMITIVE MAN LEARNS NEW WAYS

1. At first hunters used only meat and furs from the animals they were able to kill. Then they found that they could obtain many useful materials from the bodies. The skins made good covers and containers. When cut into thin strips, they could be used like rope. When dried and stretched into leather, the skin made good clothing. The bones and the horns were valuable material for weapons and tools.

2. Long before knives were known, man found that the sharp edges of broken stones were good to cut with. He probably tried many kinds of stones. Some gave very good cutting edges. Others were not quite as good. It was found that flint, however, was the stone that could cut best.

3. Flint became a valuable and important stone to early man. Although it is very hard, it breaks easily and leaves sharp edges. He found many pieces of flint in various shapes and sizes. He was able to make flint arrowheads, knives, scrapers, daggers, and awls (to pierce with). When struck together, pieces of flint threw off sparks and thus gave man a way to make fire. Flint was one of man's most useful discoveries.

4. Although he had many tools and weapons made of wood, such as the spear with its sharpened end, the use of stone was of much greater help to him than wood. Stone was harder and could be sharpened, too. When he learned how to chip stone, especially flint, he found he could make it into whatever form he wanted. He was thus able to make better arrowheads, spearheads, and axes.

5. In trying to shape bone, man found that it was better to grind it than to chip it. Bone needles could be made in this way for use by women in the cave homes. Then man began to grind and polish stone also. He could then make stone axes and chisels with smooth and fine edges. This method of grinding and polishing became the improved way of tool making.

6. When the early hunters killed a mother animal, its young might be brought back as pets for the children. As these animals grew up they became tame. Many kinds of animals were probably brought up among the people in the tribes. Some of these animals were useless when fully grown. Others, however, were found to be valuable. Man had finally found that living animals could be useful to him.

7. Wolves or "wild dogs" became man's first tame animal. Sheep, goats, cattle, and pigs were later added to the list of tamed or domesticated animals. A few sheep or pigs would soon grow into many. Even if wild beasts became scarce, the number of tame beasts increased. Man now had an assured supply of food without the need to go hunting.

Do not lose the outlines you have just made. You will need them for your next experiment in reading.

12. OUTLINES HELP YOU TO REMEMBER

In your writing you have probably found it helpful to make an outline to keep you on the right track. Now we shall see that making an outline of what you read will make the paragraphs clear.

EXERCISE 9

Turn to the outlines you made for the last lesson, and we shall begin to give you practice and to test your ability to remember. The first paragraph has already been outlined for you. The wording may be slightly different from yours.

For Par. 1. Read this outline only once, but read with a strong effort to remember every item. Look up when you have finished, and see if you can repeat all the ideas silently to yourself.

Topic:
Hunters got useful materials from animals.
Details:
   A. Meat and furs
   B. Skins for covers and containers
   C. Strips of skin used as rope
   D. Skin made into leather for clothing
   E. Bones and horns for weapons and tools

Now cover the outline and answer these questions on your paper.

    a. How many parts of the animal are mentioned?
    b. What did hunters use for rope?
    c. What two parts of the animal did they use for clothing? (The answer comes from two parts of the outline.)
    d. What use did they make of the bones and horns?
    e. What did they do to the skin so that it could be used for clothing?
    f. What else was the skin used for?

For Par. 2. Read the outline from your own paper, but read the way you did for paragraph 1. Then look up and try to repeat mentally just the ideas, not the exact words. Use the main thought to guide you in thinking of the details. If you need a reminder, you may look down for a moment. Finally, cover your outline and rewrite it from memory on your paper. The outline form just below will help you. Do not write in this book.

    Topic:
        Man found sharp edges of broken stones good for cutting
    Details:
        A. Tried many kinds
        B. Some stones very good
        C.
        D.

For Par. 3. In this paragraph the main thought, in the first sentence, is repeated in the last sentence. Therefore, in your outline you will not need the thought of the last sentence. Now read in the same way as before and cover it up. Then try to rewrite the *whole outline without any further help.*

For Par. 4. Continue this exercise for the other outlines. Use the forms given here as your guide. Some helpful hints will be given to you occasionally.

    Topic:
        Stone of greater help than wood
    Details:
        A.
        B.
        C.

For Par. 5.

Topic:
Details:
   A. With bone, found it better to grind than to chip
      (There are four details.)

For Par. 6.

Topic:
   How animals came to be useful to man
Details:
   (There are five details.)

For Par. 7.

Topic:
Details:
   A.
   B.
   C.
   D. Even if wild beasts became scarce

READING
THE SENTENCE

In Chapter 1, you were given skills which will help you get meaning from the paragraph as a whole. You learned how to discover the details in a paragraph. You saw how a key sentence can lead you to the main thought.

When you read a paragraph with care, you follow the thread of thought from one sentence to the next. Of course you do not attempt to remember each sentence as you read it. Rather, you follow the thread from sentence to sentence to discover the meaning, to gain ideas. On the next page is a Greek legend that tells about Theseus and the Minotaur. See how well you can follow the thread of this story.

1. CAN YOU FOLLOW THE THREAD?

Theseus (Thē′si-us) was a Greek hero, and the Minotaur (Min′o-tor) was a huge beast, half man, half bull. The beast lived in a mysterious cavern, whose secret passages were always in complete darkness. Theseus was given the task of killing the Minotaur. Supposing he should succeed in finding the beast in this cavern and slaying it, how would he ever be able to find his way back through the darkness? From the goddess Ariadne (Ar′i-ad′ně), he learned of a way to solve his problem. He started his journey into the black passages with a large spool of thread. He fastened the end of the thread at the entrance and then unwound it as he went along. At last, after he had killed the Minotaur, all he had to do was to follow the thread, and he would find his way out of the cavern. Thus Theseus solved his difficulty and became a hero at the same time.

That expression, **to follow the thread,** now means "to follow the meaning through a passage of speech or writing." If you can read a difficult paragraph or a long sentence with understanding, we say that you can follow the thread.

Short and Long Sentences

Some sentences that you meet in your reading are short and easy to understand, like these:

> Mary stumbled. She fell. She hurt herself. She screamed. Help came.

These sentences were too short and too easy to interest you, yet each one was a complete sentence. It gave you a complete thought. It told you something about a person or thing. The first sentence told you what Mary did. She stumbled. The second also told you what she did. She fell. Each sentence gave you a little story, even though it omitted any details. Even two or three words may be enough to give you the thought if they are the framework words of a sentence.

But some sentences are long and full of details. It is possible that you might *lose the thread* before you come to the end of them. Let us find out what makes the difference between a short sentence and a long one.

We will start with this easy sentence:

She fell.

We are going to see how this simple sentence can become long and complicated if we add enough details. For instance, we shall add *when* she fell.

> *Yesterday afternoon, while Mary was on her way home from school*, she fell.

Then we shall also add *why* she fell.

> Yesterday afternoon, while Mary was on her way home from school, *her foot caught in a dead branch lying across the road* and she fell.

The sentence has now become longer. But you can still "follow the thread" as long as you can keep your mind on those two important words, *she fell*. We shall make the sentence even longer by telling *where* she fell.

> Yesterday afternoon, while Mary was on her way home from school, her foot caught in a dead branch lying across the road and she fell *on the dusty surface*.

You can see that the entire sentence is really a long way of saying merely, "She fell." With a little skill and practice you can easily follow the thread through sentences of this kind.

2. THE MOST IMPORTANT WORDS

Long sentences, like the one about Mary, are likely to contain many details. You can follow the thread much better if you recognize which parts are only details. Some of them, for instance, might be details about how, or when, or where, or why. But it takes only a few important words to help you understand the important thought. In a newspaper such words might be used for headlines.

The headline "Fire Destroys Hospital" comes from this sentence:

> During the early hours of the morning a great roaring *fire destroyed* nearly all of the new three-story *hospital* at Allenville today.

35

The headline "Police Capture Bandit" is a short way of expressing this sentence:

> After searching throughout three states for a week, the *police* finally *captured* the *bandit* who shot the bank teller in a hold-up attempt.

When you pick out the fewest possible words that give the thought of a sentence, you have the **core thought** of the sentence, and you will then be able to understand it. Every sentence must contain at least one thought, and that thought will have a core, or framework, of at least two or three words.

The framework of a sentence might be compared to the framework of a house. When the house is being completed, details are added to the framework—details such as shutters, window boxes, sidewalks, and shrubbery. All sorts of details may be added, but the framework remains. So it is with a sentence.

To make a complete sentence we may add details to the framework, or core thought. Then if we take away the details of the sentence, the framework or core thought remains.

3. JUST ENOUGH GRAMMAR TO HELP READING

Please understand that this book does not intend to teach you grammar. However, if a little grammar will help you to understand difficult sentences with ease, then it is worth while to include some grammar here.

The Two Main Core Words

One of the most important words in a sentence is the word that usually shows action. It is called the **verb.** It generally tells what some person or thing did or is doing.

Here are several sentences as examples. The verbs have been marked for you.

> The boys <u>fought</u> each other.
> The fire <u>started</u> in the cellar.
> He <u>moistens</u> the postage stamp with a sponge.

Another very important word is the **subject.** It tells what person or thing performs the action shown by the verb.

You have already seen that in the sentence "The boys fought each other" the action word is *fought*. Now ask yourself, "Who did it? Who fought?" The answer will give you the subject: The *boys* fought.

The other two sentences also contain core words, as shown here. Those two words carry the chief idea of the sentence.

> The <u>fire</u> <u>started</u> in the cellar.
> <u>He</u> <u>moistens</u> the postage stamp with a sponge.

EXERCISE 1

Remember that you can find the subject by asking Who did it? or What did it? First, find the verb; then ask *who* or *what* before the verb. Be careful. Sometimes the verb is far inside the sentence. Sometimes the subject and verb are not close together.

Directions: Number your paper 1–10. Make two columns, heading one *Subject* and the other *Verb*. Write the subject and verb from each sentence on the next page. The first two sentences are marked for you.

1. In a London fog, <u>people</u> often <u>move</u> very slowly.
2. In a large glass bowl on the center of the table the sleek <u>goldfish</u> <u>swim</u> lazily back and forth. (You had to read far into the sentence to find the verb *swim*.)
3. The tallest giant in the world stood alongside the smallest midget.
4. The early Christians, out of sight in their catacombs, or great underground caverns, hid from the Romans for years. (The verb, *hid*, is near the end of the sentence. Be sure to get the correct subject. *Who* hid?)
5. On page 1 of the paper, a strange headline appeared.
6. The jet plane, with its full load of one hundred passengers, shoots like a rocket up toward the clouds.
7. The little fellow, tired and hungry after his adventure in the woods, slept all through the lesson.
8. Through the wet window, the old man appeared like a wriggly black shadow in the mist.
9. Your mother, always thoughtful about you, prepared all day for your birthday tomorrow.
10. The owner of the stationery store occasionally rests for a day from his work.

The Third Core Word

Two words are not always enough to give you the core meaning. Here is an example.

(The) fielder caught

This leaves you puzzled. It certainly does not sound complete. You keep wondering, "The fielder caught *what*?" Let us first look at the whole sentence to see what is missing.

The fielder, leaping high, caught the ball just in front of the fence.

Now we can answer the question, "The fielder caught *what*?" He caught the ball. We can see the need in some sentences, therefore, for a third core word. That word is usually called the **complement,** and we can find it merely by asking "What?" after the verb.

Verb: caught   *Subject* (who caught?): fielder
Complement (fielder caught what?): ball

If you were to mark the sentence for the core words, it would look like this:

> The fielder, leaping high, caught the [ball] just in front of the fence.

There is an easier way to find the core, and you are now ready to use it. For every sentence, ask yourself "What happened?" or "What is happening?" Then find the words that answer the question, and you will have the core of that sentence. Remember that you will not need more than two words if the two words sound complete.

The boy caught...

EXERCISE 2

This short exercise will give you practice in selecting cores and in deciding whether they consist of two or more words. Make sure by asking yourself "What happened?" or "What is happening?"

Directions: Copy the sentences on your paper. Put a single line under the subject, a double line under the verb, and brackets around the complement if there is one. Brackets look like this: [ ] Five sentences have been marked to guide you.

THE GUINEA PIG

1. Some animals got their [names] in peculiar ways. 2. For instance, squirrel originally meant [shady tail]. 3. You can easily see the [reason]. 4. Hippopotamus comes from two Greek words, *potamos* and *hippos*. 5. They mean [river] and [horse], or river-horse. 6. The lyre bird's tail, when spread, resembles

a musical instrument, the lyre. 7. But the guinea pig has no good reason for its name. 8. It comes from Guiana (pronounced Gee-anna), not Guinea. 9. It belongs to the rat family, not the pig family. 10. Its original name was *Guiana cava*. 11. That means "rat from Guiana." 12. Then someone translated it wrongly into English. 13. He wrote it as "Guinea pig" or "pig from Guinea." 14. He made two mistakes in his translation. 15. But then the wrong translation became the accepted name. 16. Now very few people know anything about the mistake.

Some Other Words Are Important, Too

The core words are absolutely necessary to ensure your understanding of the sentence. Yet each sentence has its own special meaning, and often additional words are needed to make that meaning clear.

Note the following two sentences. The core words are exactly alike, but how completely different the special meanings are!

    a. He strolled happily through the pleasant field.
    b. He strolled fearlessly among the lions in the great cage.

Surely it becomes important to show those differences in the core, although we should generally do it with as few words as possible. It can be done in this way:

    a. He strolled happily through the pleasant field.
    b. He strolled fearlessly among the lions in the great cage.

In each of these sentences one word tells *how* the man strolled, and word groups like *among the lions* tell *where* he strolled. These words are modifiers.

Clearly, modifiers make a great deal of difference in the meaning of a sentence. For another example, it makes a great deal of difference whether the wind blows *gently* or *fiercely*.

GENTLY   FIERCELY

EXERCISE 3

Now try your skill in selecting the core words plus *important modifiers*. Select only the words that are important to the thought. Your classmates may not agree with you on the important words. Be ready to defend your opinion.

Directions: Make four columns on your paper, heading them Subject, Verb, Complement, Modifiers. List the numbers 1 to 15 down the left side of your paper, and write the important words from each sentence in the proper columns. The entries for the first two sentences have been done for you to show you how.

	Subject	Verb	Complement	Modifiers
1.	sun	shone		hot, bright, all day on the sweltering crowd
2.	boy	wiped	perspiration	away

1. The sun, hot and bright in the cloudless sky, shone all day on the sweltering crowd.
2. The boy wiped the perspiration away from his brow.
3. His hand, though tired and moist, still gripped his fishing-rod firmly.
4. He waited long and patiently for just a nibble.
5. Only one fish bit on his bait that day.
6. At last the boy, in disgust at the fish and the heat, threw down his rod angrily.
7. He turned away from the lake with a feeling of great disappointment.
8. Suddenly, without warning, a fish leaped out of the water straight toward him.
9. It fell on the ground near the boy's feet.
10. He forgot completely about the heat.
11. He flung his arm out quickly toward the fish on the ground.
12. But he swung too hard.
13. His careless action flipped the fish back into the water.
14. He glared with bitter exasperation at the rapidly disappearing fish.
15. Now the fish awaits a more careful fisherman.

4. RECOGNIZING THE MEANING OF A PHRASE

The core words alone, as you have seen, are not always enough to give you the proper meaning of a sentence. There are other words that **describe,** that tell **what kind;** or they may tell **which one.** These words can make a great difference in a sentence. You can see that difference in the two sentences below.

> **a.** Ann wore a *gold* ring.
> **b.** Mary wore a *brass* ring.

If the words *gold* and *brass* were left out of the cores, then we might think that Ann and Mary were wearing the same kind of rings. Since the rings are quite different, however, we need to show that difference. We therefore include the words that tell us what kind of ring.

There is another way of describing the ring. Instead of *gold ring* we might say *ring of gold.* Instead of *brass ring* we could say *ring of brass.* Instead of one word to tell "what kind," we can use a combination of words. That combination is called a phrase. "Of gold" and "of brass" are phrases.

Pay particular attention to the last word in the phrase. That is almost always the important word. Notice it in these examples:

> **a.** the friend of my sister . . . . means . . . my sister's friend
> **b.** the dress of satin . . . . means . . . the satin dress
> **c.** the man with the umbrellas . . . . means . . . the umbrella man
> **d.** a trip during the summer . . . . . . means . . . a summer trip
> **e.** a ring of great expense . . . . means . . . an expensive ring

Did you notice in the examples above that the phrase appears *after* the word it modifies? Knowing this will help you keep together the words that belong together in your reading. Usually a one-word modifier like *sister's* comes before the word it modifies.

It is not always possible to change a phrase to a one-word modifier.

> You can say: The man *near the door* has my ticket.
> But not: The near the door man has my ticket.
> You can say: The woman with the green car returned.
> But not: The green car woman returned.
> You can say: We asked the people just off the train.
> But not: We asked the train people.

EXERCISE 4

Directions: Number your paper 1–10. Make four columns, heading them Subject, Verb, Complement, Other Important Words. Under this last heading you will place phrases that are important. Be ready to tell which word each phrase belongs to.

1. My cousin from France found a bicycle with a missing pedal.
2. The uniform from my scout troop fitted Tom perfectly.
3. I discovered the rest of the money today after breakfast.
4. My mother quickly ironed the entire pile of clothes.
5. The gifts for Helen came from a very fashionable shop for girls.
6. The silk glove covered a hand of steel.
7. A man with a bass fiddle passed me on the stairs the other day.
8. My father's friend from England stayed with us for a few days.
9. His work at school showed great improvement week after week.
10. He greatly appreciated his first week at camp.

5. HELPING VERBS

You will often find sentences in which the verb is made up of two or more words. Some of these will be **helping verbs.** There are only a few of these in our language. They usually appear before the main verb, and that makes it easy to recognize them.

Any main verb can be "helped" by all these helping verbs. You often use them in your conversation, and you meet them constantly in your reading. Suppose, for example, you come upon this sentence:

Mary will sing today.   **HELPING VERB**

You can see at once that the complete verb is not "sing" but "will sing." Yet it might appear in any one of these other ways:

shall sing	can sing	might sing
must sing	should sing	could sing
may sing	would sing	does sing

Some of the other helping verbs require a change in the main verb:

am singing   are singing   were singing
is singing   was singing

Several helping verbs require another kind of change in the main verb:

has sung   have sung   had sung

Notice that it would have been incorrect to say "has sing" or "has sang."

6. WHERE THE NEGATIVE IS PLACED

The opposite of *Yes* is *No*. The opposite of "He has money" is the statement "He has **no** money."

There are several ways of making negative statements. Note these two:

a. Mr. Tanaki speaks **no** English.
b. Mr. Tanaki does **not** speak English.

You can observe two things in **b:**

1. The sentence uses *not* instead of *no*.

2. The negative breaks into the verb. It is placed between the helper and the main verb. That is the usual way of speaking or writing negative statements. You will find this separation of the two parts of the verb in most of the negative expressions you will meet in your reading.

"THEY HAVE NO MONEY"

"NO ONE HAS ANY MONEY"

"NOBODY HAS MONEY"

You were just reminded of two negatives, *no* and *not*. You know them well. There are other negatives that you know also, and you have used them often. They include *not ever, never* (it means *not ever*), *none, no one, nothing, nobody.*

Watch for these negatives in the sentences that follow, and take special note of where they are placed. Some of them will occur between the two parts of the verb. Which negatives are they? Others will be used in sentences that do not have any helping verb. Which negatives are those?

a. 1. The soldier guarded the guns.
   2. The soldier did *not* guard the guns.

b. 1. The pirate found gold in the cave.
   2. The pirate did *not* find gold in the cave.

c. 1. The invalid saw many visitors all week.
   2. The invalid saw *no* visitors all week.

d. 1. My father likes toast for breakfast.
   2. My father does *not* like toast for breakfast.

e. 1. I can work this lock by myself.
   2. I can *never* work this lock by myself.

f. 1. They all came to my birthday party.
   2. *Nobody* came to my birthday party.

Contractions

You have frequently seen the expressions *can't, won't, wouldn't,* and others like them. They are all negatives, too, but they are **contractions** of *cannot* (can't), *will not* (won't), and *would not* (wouldn't). None of them will cause you any difficulty in your reading.

However, there are contractions which include helping verbs. These will require careful attention. The following table will help to clarify them for you.

Sentence with Contraction	*Meaning*
I'm not feeling well today.	I am *not* feeling well today.
They've been lost.	They have been lost.
I've not heard about it.	I have *not* heard about it.
He's found it already.	He has found it already.

45

EXERCISE 5

Directions: Number your paper 1 to 10. Write on your paper the subject, the verb, and the negative (if any) for each sentence. Write the words in full, without contractions. Underline the full verb once and the negative twice.

1. He hasn't any paper left.
2. I'm not going with you today.
3. The ropes aren't hanging properly.
4. That girl never admits her mistakes.
5. No one saw the scared look on his face.
6. I'll never forgive you for that mistake.
7. I won't forgive you for that mistake.
8. Sally wouldn't go by herself.
9. Dan should not worry about the examination.
10. The doctor can't find anything wrong with Billy.

YOU SHOULD ALWAYS THINK

7. DIVIDED VERBS

Frequently the two parts of the verb appear together and can be recognized at once. But there are times when the two parts are separated from each other by a word or two. Still, they should be easy to recognize. Here is an example of this separation:

I *can* never really *forget* your kindness to me.

EXERCISE 6

Directions: Copy the following sentences on your paper. Underline the two parts of the verb. Do not underline the words that separate them.

1. The band will now play patriotic songs for us.
2. We can never really thank you enough for your help.

3. When danger threatens, you should always think before you act.
4. The pitcher could certainly throw fast balls.
5. The beginning of the parade was now approaching us.

Longer Separations

Surely those sentences gave you no trouble. However, in many sentences there is a long separation between the helping verb and the main verb. In such sentences you may "lose the thread" somewhere between the two parts of the verb. Therefore you must be doubly careful to recognize both parts.

Notice these examples:

1. Tommy *will* always, as long as he lives, *remember* that night alone in the forest.
2. Aunt Hattie *had* never, in spite of all her experience with children, *seen* any boy so bespattered with mud as was James.

Would you have recognized the complete verbs if they had not been italicized? If so, you have shown excellent understanding, and you are ready for the next exercise.

EXERCISE 7

Be prepared to give the core meaning of each sentence below. Some of the sentences have already been marked for you.

Directions: Copy the sentences on your paper. Draw a single line under the subject and a double line under each part of the verb. Put brackets around other important words.

1. Many Indian tribes in the southwest live on parched land.
2. They have during every dry season prayed [for rain].
3. Their prayers have taken the form of religious dances.
4. [However,] in spite of their long dances and their patience, the prayers have [not always] succeeded in bringing rain.
5. Numerous tourists have visited these tribes.
6. They came only to witness the dances.
7. They did not in any way show the slightest interest in the hardships of the Indians.
8. Perhaps scientists will some day solve the water problems for these tribes.

BABE RUTH WAS **A MIGHTY BATTER.**

BABE RUTH IS **FAMOUS.**

8. LINKING VERBS

Up to now, the verbs in this chapter on understanding sentences have been words of action. They showed what someone did or was doing. The sentences answered the question "What happened?" or "What is happening?"

In the sentence, "The Scouts explored the island," *explored* certainly shows action. Something happened.

But in the sentence, "The Scouts were good explorers," nothing is happening. *Were* does not show any action, yet it is a verb. It merely **connects,** or **links together,** two words that mean the same person.

Sometimes such verbs join together the subject and a word that describes it. "The Scouts were weary" really says "the weary Scouts." Nothing happened in this sentence. The verb *were* does not show action. Its purpose is only to join two words that belong together in meaning.

All the verbs that come from "is" or "was" are **linking verbs,** and they may have helping verbs also, just like verbs of action.

As you read the sentences in the short list below, you will notice the linking verbs there. You will also notice that these verbs are important in getting the core meaning of a sentence.

a. That young man *is* a lawyer.
b. All the campers *were* good swimmers.
c. The boys in that class *are* all honor students with marks of at least B+.
d. From the first day the dog *was* very happy in his new ｝ome.

(Notice that in sentence **d** *happy* is not part of the verb. It merely describes "dog.")

e. The bicycle *will be* a very welcome present next Christmas.

(Notice the helping verb.)

f. My favorite pets *have* always *been* wire-haired terriers.

(The two parts of the verb can be separated.)

g. My little brother *was* just *being* stubborn that day.
h. Every verb in these sentences *has been* a linking verb.
i. Some pears *become* yellow as they ripen.
j. A rainy day *can seem* dull and dreary.
k. The apple *looked* good, but it *tasted* sour.

(*Become* and *seem* also are linking verbs. Other similar linking verbs are *appear, sound, taste, feel.*)

THE APPLE **LOOKED** GOOD BUT **TASTED** SOUR

Linking verbs often appear to be small and modest, but we must not forget how important they are to the sentence. We cannot obtain the core meaning unless we recognize them. Here is a sentence taken from the last list.

> The boys in that class are all honor students with marks of at least B+.

What is the sentence saying? The answer is: boys   are   honor students.

Now let us mark the sentence for the longer form of the core.

> The <u>boys</u> in that class <u>are</u> all [honor students] with marks of at least B+.

EXERCISE 8

Directions: Number your paper 1 to 8 and list the verbs from the following sentences. Do not forget the linking verbs and the helping verbs.

1. Timmy was the bully of our class.
2. He was tall and strong for his age.
3. Yet he might be no older than the rest of us.
4. He could sometimes be quiet and peaceful.
5. But he usually seemed very angry over something.
6. His voice was generally harsh and loud.
7. He would always be hardest on the smallest boys.
8. Since his arrival we had been afraid of him.

EXERCISE 9

In this exercise you will find both action verbs and linking verbs. Some verbs will appear in two parts. Some will be separated, either by single words or by a number of words. Do not depend on guessing. If you are not sure in some cases it will be better to leave them unmarked.

Directions: On your paper make four columns, as follows: Verb, Subject word, Complement, Other important words. At the left, number your paper 1 to 16. Then write the proper words from each sentence in the appropriate columns.

1. Tom was feeling unhappy about the test. 2. Yet he had, until that morning, been full of confidence about it. 3. In full preparation for it, Tom had invited two of his classmates to his home for the entire day. 4. With the radio off and the TV far away in another room, they had worked together over their books and notes. 5. They had not wasted a single minute of their time. 6. Every chapter was carefully reviewed. 7. They had even quizzed each other about the topics. 8. The next morning, however, Tom felt shaky. 9. He had lost his confidence. 10. The examination questions seemed strange to him. 11. He was answering them now, but with many doubts. 12. He finally turned in his paper with a heavy heart. 13. The marks were of course posted on the bulletin board the next day. 14. Then Tom received a great shock. 15. He was looking at his mark with much surprise. 16. He had passed with a high rating!

9. WHAT TO DO WITH QUESTIONS

It is very interesting to see what happens to a sentence when it becomes a question. Consider this sentence:

Danny is going swimming today.

Now see it in question form:

Is Danny going swimming today?

This is how the sentence was changed:

1. The two parts of the verb became separated.
2. The subject took the place between the main verb and its helper.

What is the whole core of the sentence? The sentence is very short, and every word in it is important enough for the core meaning. Let us see what to do, however, when the question is long and somewhat more complicated. Here is such a sentence. See how quickly you can find its meaning.

How in the world did Susan, the laziest girl in the entire class, ever finish the homework for tomorrow so quickly?

One way to make sure of the meaning is to do what you have done with all the sentences in this section.

1. Look for the verb. The verb is *finish*.
2. Does it have a helper? Yes, the word *did*.
3. Ask yourself "Who did finish?" and you find the subject, *Susan*.
4. These words, "Susan did finish," sound incomplete, so you ask, "Susan did finish *what*?" and the answer is *homework*.
5. Finally, you decide on other important words that add the special meaning, and you get something like this:

How in the world did Susan, the [laziest girl] in the entire class, ever finish the homework for tomorrow [so quickly]?

By itself, the whole core would appear as:

How did Susan, laziest girl, finish homework?

51

When you select the core words as you did on page 51, you are sure of understanding the sentence well. However, it took many steps to do this. Surely it would take too much time if you always stopped in your reading to pick out the core.

You need to go slowly only while you are *learning* about it. Very soon, with a little practice, your eye will catch these important words without stopping for them, and your mind will recognize the core meaning at once. Then the only time you may have to pause and think will be over a particularly long sentence.

We shall begin to practice, therefore, with shorter questions. You will note that questions begin, almost always, with special question words like *how, when, where, why, who, whom, what,* and *which.* These important words can never be omitted from the core.

When did he leave?
Where did she find the money?
Whom shall we see at the party?
Why is the bank closed so early?
Which team will win the pennant?
In *which* drawer should I look for the stockings?

EXERCISE 10

Directions: Are you ready to try some questions by yourself? Prepare your paper by writing the numbers from 1 to 8 in a column at the left. Then, for each sentence, write out only the important words you select, not the whole sentence. Mark the subject with a single underline, the verb with a double underline, and the object or complement with brackets. Circle the question word.

1. Why are the scientists of the world so interested in outer space?
2. What are scientists doing to conquer outer space?
3. Have all the rocket tests been successful?
4. Will a rocket reach the moon?
5. When will rocket ships make regular trips to the moon?
6. What dangers have the spacemen encountered on these flights into outer space?
7. How can passengers on long moon trips protect themselves from the bitter cold of outer space or the burning heat of the direct rays from the sun?
8. Which planet would be your choice for your first voyage in a rocket ship?

10. WHEN THE POSITIONS ARE CHANGED

Sometimes a sentence can be made to sound more interesting if the subject is taken out of its usual place and put after the verb. Here is a sentence in the usual form:

> The shrouded <u>ghost</u> <u><u>glided</u></u> through the deserted house at midnight.

Here is the same sentence in a new form:

> At midnight through the deserted house <u><u>glided</u></u> the shrouded <u>ghost</u>.

A sentence often has a stronger effect if the subject is removed from its usual place and shifted toward the end of the sentence. This kind of arrangement is called the **inverted form.** It should not give you any trouble if you will remember to look first for the verb and then for the subject in the usual way.

Now for some examples. Be on your guard. Not all of them will be in the inverted form.

1. Far overhead, up toward the fleecy clouds, soared the tireless sea gulls. (Direct order: <u>sea gulls</u> <u><u>soared</u></u>)

53

2. All over his forehead there appeared little beads of per- spiration. (<u>beads</u> <u>appeared</u>)

3. From far-off Tibet came two new pupils to our school. (<u>pupils</u> <u>came</u>)

4. In spite of his desperate efforts, the canoe overturned. (<u>canoe</u> <u>overturned</u>: Was that the inverted form?)

5. At the tunnel there was found the ancient Egyptian mummy. (<u>mummy</u> <u>was found</u>)

EXERCISE 11

Now try the following sentences on your paper. Underline subject and verb as in the examples above.

1. Dark and piercing eyes had he.
2. Up and down the sand hills of the desert marched the tired, perspiring troops.
3. Only brightly colored pebbles did he find.
4. What an unexpected surprise he found at the turn of the road!
5. Proudly at the head of his regiment rode the colonel.

11. SENTENCES WITH COMPOUND PARTS

A sentence may have more than one subject. In the sentence "Jack went up the hill," one person went up the hill. The subject is *Jack*. But in the sentence "Jack and Jill went up the hill," two persons went up the hill. They are Jack and Jill. Those two words are the subjects of the sentence. They are joined by the connecting word "and."

The sentence will become even clearer if we show it in a kind of diagram.

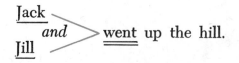

This seems so simple that you may wonder why we take time to explain it. It will not seem quite so simple when the sentences are longer and more complicated. Yet the core meaning can be found in the same way as for all the sentences in the previous exercises.

We shall now examine a long sentence. You will notice that even in a long sentence the core is not difficult to find.

> The leading tennis player in Australia and the winner of the United States tournament met for a final contest of skill in New York City.

If you ask "What happened?" or "Who met?" you can find the subjects and untangle the core from the whole sentence.

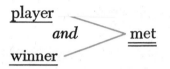

Now mark those words in the complete sentence, and also underline a few important words, and you will have the whole core. You will also have a perfect understanding of the thought. Look for it in this sentence:

> The <u>leading</u> <u>tennis</u> <u>player</u> in <u>Australia</u> and the <u>winner</u> of the <u>United</u> <u>States</u> <u>tournament</u> <u>met</u> for a <u>final</u> <u>contest</u> of skill in New York City.

You should be prepared to find other connecting words than "and." The following diagrams will permit you to see how they may be used.

Either
Samuel
     or >can go to the game, not both.
his brother

Neither
Mrs. Thompson
     nor >is coming here to night.
Mr. Thompson

Not
wealth
     but >is your most precious possession.
health

A sentence may have even more than two subjects, as shown in this diagram:

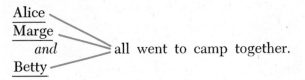

Verbs, too, may often be found in compound form.

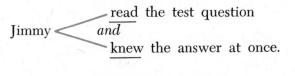

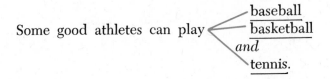

We may even have compound complements.

Some good athletes can play

baseball
basketball
and
tennis.

EXERCISE 12

Directions: For each of the following sentences make a diagram on your paper like those in the examples. Use only the core words that carry the important meaning. Be ready to tell whether the compound part is the subject or the complement or the verb, and how many persons or things are mentioned.

1. Andy gets up late every morning but always arrives at school just in time for the bell.
2. He enjoys the pleasure of sleeping late but not the rush to school afterward.
3. His kind mother and forgiving father have finally lost all patience with him.
4. Every day for months they tried many ways of helping him and many methods of breaking his bad habit.
5. Even his friends as well as his teachers became disgusted with him.

6. One day, much to everyone's astonishment, Andy arose early and finished his breakfast before 7 A.M.
7. Neither his mother nor his shocked father could believe their eyes.
8. His classmates at school congratulated him on his change and slapped him on the back with genuine admiration.
9. Andy found their admiration very pleasant and continued his early arrivals.
10. Now he criticizes other boys and girls for their lateness.

12. WHAT HAVE YOU LEARNED ABOUT SENTENCES?

1. A sentence may be very short or very long, but it must contain at least **one complete thought**:

    a. Fish swim.
    b. In a large glass bowl on the center of the table the sleek goldfish swim lazily back and forth.

2. You can be sure of the meaning if you can select the important words. The most important are the **subject**, the **verb**, and the **object** or **complement** if there is one.

3. The verb is frequently an action word. The sentence tells what happened or what is happening in two or three words:

swim   lose   stood   hid

4. The subject is the word that shows who or what is doing it or did it:

Fish swim.   *People* lose.   *Giant* stood.   *Men* hid.

5. Some words are **linking verbs.** They do not show action. They merely link the subject with another word that means the same thing, or that refers to it. In such sentences you should ask yourself, "What is the sentence saying?"

    The young man *is* a lawyer. (The lawyer is the young man.)
    The girl *seems* happy. (The happy girl)

6. Verbs may have helpers:

    will swim   did lose   is standing   has lost

7. The two parts of the verb may be separated by other words.

> She *will* never *forget* that day.
> Everyone *must,* according to law, *obey* traffic signals.

8. In a **question,** the subject is usually shifted from its place in front of the verb to another position.

> Does the *doctor* still live here?
>
> When will a *rocket* reach the moon?

9. In **inverted sentences** the positions of subject and verb are changed.

> Far overhead *soared* the tireless *sea gulls.*

10. Besides the subject and the verb, some other important words will be needed to get the core meaning of a sentence.

> Aunt Hattie had never, in spite of all her experience with children, seen any boy so bespattered with mud as was Jimmy.

11. A sentence may contain **compound parts,** whether subject, verb, or complement.

> plays badminton
> Mary   *and*
> swims on the team, too.

FAIR AND WARM

FAIR FIGHT

UNDERSTANDING WORDS 3 THROUGH CONTEXT

What can you do when you meet a strange new word in your reading? You can skip it and try to get the meaning of the sentence without the word. Skipping will not do, however, if the word is important in the sentence. If there is a dictionary close at hand, you can interrupt your reading and find the exact meaning of the word for the sentence you are reading.

But suppose you are making use of odd moments for reading. Suppose you are reading on a bus or in a cafeteria, where there is no dictionary. What else can you do about the strange new word? You can get clues to its meaning from the **context.**

The context of a word is what is written or spoken together with the word; in short, the other words around it.

In this chapter, we will learn how to get clues to the meaning of a strange word from the other words around it.

1. CONTEXT DECIDES WHICH MEANING APPLIES

For a few simple examples of the use of context take the words *glasses, car, rose, bill, hands.* Even though these are easy words, you cannot know their exact meaning till you read them in context. What is the meaning of these words in the sentences below? The context will tell you.

1. She bought six water *glasses.*
2. The last *car* left the tracks.
3. Jim *rose* from his chair.
4. A duck has a flat *bill.*
5. The clock's *hands* were broken.

What clue in the context helped you find the exact meaning of each word? What other meanings do you know for these words?

In this chapter you will also learn how to get context clues to the meaning of a strange word. Some of the words in the paragraph below may be strange to you. Read the paragraph and decide for yourself the meaning of each underlined word. Look for clues in the context.

OUR GYM CLASS

We all enjoy our gym class. Our <u>coach</u> is always there to <u>instruct</u> us. Sometimes he teaches us <u>rhythm</u> exercises. For these he counts, or we use the piano to get the timing or beat. When the weather is good, we play outside, but when it is <u>inclement</u> we stay indoors. We like to play softball. Almost the whole class can <u>participate</u>. Our coach is <u>ambidextrous;</u> he can throw a ball straight with either hand.

Were any of the underlined words strange to you? What clues helped you find the meanings?

Choosing the Meaning

Oddly enough, you will face the problem of choosing the right meaning with familiar, commonplace words as often as with strange, new words. Notice the word *flat* in this sentence:

His answer to her request was a *flat* refusal.

You know that *flat* means smooth and level, but this does not seem to describe a refusal. When you turn to your dictionary you will find many meanings for this word.

flat: 1. smooth, level; 2. spread out; 3. not very deep or thick; 4. not shiny or glossy; 5. not to be changed; 6. a musical symbol; 7. set of rooms.

You will see that definition number 5 is the one that fits the sentence best and makes sense. The meaning of the sentence decides which word fits. This is what we mean in saying that context decides the meaning of a word. The dictionary tells you what meanings a word has, but it is up to the reader to select the right one. He can do this only by matching a meaning with the surrounding words of a sentence, the context.

EXERCISE 1

Directions: Number your paper 1 to 11. Read the dictionary meanings for *point* and *court* that are given below. Then write the number of the definition of *point* which fits the context for sentences 1 to 6. Do the same with *court* for sentences 7 to 11. This exercise will give you practice in selecting the proper meaning. It will also show you how the context helps you to choose the meaning.

point: 1. a unit of scoring; 2. a particular time; 3. a small mark or dot; 4. a sharp end; 5. an item; 6. the main idea.

1. I missed the point of your story.
2. We needed one more point to win the game.
3. At that point, the child fell asleep.
4. Point by point, he answered the argument.
5. The pencil had a sharp point.
6. Jim forgot to add the decimal point.

court: 1. a space between walls; 2. place where justice is given; 3. attention paid to win favor; 4. followers of a royal person; 5. area marked off for a game.

7. The lawyer said the case would be tried in court.
8. The court had assembled by the time the king arrived.
9. The young man was paying court to the new girl.
10. A breeze blew briskly through the court.
11. Tennis is played on a tennis court.

EXERCISE 2

There are three numbered sentences below. In each there is an italicized word, used with one particular meaning. In the lettered sentences under it, the same word is used. Find the sentence in which the word has the same meaning as in the numbered sentence.

1. The sailor kept a *fast* grip on the rope.
   a. The tree was held *fast* to the ground by its roots.
   b. The messenger had to be a *fast* runner.
   c. He was pale and thin after his long *fast.*
2. The hunter began to *stalk* the deer through the forest.
   a. There wasn't a *stalk* left in the cornfield.
   b. The tiger *stalked* silently through the forest.
   c. Do you care for a *stalk* of celery?
3. They *bore* their hardships bravely.
   a. Doesn't he *bore* you with his dull talk?
   b. The carpenter will *bore* a hole through the door.
   c. The pain was great but the child *bore* it without a whimper.

2. SOME WORDS HAVE DIFFERENT MEANINGS

There are many common words that have a great number of different meanings. The meaning differs from one context to another. You must therefore use care in reading the context. Otherwise you may get a meaning that was not intended by the author.

Little Tommy's father had been ill with asthma. When Tommy, who was just three years old, inquired what that meant, his mother explained patiently, "It means that Father can't draw his breath." "Oh," he answered quickly, "I can help him. I will bring him my new pencil."

Here are some other examples of common words used with different meanings.

A

1. Danny was the *guard* on his basketball team. (Danny was a player in a special position.)
2. The commander called on the *guard* to parade in the President's honor. (A special group of soldiers to escort an important official.)
3. The state troopers were sent out to *guard* the bridge. (To defend)
4. There was no one on *guard* when fire broke out. (On post)
5. Every dangerous tool on a machine must have a safety *guard* in front of it to protect the worker. (Any device, such as a screen or bar, to keep the worker's hand out of danger)

B

1. A southern mansion looks very attractive with its tall *columns* in front of the porch. (Tall, slender pillars)
2. There was nothing that morning in the *columns* of the newspaper about the accident the day before. (A narrow strip of printed material)
3. A single *column* of American troops came swinging through a narrow street in Paris. (Any arrangement of people in a row)
4. The *column* of figures was too long to be added up easily. (A vertical row of numbers)

You could tell very readily, from the context, that the word *guard* or the word *column* means something different in each sentence. If a reader is hurried or careless, he may not pay enough attention to the context to recognize the different meanings of common words.

EXERCISE 3

A. Here are several meanings of the word *rest*. Decide which meaning fits each numbered sentence below.

> **a.** to stop activity and relax
> **b.** to stand on or lie on
> **c.** remainder
> **d.** to lean
> **e.** a mark in music to show a pause

1. After she had been practicing for an hour her fingers were tired and she stopped to *rest* them.
2. He played the right notes, but the song sounded all wrong because he neglected to stop at the *rests*.
3. Johnny slouched in his seat and *rested* his head against the back of the chair.
4. The tall building *rests* on solid rock.
5. "I've done enough for today," he stated. "The *rest* will have to wait till tomorrow."

B. Do the same for the word *show*.

> **a.** to explain   **e.** to display
> **b.** to point out   **f.** a pretense
> **c.** to prove   **g.** a performance
> **d.** to direct

1. The stage *show* was thrilling and had a happy ending.
2. I'll *show* you that I really mean it.
3. Let me *show* you my collection of butterflies.
4. "Sally," said Mother, "please *show* Mr. Drake the way to the drug store."
5. "I shall now *show* you how to work this problem," said the teacher.
6. The guide *showed* the tourists the peak of Mount McKinley in the distance.
7. The little fellow made a *show* of being in pain, although he was not really hurt at all.

EXERCISE 4

There are two groups of sentences in this exercise. All the sentences contain the word *order*, although it has many meanings here. Look for a sentence in Group **B** that uses *order* in the same way as a sentence in Group **A**. Then be ready to explain the meaning in each pair of matched sentences.

A.
1. Upon the *order* to halt, the soldiers snapped to a stop.
2. The class was somewhat out of *order* until the teacher arrived.
3. The policeman *ordered* the suspect to empty his pockets.
4. The president of the firm left an *order* for three new machines.
5. All the books were arranged in perfect *order*.

B.
1. Mrs. Jones *ordered* a supply of meat from her butcher.
2. The excited mob came to *order* as soon as the police appeared.
3. The teacher *ordered* the class to prepare for the fire drill.
4. The books were scattered about without any appearance of *order*.
5. The gunner awaited the *order* to fire.

EXERCISE 5

There are six sentences under **A** below. Each contains the word *band*. There are four meanings for *band* under **B**. Choose the meaning that fits each sentence under **A**.

A.
1. A *band* of robbers surrounded the travelers in the desert.
2. The bride blushingly showed the gold *band* on her finger.
3. The box was securely bound with *bands* of copper.
4. The children's *band* played the National Anthem.
5. The road stretched across the fields like a *band* of ribbon.
6. There was a bright *band* of white around the blue vase.

B.
1. A group playing varied musical instruments
2. A small group of people joined together for any purpose
3. A thin, flat strip of metal or other material
4. A stripe painted around something

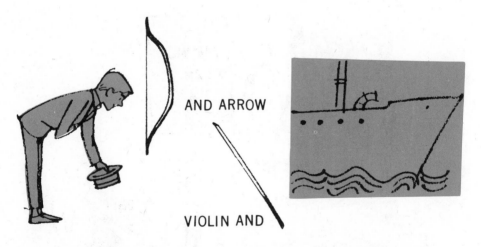

AND ARROW

VIOLIN AND

3. CONTEXT DECIDES ACCENT AND PRONUNCIATION

Many common words not only have different meanings; they also have different pronunciations. If you see the word *wind*, what do you think of? The north wind? Or do you think of the way you might wind a string around your finger? The only way to decide how it should be pronounced, of course, is to know the context in which it is used.

How many meanings do you know for the word *bow*? Are you sure you can pronounce it properly to fit each meaning? You will notice that the dictionary uses pronunciation marks to help you with each meaning. If you look up the word *desert* you will see that it may be pronounced DESert or deSERT, according to the way it is used. How is the word pronounced in these three sentences?

> The captain refused to desert his ship.
> The travelers were lost in the desert.
> The Sahara is a large desert in Africa.

EXERCISE 6

In each group of sentences below, the same word is used with different pronunciation and different meanings. For each sentence decide how the word is pronounced and which meaning makes sense.

A

a. bass (băs): a kind of fish
b. bass (bās): low or deep in sound

1. Joe has an excellent *bass* voice.
2. The big black *bass* put up a terrific struggle.
3. The *bass* section of the orchestra took their places at the left of the stage.

B

a. con'tents: what is contained
b. con tents': satisfies; pleases

1. They examined the *contents* of the box carefully.
2. My cat *contents* herself with napping before the fire.
3. We shook the can and guessed at its *contents*.

C

a. ob'ject: purpose; any article that can be seen or felt by touching
b. ob ject': to show strong disapproval

1. The *object* of the puzzle was to take the two rings apart.
2. Does anyone *object* to eating ice cream?
3. The *object* in Aladdin's hand was an old brass lamp.

67

D

a. re fuse': to deny a request; to reject an offer; to say "no"
b. ref'use: rubbish; useless waste

1. The prisoner *refused* to answer any questions.
2. *Refuse* from the kitchen should be placed in tightly covered cans.
3. Although the man seemed to be seriously ill, he *refused* any assistance.

E

a. con'duct: a way of acting; behavior
b. con duct': to guide or lead

1. Mr. Smith *conducts* his business very profitably.
2. The *conduct* of the boys on their excursion was admired by all the grown-ups.
3. A famous visitor from France will *conduct* the orchestra today.

4. HOW TO USE CONTEXT CLUES

You have seen how context decides which meaning of a word—and which pronunciation—fits a particular sentence. You have also seen how the context in a paragraph helps you decide on the meaning of a word. It is clearly important to keep the context in mind as you read along.

There is nothing unusually hard about doing this. In fact, it is what you have to do to make sense of your reading. Every word in a sentence contributes something to the meaning of the sentence. You build up the meaning word by word as you go along. You do not get the whole meaning until you come to the end of the sentence. For this reason, you must hold the whole meaning in mind from the start of the sentence to the end.

It is fortunate that you have learned to do this, because it helps you select the right meaning for words as you go along. Most of the time you select meanings almost automatically. There is a danger here, of course: the danger of taking the first meaning that comes into your head. You will avoid this danger if you insist that the sentence must make sense. If you feel doubtful about the meaning of words or of a sentence, you may have made a wrong choice.

If a sentence doesn't seem to make sense, do not assume that the writer made an error. Try to figure out the meaning. Try a different meaning for key words. And try to figure out the meaning of strange new words.

The context often gives you clues to the meaning of unfamiliar words. It will provide enough meaning to permit you to go on with your reading. Later you can check your meaning with the dictionary. In the rest of this chapter we shall learn several ways in which context helps give meaning to words.

Definition and explanation

Sometimes a writer takes the trouble to define or explain an uncommon word.

> The hardened remains of animals are called *fossils*.
> The *nucleus* is the center of the atom.

These are outright definitions. The writer tells you what fossils are and what a nucleus is.

Sometimes, instead of defining, the writer will restate the meaning in other words. In doing so he may use the word *or*, as in the following sentences.

> The savage believed that a *demon*, or evil spirit, lived in the mountains.
> These planes fly right into the *eye*, or center, of the hurricane.

The explanation can be given also without using the word *or*.

> We will meet you in the *foyer*, the entrance hall of the theater.
> My grandfather had a horse and *buggy*, a light four-wheeled carriage with a single seat.

There are other ways in which writers provide an explanation for the words they use. You will see them in the following sentences.

> *Arid* lands, because they are dry and barren, are useless for farming.

(The author has described the lands so that you will know what *arid* means.)

They ate in the *automat,* where they got sandwiches from little compartments that open when coins are put in the slots.

(Since you are told what happens at the automat, you can tell what kind of place it is.)

The guards were ordered to be *neutral;* that is, they were not to take sides in the fight.

(By telling you how the men were to act, the author is giving you the meaning of *neutral.* The words *that is* very often introduce an explanation. Watch for them.)

She was a *fastidious* young woman, who never permitted her fingers to remain soiled or her hair to be in disorder.

(By telling you about the young woman's habits, the author lets you guess the meaning of *fastidious.*)

EXERCISE 7

There are ten sentences below, each with a word in italics. After the sentences there is a list of ten meanings. Using context clues, select the meaning for each italicized word.

Directions: Number your paper 1 to 10. Write the letter that appears before the right meaning for each italicized word.

1. The little girl was so *inquisitive* that she opened the box as soon as her mother's back was turned.
2. *Disaster* struck the town when the hurricane arrived with violent winds that shattered everything in their path.
3. To be *diplomatic* you must appear to be friendly even if you do not feel like it.
4. The *preliminary* chapter was easier than the later ones.
5. The flashlight suddenly *illuminated* the cellar.
6. The boy leaped across the fallen branches with the *agility* of a deer.
7. The vase was so *fragile* that it shattered into a thousand pieces at the first touch.
8. The *fatal* accident occurred at a sharp bend in the road.
9. We had to work our arithmetic problems with great care to make sure that our answers were *precisely* correct.
10. The earth spins around its axis with one *rotation* every twenty-four hours.

THE MEANINGS (FOR EXERCISE 7)

a. first, or beginning
b. turn
c. an event that causes great destruction
d. quickness, nimbleness
e. curious
f. easily broken
g. exactly
h. bringing death
i. showing courtesy in relations with other people
j. lit up

When the clue is an opposite idea

Another way in which the author helps you with a new word is by giving an opposite idea in the same sentence or near by. There is often some **signal word**, such as "but," which shows that you may expect an opposite meaning. This will guide you toward the meaning of the new word. The following sentences will provide you with several examples.

1. The older folk were eager to go home, **but** the children were *reluctant* to leave the beach.

(Since you know what *eager* means, you can see that reluctant means *not* eager.)

2. Some of the homes in the village were clean, well-built cabins; **others** were nothing but *hovels*.

(What kind of homes are *hovels* if they are different from "clean, well-built cabins"?)

3. Our visitors were so quiet and well-mannered **that** we were ashamed of our *boisterous* behavior.

(Does the first part of the sentence help you to understand the meaning of *boisterous*, which is just the opposite?)

4. **Although** the mountain goat looks clumsy, he is remarkably *nimble*.

(*Although* is a clue that an opposite idea will be expressed. Which word is the opposite of *nimble*? Can you think of any other word that means the opposite of clumsy?)

EXERCISE 8

In each of these sentences the hard word is italicized. There is also a word or phrase that is opposite in meaning. Look for this opposite. It will be a word or phrase that you know. It will suggest the meaning of the italicized word.

1. The tiger ate *voraciously* until nothing was left of the carcass. Then he had no appetite for the next day.
2. He was usually friendly and peaceful; however, he could suddenly become very *aggressive*.
3. "These look like genuine rubies," said the jeweler. "But they are *synthetic*."
4. Everyone in the crowded stadium waited quietly while the pitcher prepared to throw the ball, but the moment the ball was hit the crowd exploded into a *tumult*.
5. The prisoner did not give the impression of honesty, but the jury finally became certain of his *veracity*.
6. In some countries a great many people are *illiterate*, but much is being done to teach them to read and write.
7. The police do not permit people to gather at the scene of an accident. Their first duty is to *disperse* them.
8. The old lady enjoyed the company of children if they were neat and clean, but she *abhorred* them if they were dirty.

MEANING THROUGH WORD PARTS

4

No matter how well you can grasp the thought of sentences and paragraphs, you will sometimes find your reading blocked by a single word. It may be a word you have never seen or heard before. It may even look slightly familiar and yet have no meaning for you.

Suppose you are reading about a painting, and you meet this sentence:

They thought the painting was <u>incomparable</u>.

What does this mean? Does it mean the painting was bad, or crowded, or cheap? Because of one word, you fail to get the meaning of the sentence. Without this sentence the paragraph no longer makes sense, and even the next paragraph may be hard to understand.

When something like this happens, what can you do? You might give up completely and go on to something else. This is not a very practical thing to do, because as you go along in your reading you are going to meet more and more unfamiliar words. If you skip them all you won't get much out of your reading and study.

The best thing to do, of course, is to go to a dictionary. But if you are reading in some place where a dictionary is not at hand, you can make a note of the word and look it up later. Meantime you still want to get on with your reading. Is there anything you can do by yourself to work out the meaning of the unfamiliar word?

APPEAR   DISAPPEAR   REAPPEAR

Fortunately there are two things you can do. Either of them may give you enough meaning for a word so that you can go on with your reading. First, as you know, you can find clues to the meaning of a word from its context; that is, from the other words with which it is used. Second, you can find clues to meaning in the word itself. This chapter will deal with the clues to meaning that you can find in words themselves.

1. RECOGNIZING THE ROOT WORD

One way to understand a new word is to recognize in it a word you already know. In the word *incomparable* you can see the word *compare*. You will notice that *in* has been added at the beginning, and *able* has been added at the end. Together those three parts simply mean "not-compare-can be." In *sensible* English the whole word means "can not be compared." Therefore the whole sentence can now be understood. "They thought the painting was so good that *it could not be compared* to any other."

If you have the skill to take words apart, and if you know the meaning of the parts, a great many new words will become clear to you with hardly any effort. This skill requires you to recognize the **structure** of words, that is, to see how they are constructed or built up.

You will notice that many words which appear to be rather long are really short words with syllables added to them. Sometimes there is a **suffix,** or an ending part, as in these words:

attend + ance = *attend*ance
person + al + ity = *person*ality
arrange + ment = *arrange*ment
fool + ish + ness = *foolish*ness

Sometimes a **prefix,** or a beginning part, has been placed before a simple word:

dis + appear = dis*appear*   trans + plant = trans*plant*
in + come = in*come*   un + happy = un*happy*

75

Sometimes parts have been placed both before and after the word:

trans*continent*al	un*fashion*able
dis*agree*ment	un*change*able

The original, shorter word, before other parts have been added, is called the **base word,** or **root word,** or just **root.**

Altogether there are more than 600,000 words in the English language. One reason for that vast number is that we make many, many new words by adding parts to short, familiar words.

Take the simple word *act,* for example. How many words do you think you can make from it? The list below is just a start. With this beginning, you could go to the dictionary yourself and make the list grow. If you do this, you could also take time to find out what the new words mean.

act	actor	active	action	
react	reactor		reaction	reactionary
		inactive	inaction	

You can see that some of these words are made by adding a prefix. Others are made by adding a suffix. Some words are made by adding both a prefix and a suffix. It will help you to discover the meaning of long words more easily if you learn to look first for the root of each word.

EXERCISE 1

Directions: On your paper number a column from 1 to 20. Write the root word that you find in each of the words below.

1. irregularity	11. statehood
2. uncertainty	12. foreseeable
3. needless	13. fortify
4. improperly	14. submarine
5. unwisely	15. tirelessly
6. unattractive	16. infielder
7. derailment	17. vaporize
8. misstatement	18. transplantation
9. information	19. unreasonable
10. impression	20. unplanned

HAPPY ✚ NESS ═ HAPPINESS

MERRY ✚ LY ═ MERRILY

THROB ✚ ING ═ THROBBING

2. CHANGES IN SPELLING

It is not always easy to recognize the root word, because the spelling is sometimes changed when an ending is added. For instance, when we *admit* a mistake, we are making an *admission*. A person who achieves *fame* has become *famous*. When we hear something *explode* we hear an *explosion*. We change *deceive* to *deception; miracle* to *miraculous*.

Do you think you could recognize that the root word in *destructive* is *destroy?* Or that the root in *mischievous* is *mischief?* Those spelling changes for adding a suffix are difficult. It is much easier to see that *daring* contains the root *dare,* or that *funnier* contains the root *fun.*

The following review will show some of the easier spelling changes when suffixes are added.

1. When a suffix is added to a word ending in *y* with a consonant before it, the *y* is changed to *i.*

merry + ly = merrily	heavy + est = heaviest
happy + ness = happiness	pity + able = pitiable

If the suffix is *ing,* the *y* does not change. We do not write *worriing,* but *worrying,* because two *i*'s together would be confusing.

2. Some one-syllable words end in a consonant that is preceded by one vowel: *plan, throb.* When a suffix beginning with a vowel is added, the consonant is doubled.

grin + ed = grinned	hop + ing = hopping
plan + ed = planned	bag + age = baggage
throb + ing = throbbing	

3. When a suffix beginning with a vowel is added to a word ending in *e*, the *e* is dropped.

hope + ing = hoping   ice + y = icy

Sometimes when a suffix is added there is really no change in spelling, yet the appearance of the word is changed considerably. Don't be misled. Notice the words below.

actual + ly = actua*lly*   real + ly = rea*lly*
thin + ness = thin*ness*   clean + ness = clean*ness*

EXERCISE 2

Write the numbers 1 to 10 on your paper. Add the suffix given, make the spelling change if one is needed, and write the new word alongside the proper number.

1. hot + er
2. beauty + ful
3. library + an
4. write + ing
5. cruel + ly
6. imagine + ary
7. style + ish
8. courage + ous
9. dim + er
10. trap + ing

EXERCISE 3

Now you are being asked to do something that is important for you as a reader. You are going to pick out the root word from longer words. Notice where the spelling has been changed.

Directions: Write the numbers 1 to 20 on your paper. Find the root in each word listed below, and write that root alongside the proper number. Remember that the root must be spelled correctly as a real word.

1. rearranging
2. defacing
3. confusion
4. defiant
5. formation
6. carrier
7. injury
8. evaporate
9. mannish
10. mentally
11. indefensible
12. historical
13. mysterious
14. immovable
15. displeasure
16. nationality
17. international
18. removable
19. fearless
20. observation

More Difficult Changes

As you have seen, there are some words that go through unusual spelling changes when they add a suffix. Here are some examples. Give them your careful thought. Refer to them again as you do Exercise 4.

a. admit   + ion *changes to* admiss   + ion = admission
b. receive   + ion *changes to* recept   + ion = reception
c. decide   + ion *changes to* decis   + ion = decision
d. reduce   + ion *changes to* reduct   + ion = reduction
e. miracle   + ous *changes to* miracul + ous = miraculous
f. expel   + ion *changes to* expuls   + ion = expulsion
g. piano   + ist *changes to* pian   + ist = pianist
h. grammar + ical *changes to* grammat + ical = grammatical
i. science + ific *changes to* scient   + ific = scientific

EXERCISE 4

Directions: Study the changes shown above. Add the suffix to each word as shown below. Write the new word and number it.

1. permit + ion	10. produce + ion
2. remit + ion	11. induce + ion
3. commit + ion	12. fable + ous
4. deceive + ion	13. particle + ar
5. perceive + ion	14. compel + ion
6. describe + ion	15. explain + ation
7. explode + ive	16. deep + th
8. offend + ive	17. peace + ify
9. respond + ive	18. explode + ion

3. THE WORK DONE BY SUFFIXES

There are certain suffixes that are used to make nouns. Others are used just to make adjectives or verbs. These suffixes add little meaning to the base word, or root. Their purpose is to let us use the word in a different way. If you know these part-of-speech suffixes you can separate them easily from a long, unfamiliar word and get at the root word.

(If you are not sure of nouns, adjectives, and verbs, you may wish to review them before going on in this chapter.)

Noun suffixes

The suffixes *-er, -ness, -ment, -ity, -ation* (also *-tion* and *ion*), are the common ones. They add little meaning to a word; they just permit us to use the word as a noun. We know how a man is acting when we say he *argues*. When we give a name to that action we call it his *argument*. Here are several other such changes.

$$Verb \ + suffix = noun$$
advance + ment = advancement
construct + ion = construction
consider + ation = consideration

We may say that a man is *honest*, or we may speak of a man's *honesty*.

$$Adjective + suffix = noun$$
honest + y = honesty
sane + ity = sanity
weak + ness = weakness

Adjective suffixes

The suffixes *-ive, -al,* and *-ous* are used to make adjectives out of nouns or verbs.

$$Noun \ + suffix = adjective$$
courage + ous = courageous
nation + al = national

$$Verb \ + suffix = adjective$$
create + ive = creative
divide + ive = divisive

Now let us see just how such changes are used in actual sentences.

a. When you *pay* the grocer you are making *pay*MENT to him.
b. One who *considers* the feelings of others is *consider*ATE.
c. A *friend* acts in a *friend*LY manner.
d. If he is very *kind* he always shows *kind*NESS.
e. Actors who *perform* are giving a *perform*ANCE.
f. A *decorat*ION is pinned on a soldier when the general *decorates* him.
g. We may say that a man *explores* new territory, or he makes an *explor*ATION.

The noun suffixes you have just studied give no clue to the meaning of the words. However, by dropping them off, you can find the root words, whose meanings we often know.

EXERCISE 5

In each **a** sentence below, the simple form of a word appears in italics. In each **b** sentence there is a blank into which another form of the word will fit.

Directions: Number your paper 1–10. Select the right suffix, add it to the word, and write the new word. Make every spelling change that is required.

SUFFIXES: -ion   -ous   -ation   -ence   -dom   -ly

1. **a.** You will have to *decide* between these two pictures.
   b. What is your _____?
2. **a.** The immediate cure was a *miracle*.
   b. Everybody kept saying that it was _____.
3. **a.** It is easy for Bobby to *imagine* that a fairy brought him a Christmas present.
   b. He has a strong _____.
4. **a.** We should never *tempt* anyone.
   b. _____ is hard to resist.
5. **a.** Sometimes it is a waste of time to *explain* a mistake.
   b. Very few people care to listen to an _____.
6. **a.** Solomon was a *wise* man.
   b. The Bible contains many stories about his _____.
7. **a.** The dynamite *exploded* with a noise like thunder.
   b. The _____ was heard miles away.
8. **a.** The boy did not *confide* in his mother.
   b. He did not have enough _____ in her.
9. **a.** Jimmy felt lonesome without *friends*.
   b. But the others did not feel _____ toward him.
10. **a.** Arthur thought he could *deceive* his parents about his marks.
    b. But his _____ was soon discovered.

EXERCISE 6

In the words on the next page, every root went through an unusual spelling change when a suffix was added. Now see if you can recognize the original spelling of each root.

Directions: Number your paper 1 to 20 and write the root words alongside the proper numbers. Be sure to spell each root word correctly. If you are not sure of the spelling or meaning, look it up in a dictionary.

1.	admission	11.	permission
2.	reception	12.	scientific
3.	description	13.	fabulous
4.	pianist	14.	deception
5.	explanation	15.	explosion
6.	depth	16.	offensive
7.	grammatical	17.	production
8.	miraculous	18.	expulsion
9.	decision	19.	particular
10.	reduction	20.	pacify

4. SUFFIXES THAT ADD MEANING

In Section 3 you met suffixes that add little meaning to words. They are used chiefly to change a word into another part of speech. When this happens, the meaning of the root word carries over into the new word.

Now we come to suffixes that do add meaning to root words. A few will be presented here; you will meet others as you go along through school. Perhaps you will discover some suffixes by yourself. If you do, you should go to a good dictionary to find out their meanings. You will discover that many of them have several different meanings. Those that you will study here have only one meaning.

Word suffixes

There are several short words that are used as suffixes. Since you know their meanings, you can understand them easily in the words in which they appear.

-less = lacking or without, as in *hopeless*
-most = the most, as in *northernmost*
-able = able to or able to be, as in *payable*
-like = similar to, as in *childlike*
-ward = in the direction of, as in *eastward*

Suffixes added to nouns

Several noun suffixes have the meaning of "one who," as in *actor*, "one who acts." This particular suffix, -or, may also mean "a thing that," as in *elevator*, "a thing that elevates or lifts." The following noun suffixes usually refer to people.

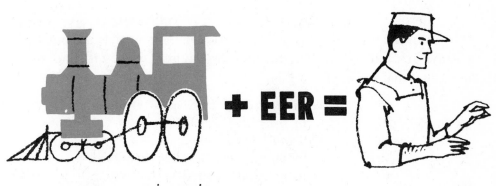

-eer   as in *engineer*
-ess   as in *waitress*
-ier   as in *furrier*
-ist   as in *chemist*

There are other noun suffixes, each with a different meaning. You will find them in hundreds of English words.

-archy = ruling, or that which is ruled: *monarchy*
-cide = killer or killing: *germicide; insecticide*
-graph = something written: *autograph*
-gram = something written or drawn: *cablegram*
-itis   = inflammation: *tonsilitis*
-meter = a device for measuring: *speedometer*
-ology = a branch of learning: *geology*

Adjective suffixes

There are several adjective suffixes that mean "full of" or "abounding in." The two most frequently used are:

-ous, as in *humorous*
-ful, as in *careful*

No English words end in *full*. The suffix has only one *l*: *ful*, as in the word *spoonful*.

There is another group of adjective suffixes that are closely related in meaning. It is hard to pin down their meanings, but they all say "related to, tending to, like, or having." You will find them in a great many words.

-ive	as in *attractive:* tending to attract
-ish	as in *waspish:* like a wasp
-ious	as in *ambitious:* having ambition
-ative	as in *informative:* tending to inform
-al	as in *national:* related to the nation

EXERCISE 7

Directions: Number your paper 1 to 13. Write alongside each number the suffix that matches the meaning given in the column at the left. For one of the meanings there will be four suffixes, therefore four answers.

1. one who, or a thing that	-less
2. a branch of learning	-ward
3. able to, or able to be	-or
4. a device for measuring	-archy
5. one who	-ology
6. in the direction of	-most
7. similar to	-able
8. the most	-ist
9. inflammation	-gram
10. lacking, without	-like
11. a ruling, or thing ruled	-cide
12. something written or drawn	-eer
13. a killing or killer	-itis
	-ess
	-meter
	-ier

5. HOW TO USE YOUR KNOWLEDGE OF SUFFIXES AND ROOT WORDS

There are many new words that you will now be able to understand by putting together the meaning of the root word and the suffix. For example, you know what a *thermometer* looks like, but you get the meaning of the word itself from its parts: *thermo* (heat) and *meter* (measure). A thermometer is "something that is used to measure heat."

When a new word is in a sentence, the surrounding words also help you to turn the exact meaning into a common-sense meaning. Here is an example.

He reached the *uppermost* rung of the ladder.

Uppermost is composed of *upper* and *most*, or the *most upper*. The sentence means "He reached the most upper rung." Turning this into a common-sense definition, we would say, "He reached the *top* rung."

Let us examine a few more new words that we can now explain. We shall begin with the sentences and explain the words later.

1. The singer brought her own *accompanist* to the theater.
2. He sent his wife a *radiogram* from the ship at sea.
3. The newspaper reported an *infanticide* in the neighboring town.
4. After hoisting sail the schooner turned *seaward*.
5. The teacher offered some *constructive* ideas for the trip her students were going to take.
6. He was foolish in displaying a *contemptuous* attitude toward the new boy's suggestions.
7. There was much *sociability* after the meeting.
8. The events in the story were all thrilling but the story had no *continuity*.
9. The minister's sermon was especially *inspirational* last week.
10. The *observance* of Thanksgiving Day is proclaimed by the President every year.

THE DEFINITION

1. a. *accompanist* = accompany + ist = accompany + one who
   b. The singer brought the *one who accompanies* for her.

85

2. **a.** *radiogram* = radio + gram = radio + something written
   b. He sent his wife a *message through the radio.*

3. **a.** *infanticide* = infant + cide = infant + killing
   b. The newspaper reported the *killing of an infant* in the neighboring town.

4. **a.** *seaward* = sea + ward = sea + in the direction of
   b. The schooner turned *toward the sea.*

5. **a.** *constructive* = construct + ive = adjective form of *construct*
   b. The teacher offered some ideas that would *build up* or *help* the students on their trip.

6. **a.** *contemptuous* = contempt + ous = contempt + full of
   b. He was foolish in displaying an attitude *that showed contempt.*

7. **a.** *sociability* = sociable + ity
   b. (Give the word in a sentence.)

8. **a.** *continuity* = continue + ity
   b. (Give the word in a sentence.)

9. **a.** *inspirational* (explain its parts)
   b. (Give the word in a sentence.)

10. **a.** *observance* (explain its parts)
    b. (Give the word in a sentence.)

6. WHAT DO PREFIXES MEAN?

You have seen that suffixes such as *-ment* and *-ness* add little or no meaning to a word. Many prefixes, by contrast, have more than one meaning. And in many words the prefix adds meaning to the root word. It is important, therefore, to know what these prefix meanings are. Knowing them will help you unlock the meaning of many unfamiliar words.

There are at least 68 common prefixes that appear frequently in English words. We shall meet only a few of them here, and we shall begin with those that have just one meaning. Because they have only one meaning, you can depend upon them whenever you meet them.

No doubt you often read words with these prefixes without giving any thought to the exact meaning of the prefixes. As you study them separately, their meaning will become clear.

auto = self or self-propelled, as in *automatic*
bio = life, as in *biology*
micro = small, as in *microfilm*
mono = one or alone, as in *monotone*
mal = bad, as in *maltreat*
mis = wrong, as in *misspell*
non = not, as in *nonsense*

EXERCISE 8

From what you know of word parts, can you figure out a meaning for each of the following words?

1. autograph
2. monogram
3. monologist
4. micrometer
5. biology
6. biography
7. monotonous
8. misstatement
9. malodorous
10. nonexistent

Prefixes with more than one meaning

Now we come to prefixes that have more than one meaning. The prefix *in-*, for example, sometimes means *in* and sometimes means *not*. When you meet an unfamiliar word beginning with *in-*, how can you tell which meaning the prefix has? Sometimes you cannot tell. But usually the meaning of the root word will give you a clue, as will the rest of the sentence.

Notice the use of *inaccessible* in this sentence: "Because of heavy snows and poor roads the mountain park is *inaccessible* in winter." You would know that heavy snows and poor roads might not permit travel. The suffix *-ible* means "able to be." You might then decide that heavy snows and poor roads made the mountain park "not able to be traveled." You would be right. In this word *in-* means "not." Do you know what *access* means?

The prefix *in-* changes to *ir-* before words beginning with *r*: *irresponsible*. It changes to *il-* before *l*: *illegal*; and to *im-* before *m* and *p*: *immature, impossible. Il-, ir-*, and *im-* all have the same meaning.

in-
ir-   1. *not*, as in *injustice, irresponsible, illegal*, and *impossible*
il-   2. *in*, as in *ingrown, impress*
im-

un-   1. *opposite of*, as in *untie*
           2. *not*, as in *unimportant*

Another very useful prefix is *un-*. Basically it means "the opposite of." Thus "to untie" is the opposite of "to tie." But *un-* may also mean "not," as in *unimportant*, "not important." With *un-*, try the meaning "opposite of" first. If that doesn't make sense, try "not." What does it mean in *unseat*? In *unnecessary*? Indeed, this is the way to try all of the following prefixes that have more than one meaning:

anti- 1. against, hostile to, as in *antislavery*
        2. preventing or curing, as in *antifreeze, antitoxin*
dis-   1. the opposite of, as in *disarm*
        2. not, as in *discourteous*
pre- earlier in time, as in *preview*
pro- favoring, as in *prolabor, pro-American*
re-   1. back or away, as in *repay, remove*
        2. again, as in *reprint*

EXERCISE 9

A. Find one meaning for each of the following words by using the clue in the prefix. Use this form on your paper:

replace: to place back (re = back)

1. prearrange	11. distrust
2. immodest	12. disarm
3. illegible	13. dishonorable
4. improper	14. preview
5. inborn	15. prehistoric
6. unborn	16. re-enter
7. intake	17. reform
8. antiknock	18. retrace
9. antirust	19. unbind
10. antiwar	20. uncomfortable

B. Now try your skill with some longer words. Look first for the root, or base word, then the prefix, and finally the suffix. Put together all of the knowledge you have gained in this chapter about word parts. Use this form on your paper:

Word	*Prefix*	*Suffix*	*Root*
incomprehensible	in	ible	comprehend

Meaning: not able to be comprehended

1. immeasurable	6. restatement
2. uncontrollable	7. unpleasantness
3. disadvantageous	8. unattractive
4. disagreeable	9. reformation
5. nonresidential	10. illegality

7. STEMS FROM FOREIGN WORDS

When you know the meaning of a word at once by recognizing the familiar root, prefix, and suffix, you have learned the first method of word attack. But you will find many words which are built from roots that are not true words. Let us call them **stems** instead of roots. Suppose we take the word *incredible*. You recognize immediately the prefix *in-* and the suffix *-ible*. But *cred* is not an actual word. It is a "word part" that comes from another language. In Latin *cred* means belief. You can see now that if something is incredible, it is something which cannot be believed.

This does not mean that you must learn foreign languages to recognize stems. You will find that many of our English words come from just a few stems. Therefore when you learn one of them, you will soon recognize many related words. The *cred* family, for instance, includes such familiar words as *credit, creed, credentials.*

Can you see how they are related?

When you know that *aud* means *hear,* can you make up your own definition for the words in italics?

> Those who came to hear the address were a fine *audience.*
> They heard the address in the *auditorium.*
> She spoke so softly that her voice was barely *audible.*

Most of the stems are borrowed from the early Greek and Latin languages. A few of them are particularly important for us to know, and we can learn them quickly without having to study either Latin or Greek.

The stem *port* comes from Latin and means "to carry." Thus a *portable* radio is one that can be carried. Your *deportment* has something to do with the way you carry yourself.

EXERCISE 10

A. Use your knowledge of the stem *port* to answer the following questions.

1. A criminal who has entered this country illegally may be *deported.* What will happen to him?
2. A committee *reports* its work to the class meeting. The prefix *re-* here means "back." What does the committee do?
3. There are certain products that we do not grow in the United States. We must *import* them from abroad. What do we do with them?

B. The stem *mono* means *one*. When an actor gives a monologue, he alone (one) is talking.

1. *Monotone* means *one tone*. Why would a *monotonous* speech be boring or tiresome?
2. The owner of the invention would not take any partners into his business. He wanted it to remain a *monopoly*. How many people owned that business?
3. Many years ago, if a patient was nearsighted only in one eye the oculist (eye doctor) would fit him with a *monocle*. How many lenses does a monocle have?
4. The early airplanes had two levels of wings. All the airplanes of today are *monoplanes*. What is a monoplane?

8. ONE WORD CAN DO THE WORK OF MANY

Read these two sentences and tell which sounds better.

a. He is a *man who carries back news* for the *Evening Gazette*.
b. He is a *reporter* for the *Evening Gazette*.

Surely you can see how much better it is to use only one word if it can do the work of many. That is the advantage of adding suffixes and prefixes to simple words.

EXERCISE 11

In this chapter you met many of these longer words. This is your chance to see if you can use them. The sentences below are in pairs. The first in the pair uses a long phrase. The second has a blank where *one word* that can take the place of that phrase belongs.

Directions: Copy each **b** sentence. Insert one word in the space left blank. Do not write in this book.

1. **a.** The driver committed an act which was *not legal* when he passed the red light.
   b. The driver committed an _____ act when he passed the red light.
2. **a.** The Cave Dwellers were groups of primitive people who lived in the days *before the beginning of history.*
   b. The Cave Dwellers were groups of primitive people who lived in _____ days.

3. a. When he realized the trouble he caused he was a boy *full of sorrow.*

   b. When he realized the trouble he caused he was a _____ boy.

4. a. If you wish to have friends you must be a person *who considers other people.*

   b. If you wish to have friends you must be _____.

5. a. His knowledge of science was very much *like a miracle.*

   b. His knowledge of science was _____.

6. a. It is only after you prove *you are sincere* that you will always be trusted.

   b. It is only after you prove your _____ that you will always be trusted.

7. a. The boy practiced for weeks before he was ready to give his *talking act by himself.*

   b. The boy practiced for weeks before he was ready to give his _____.

8. a. The audience soon became tired of the speaker because his voice seemed to be *all on one tone.*

   b. The speech at the club was _____.

9. a. The partners finally found a business *that would bring in profits.*

   b. The partners finally found a _____ business.

10. a. The story of her adventure was so strange that it *could not be believed.*

    b. The story of her adventure was so strange that it seemed _____.

To Find the Meaning of a Word from Its Parts:

1. Look for a familiar root word.
2. If there is no root word, look for a stem.
3. Note spelling changes in root or stem.
4. Find the prefixes and suffixes.
5. Rearrange the meanings of prefix + root + suffix to make sense.
6. Restate the meaning of the word to fit the rest of the sentence.

STREAMLINED READING

5

If you were to ask a good automobile driver, "What is your driving speed?" he could not give you an exact answer. He would probably say, "Well, that depends. It depends on where I happen to be and on my reason for driving."

In a crowded city he drives slowly. On a narrow and twisting road he drives carefully. On a super-highway he drives as fast as the law allows. If he wishes to enjoy the scenery, he ambles along and even stops occasionally. If he wants to get to a distant city before night, he will drive fast and pay not the slightest attention to the beautiful views.

Reading is somewhat like driving. When you are reading a page that is crowded with thoughts, and when it is your purpose to understand them or study them, you will have to read slowly and carefully. If the material is easy, you can read it faster. But if you are looking only for some special fact and the rest of the content is of no value to you, then you should read at top speed. You are **skimming** when you permit your eyes to move rapidly over the page without actually reading all the words.

There are several kinds of skimming because there are several reasons for skimming. All skimming is fast, but one kind is extremely rapid. Another kind may require moderately rapid reading.

1. SKIMMING THROUGH A LIST

You can skim most rapidly when you are looking for one name or word in a list. Your eyes do not even have to move across the line from left to right as they do in ordinary reading. They may glance up and down the page or skip from place to place. Since your purpose here is to spot a certain word or term, all that is necessary is to keep that term in mind as you glance quickly over the list.

EXERCISE 1

Try your skill in this kind of skimming by using the telephone index below. Answer the questions that follow it as fast as you can. Your teacher will give you the signal to begin each question. Raise your hand as soon as you find the answer.

TELEPHONE DIRECTORY

Hill, Albert 58 Maple St ....HOward 6-2218
Hill, Bertram A 10 Fourth Ave ....ATlantic 6-2387
Hill, Charles 125 Court St ....HOward 6-3259
Hill, William 101 Broadway ....NEwton 9-3009
Hillcrest Laundry 51 State St ....WAyside 2-9000
Hillside Employment Agency 156 State St ....WAyside 2-3814
Hillside Fur Co 472 Market St ....TOwer 3-4328
Hilltop Restaurant 7 Woodlawn Rd ....NEwton 9-1005
Hilton, Anne 259 Cherry St ....HOward 6-3008
Hilton, Louis 34 Beech St ....HOward 6-4111
Himber, Paul 148 Conway St ....NEwton 9-3246
Himrod Auto Sales Co 40 Central Ave ....WAyside 2-5050
Hinderman, Joseph 136 Oak St ....HOward 6-2007
Hines, Edward 32 Meeker St ....NEwton 9-0315
Hines, Ethel 400 Carter Rd ....TOwer 3-5862
Hines, Stewart, MD 72 Lincoln St ....HOward 6-8886
Holmes, J E 29 Walnut St ....NEwton 9-1651
Home Cleaning Co 481 Market St ....TOwer 3-7100

1. How many people named Hill are listed?
2. What is the address of the Himrod Auto Sales Company?
3. Which Hines is listed first?
4. Which Hilton lives on Cherry Street?
5. What is the name of an employment agency?
6. Where is the Hilltop Restaurant?
7. What is Paul Himber's phone number?
8. Which Hines is a doctor?
9. Are there business places on Market Street?
10. On which street would you find a laundry?

EXERCISE 2

You will see that the chart below contains more information than a telephone directory does. Your eyes will have to skip over many more terms to find the one you want.

Directions: On signal from your teacher, read the first question at the top of page 96. Raise your hand as soon as you have the answer. Your teacher will give you the signal for each of the other questions.

COUNTRY	LOCATION	AREA—SQ. MI.	POPULATION	CAPITAL
Philippines, Republic of	Pacific Ocean	115,758	24,718,000	Quezon City
Poland	Europe	120,340	29,257,000	Warsaw
Portugal	Europe	35,400	9,052,000	Lisbon
Romania	Europe	91,500	18,256,000	Bucharest
Saudi Arabia	Asia	870,000	6,500,000	Mecca and Riyadh
Spain	Europe	195,500	29,203,000	Madrid
Sudan	Africa	967,500	10,000,000	Khartoum
Sweden	Europe	173,378	7,341,000	Stockholm
Switzerland	Europe	15,900	5,023,000	Berne
Thailand	Asia	200,000	21,474,000	Bangkok
Tunisia	Africa	48,313	3,783,000	Tunis
Turkey	Asia	296,500	26,880,000	Ankara
Union of So. Africa	Africa	472,500	14,673,000	{ Pretoria, Capetown
U. S. S. R.	Eurasia	4,877,600	208,826,000	Moscow
United Kingdom	Europe	94,279	51,985,000	London
United States	N. America	3,022,387	179,323,000	Washington, D.C.
Uruguay	S. America	72,100	2,615,000	Montevideo

QUESTIONS
1. What is the capital of Turkey?
2. Which country shown in the chart has the smallest population?
3. What is given as the population of U.S.S.R.?
4. Which country has an area of less than 16,000 sq. miles?
5. Tunis is the capital of which country?
6. What location is given for the Philippines?
7. Which country shown in the chart has the third largest area?
8. Quezon City is the capital of which country?
9. Which country shown in the chart has the largest population?
10. The chart is not complete. What letters of the alphabet are represented?

EXERCISE 3

The following is a schedule of ships arriving at or leaving the harbor of New York City during one week. To answer the questions you may have to keep two or three words in mind as you skim over the schedule. Work for speed!

Directions: Number your paper 1–8. Read the question, and find the answer in the following schedule and write it down. Then go to the next question.

PASSENGER SHIPS ARRIVING — NEW YORK

Ship	Line	From	Time	Pier
SUN., MON. No ships due				
TUES., SEPT. 1				
Queen Mary	Cunard	Southampton	5:00 P.M.	90
Bremen	North German	Southampton	9:00 A.M.	88
Santa Luisa	Grace	Cristobal	8:00 A.M.	57
WED., SEPT. 2				
Independence	Amer. Export	Mediterranean	8:30 A.M.	84
THURS., SEPT. 3				
Santa Paula	Grace	Caribbean	9:00 A.M.	57
Santa Sofia	Grace	Caribbean	8:00 A.M.	58
FRI., SEPT. 4				
Queen of Bermuda	Furness	Bermuda	10:00 A.M.	95
SAT., SEPT. 5				
Parthia	Cunard	Liverpool	9:00 A.M.	92

PASSENGER SHIPS LEAVING — NEW YORK

Ship	Line	To	Time	Pier
SUN., MON. No ships scheduled				
TUES., SEPT. 1 Cristobal	Panama	Cristobal	4:00 P.M.	64
WED., SEPT. 2 Queen Mary	Cunard	Southampton	5:30 P.M.	90
THURS., SEPT. 3 Bremen Britannia	North German Cunard	Southampton Liverpool	11:00 P.M. 10:30 P.M.	88 92
FRI., SEPT. 4 Independence Santa Sofia	Amer. Export Grace	Mediterranean Caribbean	Noon 11:00 A.M.	84 58
SAT., SEPT. 5 Queen of Bermuda	Furness	Bermuda	3:00 P.M.	95

QUESTIONS

1. How many ships are scheduled to leave New York on Friday?
2. At what time is an American Export ship due to arrive?
3. How long will the *Queen Mary* be in port?
4. To which pier should you go to see a friend off on a trip to Bermuda?
5. When would you go to meet a friend arriving on the *Santa Luisa*?
6. Where is the *Parthia* coming from?
7. Which of the Grace Line ships is due to arrive on Sept. 3?
8. How many ships are due to arrive Tuesday morning?

Groups of Words

With constant practice you can develop speed in skimming over charts, tables, and schedules. Glancing rapidly over lists of single words will also help you to develop real speed in skimming. There will be times, however, when your eyes will have to skip over groups of words to find the one you want. If the list does not have an alphabetical arrangement, your rate of skimming will have to be slower.

EXERCISE 4

In this exercise you are to skim through a group of titles to find those in which a word appears. The six words you are to hunt for are *Lincoln, America, children, gold, world, travel.*

Directions: Arrange a form like the following. Take one word at a time. Skim all the titles. In the squares on your form, write the numbers of the titles in which you found the word. The first has been done for you. Do not write in this book.

Lincoln	1	8	10	
America				
children				
gold				
world				
travel				

1. The Boyhood of Abraham Lincoln
2. America and Her People
3. The World We Live In
4. How to Travel on a Budget
5. The Gold Bug
6. All God's Children
7. We Dug for Gold in Alaska
8. Lincoln, the Humorist
9. Around the World by Jet
10. The Lincoln Memorial
11. Games for Young Children
12. The Geography of North America
13. Early Tales of Space Travel
14. Wonders of the Ancient World
15. The Gold Rush Days
16. Travel by Trailer
17. This Is Our America
18. Children of the Jungle

2. SKIMMING THROUGH CONTENT

The first kind of skimming was the fastest kind. You were merely looking down a list for a word, or a name, or a number. That usually takes very little time.

But now we come to another kind of skimming. This is still rapid, but not quite as rapid as the other. You will have to skim through sentences or paragraphs, not just through a list.

If skimming is to be a real time-saver in helping you with your studies, you will have to learn to skim over large areas of information to find the answer to your question. This requires more skill than glancing up and down a list of words or names. The first thing to do is to select a **key word or phrase** in the question. Then you must skim rapidly over the selection to find it. Your eyes should glide very quickly along each line because not all of the material is important to you. As soon as you find the key word, you will slow down and read carefully to find your information.

EXERCISE 5

In this exercise, the key word in each question has been selected for you. It is italicized. Use it as your guide in skimming rapidly over the sentences to find the answers.

Directions: Number your paper 1–10. Take one question at a time. Look for the answer in the sentences below. Then write only the letter that matches the sentence.

QUESTIONS

1. What is one of the most *historic* homes?
2. Who was an unusual *pirate*?
3. Where were *shells* collected?
4. What *invention* pleases everybody?
5. Which word tells what the *hawk* did?
6. Which word is used to describe *blossoms*?
7. Which *fossils* are the most famous?
8. Where is the largest *telescope*?
9. What has a new *look*?
10. About whom were *tall tales* told?

THE SENTENCES

a. With Alaska and Hawaii becoming states, the American flag has a new look.
b. Famous legends of the West include the tall tales about Davy Crockett.
c. The Chinese were skilled at painting delicate blossoms on their pottery.
d. Mt. Vernon, the home of George Washington, is probably the most famous historic home in America.
e. The world's largest telescope is said to be at Mt. Palomar, in California.

f. When she saw that the hawk had swooped down on her cat, Nancy screamed in fright.

g. While the grown-ups gossiped near the fire, the boys collected shells along the beach.

h. The most famous fossils of all are probably those of the dinosaurs.

i. One of the most colorful and unusual of all the famous pirates was the one named Jean La Fitte.

j. Fireworks are one of the few inventions of mankind which seem to give pleasure to everybody.

EXERCISE 6

The next exercise will give you practice in skimming over a larger area for more than one key word. The information is taken from a program of museum exhibits. The key words have been selected for you. They are the words that appear in italics in the questions. Write the answers on your paper.

QUESTIONS

1. Which museum shows *motion picture programs* every Saturday?
2. Which museum is located at *Fifth Avenue and 103 Street*?
3. Which museum has a *junior museum* and *gallery talks* for *children*?
4. Which museum is now in the *RCA Building* in *Rockefeller Center*?
5. In which museum were *oil paintings* of *New York* on exhibit?
6. To which museum would you go if you had questions about *man-made moons* and *ancient beliefs*?
7. Which museum has *free admission* but is closed on *holidays*?
8. Which museum has a *daily* showing of films?

Museum of the City of New York

Exhibits: *Perennial Pygmalion*, famous Greek legend as treated in various epochs; *The America's Cup Races*, yacht models, paintings; *New York in Oils*, paintings of the last 100 years. (Fifth Ave. at 103rd St., N. Y. 29. LE 4-1672.)

Museum of Modern Art

Exhibits: *Georges Seurat*, paintings and drawings, through May 11; *Juan Gris*, cubist paintings, through June 1. Gallery Talks: Friday, Saturday and Sunday at 3:30 P.M. Film Showings: Daily at 3 and 5:30 P.M. (11 W. 53rd St., N. Y. 19. CI 5-8900.)

New York Historical Society

Around New York in the Nineteenth Century, an exhibit of paintings. *Maps of American Wars, 1700–1950.* Motion picture programs every Saturday at 2 P.M. Films deal with historical subjects. (170 Central Park West, N. Y. 24. TR 3-3400.)

Brooklyn Museum

Exhibits: *Design for the Home '58,* modern home furnishings from many countries; *National Print Biennial,* outstanding prints gathered throughout the United States. *Brooklyn Bridge 75th Anniversary Exhibition* opening April 29. (Eastern Parkway and Washington Ave., Brooklyn 38, N. Y. NE 8-5000.)

Museum of Moneys of the World

Now located in the RCA Building, Rockefeller Center. Open daily from 10 A.M. to 5 P.M. Closed Saturdays, Sundays and holidays. Admission free. Curator: Vernon L. Brown. Telephone: CI 6-7400.

American Museum of Natural History

ROOSEVELT MEMORIAL HALL: *The Life of Theodore Roosevelt,* exhibit celebrating the Roosevelt Centennial Year; *Where to Go,* information service for people interested in visiting places associated with Roosevelt's life; *Exploring by Satellite,* gives the answers to many questions asked about man-made moons. HAYDEN PLANETARIUM: *Time and the Stars,* modern facts in science which have supplanted ancient beliefs, through May 5. (Central Park West at 79th St., N. Y. 24. TR 3-1300.)

Metropolitan Museum of Art

The Junior Museum is continuing its exhibit, *The Age of Discovery by Caravan and Caravel.* Film Showings, Sunday, every half hour starting at 1:30 P.M. *Southeast Asian Children's Paintings,* sponsored by the Yorkville Youth Council. Gallery Talks, for children, Saturday at 11 A.M. (Fifth Ave. at 82nd St., N. Y. 28. TR 9-5500.)

3. WHEN SEVERAL KEY WORDS ARE NEEDED

Let us suppose you have been asked to explain *what part was played by Thomas Jefferson in the struggle of the colonies for independence.* You have before you a book containing a whole chapter about Jefferson. What should you do to get the information?

One way would be to read the chapter very carefully until you find what you are seeking. But that takes time. Besides, it is not your purpose to learn everything about Jefferson but only to learn what he did in the struggle for independence. Is there a quicker way?

This is where skimming can be especially useful to you. Instead of reading through the entire selection with thorough attention to every detail, just skim along. You will actually skip a great many words without paying attention to the thought *until you reach the statements you need.*

But how will you recognize the right place when you come to it, if you have been skimming rapidly? Now you can understand the value of the key words in the question. Look again at the question. "What part was played by Jefferson in the struggle of the colonies for independence?" As you glance through the many pages, the moment your quick-moving eyes come to such words as *part, struggle, colonies, independence,* you know that you have found the right place. When skimming through lengthy material, do not depend upon *one* key word. Use *all important words* as your key words.

All those key words will help you. They are the words in the question or topic which will guide you to the answer. Up to now, the keys have been pointed out to you in every question. This time, you will select them yourself.

EXERCISE 7

Write a column of the numbers 1 to 14 on your paper. Then for your answers write the key words in each question.

QUESTIONS

1. Which of a miner's jobs is most dangerous?
2. How long does it take a ship to go through the Panama Canal?
3. What claims did the Spanish explorers make for their country?
4. On what date was the St. Lawrence Seaway opened?
5. Who was the first scientist to get useful and practical light from electricity?
6. What was the population of New York City in the census taken in 1950?
7. In what ways are cats said to be independent animals?
8. Which baseball team won the World's Series in 1940?
9. What products does the United States import from Hawaii?
10. What is the reason for our change of seasons in the Northern Hemisphere?
11. What are the names of all the planets?
12. What is the difference between a hurricane and a cyclone?
13. Which train was late in leaving Central Station yesterday morning?
14. Who put his raincoat in locker #76 on the first floor?

4. LOCATING THE APPROPRIATE PARAGRAPH

When you have chosen the key words in your question, the next step is to skim for them in the actual selection. The next exercise will test your skill in deciding at what point in the selection you will stop to read carefully for your information.

We will start with key sentences. You must imagine that each is the first sentence in a paragraph and that other sentences in the paragraph would give details.

Your problem in the next exercise is not to find answers but to find the paragraph (shown by its key sentence) where you would stop skimming and read slowly for information.

EXERCISE 8

Directions: Number your paper 1–8. Read each question to locate key words. Skim the key sentences until you find one containing the key words of the question. Write down the letter that stands before this sentence.

QUESTIONS

1. What is another name for the Pan-American Union?
2. What is the purpose of the Union?
3. List the names of the members of the Union.
4. On what date is the founding of the Union celebrated?
5. How does this organization try to promote peace?
6. Where is the headquarters for the Union?
7. Why is the Union so important to the western world to-day?
8. What other organization deals with world-wide affairs?

THE KEY SENTENCES

a. The Pan-American Union was born in the city where it still has its headquarters.
b. The day of the Union's birth is celebrated each year throughout the Western Hemisphere.
c. The Pan-American Union has come to be known by another name.
d. The members of the Union include all the republics of the Americas.
e. This organization is something like another one which deals with world-wide affairs.

f. The Union still has the same purpose for which it was organized in 1890.

g. There are a number of ways in which the organization tries to promote peace and understanding.

h. Today, the need for the Union is more important than ever before.

What Have You Learned About Skimming?

All skimming is rapid reading. There are several kinds of skimming, and each kind requires its own speed. Some skimming should be extremely rapid, as when you are looking for a word or phrase. Your eyes will hardly notice anything else.

Another kind of skimming should be only moderately rapid. In such skimming you will be looking for thoughts, not words. You will have to notice at least a few words on every line and guess at the general meaning from those few words.

KIND OF SKIMMING	PURPOSE	SPEED
Looking through a list	To find a word or phrase	Extremely rapid
Looking through a table	To find several facts	Almost as rapid
Looking through content	To find a key word or phrase	Very rapid
Looking through content	To find a thought containing several key words	Very rapid

But remember, no matter how fast you skim, the moment you find what you are seeking you should *stop skimming and read with care.*

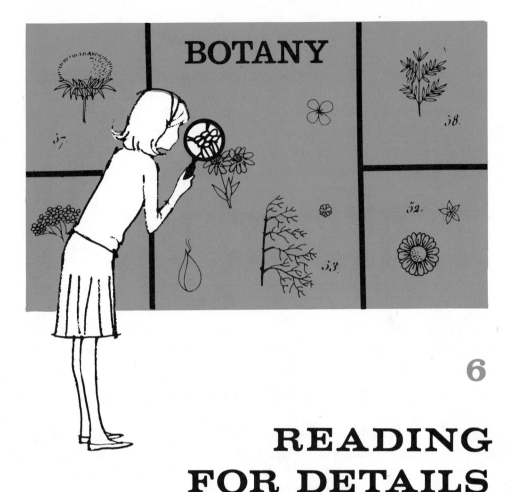

BOTANY

6

READING
FOR DETAILS

When you select a book to read, is it likely to be a book of fiction? Do you read simply for entertainment, or do you think of reading as a way of getting useful information? Librarians say that more and more students today are asking for nonfiction books, that is, books of information.

Perhaps it may come as a surprise to learn that most of the books in the world are books of information rather than of fiction. They are filled with all kinds of facts and ideas rather than with stories. As you grow older, you will gradually realize how many books of information you will need for your work and your life. Many will prove to be interesting and even exciting to read.

1. FACTS TO REMEMBER

Reading for information is not like reading stories. It requires more care and more thought. You cannot skip over words or sentences here and there as you might with a story. Every fact and every thought becomes important, like the rungs of a ladder. Each one brings you closer to the top. And every fact brings you closer to understanding the meaning of what follows.

FACTS ➡ MEANING

In the selection below, you will be able to catch the excitement of a very dramatic event if you remember to keep the facts in mind as you read on.

TWO THOUSAND MILES THROUGH THE AIR

PART I

We are so accustomed today to radio and television that we forget how amazing it is. No one stops to wonder about the magic of science that can send a voice or pictures of action across hundreds of miles of air or space. We just take these marvels for granted, like the rising of the sun every day or the running water from our faucets.

Yet up to the year 1890, people could not transmit anything at all through space, not even the sound of a little click. True, they were sending messages by telegraph and they were conversing by telephone. But those messages and voices were carried by electric waves traveling through wire. Not even in our wildest dreams could we have imagined doing this *without any connecting wire*. Who could be so foolish as to expect a message to be sent right through the air to someone miles away? Fantastic! Impossible! That kind of imagination should be left to fairy tales!

Nevertheless there were a few scientists who did have such a dream. They were the kind of people who could not be stopped by the word "Impossible." And they were hard at work trying to turn that dream into reality.

EXERCISE 1

Did you read these three paragraphs with care? Did you try to remember the facts as you read? Now try mentally to answer the following questions about them, without looking back. Cover the paragraphs to avoid temptation.

    1. Several of these statements are correct. Which are they? Which are wrong?
>   a. Before 1890 not a single message could be sent through the air.
>   b. But everybody expected it could be done.
>   c. Now everyone understands how radio and TV work.
>   d. Everyone is now accustomed to radio and TV.
>   e. Telegraph messages were transmitted through a wire.
>   f. Before 1890 no one even dreamed it could be done without that wire.
>   g. Some scientists hoped it might be done.
>   h. No scientist would bother with such an impossible experiment.

    2. Answer these questions.
>   a. What is amazing about radio and TV?
>   b. Why do they no longer seem wonderful to us?
>   c. Do you have any knowledge of how telegraph signals are sent?
>   d. What is it that travels through a wire in telegraph signals?

These questions make a very thorough examination of the three paragraphs. They help you realize how carefully you should read, during this practice period, to grasp all the facts. Now read three additional paragraphs.

PART II

One of those dreamers was a young man named Guglielmo Marconi. He already knew of something on which to base his efforts. He had learned of an experiment showing that electric waves, or some kind of invisible wave, could somehow pass through the air. A powerful electric spark at one end of a room had produced another spark between two ends of a wire at the other end of the room. The second spark was very weak, and the distance across the room was small. Nevertheless *some-*

107

thing had passed through space across that distance. Marconi was spurred on by this experiment to wonder whether this mysterious wave could be used to operate a telegraph set at any distance. *Could telegraph signals be sent without telegraph wires?*

His idea was beginning to take shape. Yet it was still a wild dream. Could it be made to work? Could it operate at a reasonable distance? This hope became Marconi's burning aim. He knew that the necessary experiments would take a long, long time. But scientists are patient people. They will work on even after failure. This man persisted in his investigations and efforts for ten weary years. He labored on through countless changes in method, countless experiments with new ideas, and countless failures. Yet he was encouraged by a few successes, though they were small. It was five years before he succeeded in producing signals that traveled across 200 feet! He had won the first round in his struggle with space.

Now came the task of improving his equipment and increasing the distance. Another few years, and his signal traveled a mile. Then ten miles. Then twenty miles. The messages were now able to reach from the shore to ships at sea. A few ship-owners recognized the tremendous value of this invention. They began to equip themselves with this new-fangled "wireless telegraph."

EXERCISE 2

Directions: **1.** List the letters *a* to *f* on your paper. Then decide whether each of the following statements is right or wrong or not mentioned. Alongside the proper letter write R for *right*, W for *wrong*, and N for *not mentioned*. Do not look back for your answers.

a. The scientist who experimented with this dream was Marconi.
b. He had never before heard of electric waves passing through the air.
c. He had seen an electric spark jump from one end of the room to the other.
d. Marconi wanted to find a way of operating a telegraph without a connecting wire.
e. The first ship that tried a wireless message did not succeed.
f. Marconi gradually increased the distance of his wireless signals from 200 feet to 20 miles.

2. On your paper list the letters from *a* to *g*. Then number them to show the order in which the events below actually occurred.

a. Marconi was not sure his dream could be made to work.
b. He wondered if he could use the spark experiment to operate a telegraph key.
c. Soon ships began to use his wireless method.
d. He realized that the spark must be sending electric waves through the air.
e. He began to work on experiments.
f. Finally he increased the distance of his signals from 200 feet to 20 miles.
g. Marconi already knew that a spark could be made to cause another spark on the opposite side of the room.

Read the paragraphs in Part III below. Then do Exercise 3, which follows on page 110.

PART III

Then came an event which made the world gasp with astonishment and gratitude. A vessel at sea received a distress signal from a sinking ship twelve miles away! The receiving vessel hastened to the rescue, and everyone on board was saved before the ship sank. For the first time in the history of the world, ships would no longer have to feel completely abandoned. They could rely on help when in peril. Other ships, though far out of sight, could be reached by the now famous S O S message, the call for help. A new age of greater safety at sea had dawned on the world.

Still, Marconi was not satisfied. His tireless energy prodded him on to efforts for ever-increasing distances. One day in 1901 he sat with an assistant in a cabin on the coast of Newfoundland. He sat in the midst of a mass of electrical equipment with a telephone receiver glued to his ear. For more than an hour he waited nervously, his face tense with anxiety, his fingers manipulating some dials. Two thousand miles away, in a little village on the coast of England, another assistant was creating tremendous electric sparks and working a telegraph key. The constant crashing of that man-made lightning was deafening and frightening.

Suddenly Marconi, in far-away Newfoundland, jumped as though he had been struck by one of those giant sparks. He had just heard three faint clicks. Just three faint clicks, repeated again and again. While the mysterious waves were speeding on their vast journey across the Atlantic, what began with shattering lightning sparks in England had dwindled down to faint clicks at Newfoundland. Previously, the world had gasped in amazement at the wireless message that brought help to a ship at sea. Now, however, it went wild with excitement and enthusiasm. Marconi's heroic labors of more than ten years were over. Wireless could span a distance of 2000 miles. It was at the service of the whole world. Who could tell what new wonders might arise from that first brilliant success in sending electricity so far through space? Who could then have predicted that it would lead to the gradual development of the more-than-magic marvels of radio and TV?

EXERCISE 3

Directions: List on your paper the letters *a* to *o*. Write the answers to the following questions alongside the proper letters.

a. How far did the wireless signal have to travel to reach the rescue ship?
b. Why was this signal a very important event for the world?
c. During the last experiment in this selection, where was Marconi waiting?
d. What was he waiting for?
e. Did he expect a strong signal or a weak one? How can we tell?
f. Where was his assistant working?
g. At what distance away?
h. What experiment gave Marconi the idea of a wireless telegraph?
i. How do you think Marconi's success with the wireless provided the idea for radio?
j. During what year did Marconi find that he could send a wireless message a much greater distance than before?
k. In what connection is the S O S message mentioned?
l. What piece of apparatus was Marconi using to help him hear the wireless sounds?
m. How many clicks did Marconi first hear in this experiment?
n. What ocean was crossed by the message and was mentioned as being between England and Newfoundland?
o. Did Marconi discover accidentally that messages could travel longer distances than before?

2. KEEPING FACTS IN THE RIGHT ORDER

The next selection is short and simple. It describes the order of business at a club meeting. The purpose of presenting it here is to have you recognize that it is not always enough to remember all the facts. In certain selections it is also necessary to remember them in their proper order.

As you read this selection, see if you can find a reason for each step in the list of facts. You should be able to see that at a club meeting **old business** should come before **new business.** You should see that **reports of committees** must precede the discussion of motions. Surely the members have a right to know what was accomplished by these committees. Then they will know whether to act on those reports.

When you finish reading the selection, stop for a moment to review in your mind all the steps of the meeting. Then proceed with Exercise 4.

The Hillsboro Girls' Club was having its fourth meeting. The girls had already learned how to conduct their meetings according to the proper order of business. First the chairman called the club to order. When everyone was quiet, she led the group in the pledge to the flag. Then the minutes of the previous meeting were read aloud. One member pointed out an error in one of the statements. After it was corrected the club voted to approve the minutes. The treasurer had a brief report on the amount in the treasury. There was no report from any other officer, and the president then called for reports of committees.

Two committees had been formed to plan future events, so their reports were now heard and discussed. It was now time for old business. But there was no old business left since the committee reports had already been discussed. Therefore the president announced that new business was now in order. A new treasurer was to be elected, because the present one was moving away. The election took only a few minutes. Then the girls discussed their plans for doing Red Cross work. A committee was appointed to make final recommendations.

The date of the next meeting was scheduled. It was to be at Ellen's house on Thursday. Since there was no further business, the meeting was adjourned.

EXERCISE 4

The steps in almost any club meeting are listed below, though not in their proper order. On your paper rewrite them in their correct order and number them. The actual reports or business transacted at the meeting are not to be included in your answer. *Do not look back at the selection.*

Reports of committees
Setting the time and place for the next meeting
Reading of the minutes
Old business
The meeting is called to order
Reports of officers
Adjourning the meeting
The pledge to the flag
New business
Correction of the minutes, if any

Order in a Longer Selection

In reading this account, notice how clear the order of events is made. Each event makes possible the next. When you finish the story see if you can recall those events mentally. Each one should remind you of the next. Do Exercises 5 and 6.

Washington Learns About a Submarine

1. During the Revolutionary War, the American army under General Washington was camped on Manhattan Island. Out in New York Harbor, the British fleet was anchored. The ships were loaded with soldiers planning to land at any time. Washington's army was not ready to fight so large a force. Some way had to be found to keep the British from landing.

Fortunately a man named David Bushnell came at that time to General Washington with a daring plan. He had invented a kind of boat that could be made to travel under water by the turning of a crank. He called it a "submarine." It was rickety, and Washington thought it was too risky to use. But Bushnell argued that a man could take a bomb with him and get to the British flagship without being seen. Then he could fasten the bomb to the enemy ship and blow it up. Washington consented to the plan when one of his officers agreed to make the attempt.

2. One dark night, a group met at a wharf where the boat was anchored. The officer lowered himself through a small trap door into the submarine, a small egg-shaped vessel. Inside this strange boat the officer began turning the crank and the vessel moved slowly away from the dock. It was towing a bomb filled with gunpowder. Soon the officer saw the hull of the *Eagle*, the British flagship he was to blow up. It was time now to submerge. He pulled a lever and his boat went below the surface and moved up to the target.

3. Then something went wrong. The officer was unable to attach the time bomb to the copper plates of the *Eagle's* hull! He was greatly distressed. It was almost daybreak and he had to give up the attempt. Just as his boat moved away from the warship, the bomb came to the surface and exploded—exactly on time but without doing any damage to the *Eagle*.

The plan had failed, but Bushnell had given future inventors an idea that would one day help them build submarines powerful enough to sail around the world under water.

EXERCISE 5

A. In this exercise, details are to be listed in the order of their occurrence in the story. A few of the details have been supplied.

Directions: Number your paper 3–16. Try to remember the details that have been omitted in the list below. Write them in the proper order. Do not write in this book.

1. Washington's army was camped on Manhattan Island.
2. In the harbor there were British ships with a very large force of British soldiers getting ready to land.
3.
4. Bushnell had a plan that would use his invention, a "submarine."
5.
6.
7.
8. One dark night a group met at the wharf.
9.
10.
11. The officer submerged as soon as he could see the *Eagle*.
12.
13. He was unable to attach the bomb.
14.
15.
16.
17. Bushnell had given the world an idea for future submarines.

B. Write the answers to the following questions on your paper.

1. Why was Washington anxious to keep the British troops from landing?
2. Why did he hesitate to accept Bushnell's plan?
3. Why was Bushnell's invention called a "strange boat"?
4. What was the name of the British flagship?
5. Why was it necessary to use a submarine boat to reach the flagship instead of an ordinary boat?

EXERCISE 6

Read the following story and list on your paper a brief statement for each event that is missing in the summary that follows it. Be sure each item is listed in the proper order.

THE WOODEN HORSE OF THE GREEKS

One of the most familiar of all the Greek legends is the story of the Trojan horse. For nine long years the Greeks had tried to conquer the city of Troy, but the Trojans held fast and the Grecian ships waited. When the Greeks knew they could not conquer their enemies by force, they thought of a plan to take the city by strategy. They set to work and built a great horse of wood, beautifully carved and hollow. Within its interior a considerable number of soldiers could be concealed. The door that would release these men was so cleverly constructed that it could not be recognized at all from the outside.

When the horse was completed, the Greeks divided their army. Some of the soldiers hid themselves with their leaders inside the horse. Then the rest of the army went aboard the ships and set sail. They did not go far, however. They anchored their ships behind a nearby island, just out of sight of the city of Troy.

The Trojans watched the ships sail away, and they rejoiced for they thought the war was over. They threw open the gates and rushed to the empty camps of the Greeks. There they found the great wooden horse.

At first they were suspicious about it, but then a Greek who had been left behind as a spy told them that the horse had been built as an offering to the goddess Athena. The Trojans thought they had captured a prize and dragged the horse inside the gates of the city. Then they began to feast in celebration of the departure of the Greek army.

In the darkness of the night, the Greeks crept from their hiding place inside the horse, and their ships returned. There was no Trojan on guard and so the Trojans were taken by surprise and their city was burned to the ground.

SUMMARY

1. Greeks fail to capture Troy.
2. They decide to use strategy.
3.
4.
5.
6. Their ships sail off, but stay in hiding behind an island.
7.
8.
9.
10. The city is destroyed by fire.

3. WHEN THE AUTHOR CHANGES THE ORDER

In the selections you have read, the steps or events were given in the order in which they happened. Sometimes, however, an author makes his story more interesting by deliberately telling events *out* of their regular order. Still, he keeps clear the order in which they actually happened. Expressions such as *meanwhile, already, long before this, after this, then,* are used as clues to show which event came before another.

Read the following selection. Then notice a way in which it might be retold.

CAPTAIN CORTEZ

Cortez found a way to keep his men in Mexico, a way that made it impossible for them to leave him. They would either have to stay and fight the Aztec Indians or be killed by them. The method Cortez used was an astounding risk, not only for all his men but for himself, too. He sank ten of the eleven ships which brought them there! When he had first entered Mexico and had seen how rich the Indians were, he determined to conquer them and make himself the owner of all their wealth. However, he had already heard grumbling among his men about their dangers and hardships. He knew they were sick of the whole adventure and eager to leave Mexico. Then he also learned that they were planning to rebel against him and return to Cuba. Instantly he made up his mind to find a way to keep them with him. It was an enormous hazard, but he was too greedy to miss any opportunity to grasp all that gold. His conquest of the Aztec Empire laid the foundation for Spanish rule in Mexico.

In the story the events are told in this order:
Cortez made it impossible for his men to leave.
Now they would have to stay and fight.
Cortez sank all but one of his ships.
He determined to conquer the Indians
    and obtain their wealth.
He heard grumbling.
He heard plans for rebellion.
He planned to keep his men with him.
It was a great risk.
He made Spanish rule possible in Mexico.

But this is the way it happened:

> Cortez determined to conquer the Indians for their
>   wealth.
> He heard his men grumbling.
> He discovered plans for rebellion.
> He determined to keep his men with him.
> He sank all but one of the ships, though it
>   was at a great risk.
> Now it was impossible for them to leave.
> He made it necessary for them to stay on
>   and fight.
> He made Spanish rule possible in Mexico.

EXERCISE 7

Directions: Read the following selection. On your paper write the events in their correct order to show that you understand what the author has told you.

> The purchase of Louisiana doubled the size of our young nation. Lewis and Clark were assigned the task of exploring this new property. Even before the purchase of this land had been considered, however, Jefferson had secretly planned to send an expedition to explore the West in search of a route to the Pacific. All of Louisiana, including New Orleans, was purchased for $15,000,000. In 1800 Spain had ceded Louisiana to the French. The purchase was made to avoid French intervention in America.

EXERCISE 8

The following is another selection in which the author expects you to visualize the events in their correct order.

> The Wright brothers were truly pioneers in aviation. On their second attempt, in 1903, they flew about 120 feet in an engine-driven glider and proved that aviation had possibilities. This flight also proved the value of sticking with an idea. The idea, in this case, went back to boyhood days, when the Wright brothers had read everything they could find about planes, and had built their own gliders. They liked to work with tools, and as early as 1892 had started a bicycle shop. By 1895 they were

manufacturing bicycles and by 1902 had designed and built an airplane engine. They had also designed propellers for their plane. It was only after hundreds of glider flights from the sand dunes along the North Carolina coast that they succeeded in their history-making flight.

In 1948 the Wright brothers' first airplane was placed permanently in the Smithsonian Institution.

If you wished to tell the story of the Wright Brothers as it happened, where would you begin? With their flight in 1903, or with their boyhood? When did they first become interested in flying? How did they learn to make gliders? Try to rearrange their story in your mind so that you may be able to tell it to your classmates just as it happened.

EXERCISE 9

The following is a long selection from a famous story, *Robinson Crusoe*. After reading this selection, see how well you can recall each step in the story. Follow the directions on the next page.

It happened about noon one day that in going toward my boat I was very surprised to see the print of a man's naked foot on the shore. How it came there I could not imagine, but I ran, terrified, to my house and fled into it like one pursued. I slept none that night.

Then one day it came into my thoughts that this might be the print of my own foot. I began to take courage and peep outside again, for I had not stirred from my castle for three days and nights and began to need provisions. I went out thus two or three days, and having seen nothing, began to be a little bolder. When I came to the place to measure the mark with my foot, I found my own foot not so large by a great deal. This made me fearful again and I went home, filled with belief that my island was inhabited.

I made my tour every morning to the top of the hill to see if I could observe any boats upon the sea. I was surprised one morning by seeing no less than five canoes, all on shore together on my side of the island. I went back and lay still in my house. I waited a good while listening to hear if they made any noise. Then being impatient, I set my guns at the foot of my ladders and climbed to the top of the hill.

I observed with the help of my glass that they were about thirty in number and that they had a fire kindled and something cooking. Then I saw two miserable creatures dragged from the boats to be killed. One fell, being knocked down by a club, while the other was left standing by himself. In that very moment, this poor wretch, seeing himself at liberty, started away and ran with great swiftness along the sands directly toward me.

I was dreadfully frightened when I saw him run my way. However, I kept my place and my spirits began to recover when I found that there were not more than three men who followed him. It came upon my thoughts that now was the time to get me a servant and perhaps a companion. I ran down the ladders, took my guns, climbed up the hill again, and crossed toward the sea.

Directions: Copy the following outline. Fill in the parts that have been left out. Be sure that all events appear in the right order.

1. Crusoe sees a footprint.
2.
3. Crusoe needs provisions so he goes outdoors.
4. He
5. He
6. He makes a daily trip to the top of the hill.
7. One morning he
8.
9. He becomes impatient.
10.
11. He sees the other victim run away in his direction.
12. He has an idea.
13.
14.

Now read over your own list of events, and be ready to retell the story aloud if you are asked to do so.

FOLLOWING
DIRECTIONS 7

Almost every day in your life you come face to face with the need to follow directions. They may be oral directions, as when your mother sends you to the store to buy a list of foods. Generally they are written or printed. At the telephone booth you may be instructed to drop a coin in the slot and to listen for the dial tone before you dial your number. The medicine bottle may direct you to stir one-half teaspoonful of medicine into a half-glass of water and to drink the dose after each meal. A road sign may direct your father to bring his car to a full stop before the railroad crossing. You are constantly meeting directions to be read and followed. Directions such as these are quite simple.

You will meet other directions that are much more complicated.

1. READING DIRECTIONS IS A DIFFERENT KIND OF READING

When you read directions, you use your eyes and your mind in a different way than when you read a story or an article in a newspaper. It takes a special ability to follow directions with thorough understanding. For one thing, you must go over them much more carefully than any other kind of material. You must be absolutely sure of each step. A small mistake in a single step of the directions may completely spoil what you are trying to do.

For instance, a messenger received instructions to deliver a package to 139 Crescent Street. He glanced at the paper hurriedly, thought he knew the number, and slipped the paper into his pocket. A half hour later he rang the doorbell at 931 Crescent Street and discovered his mistake. He had gone more than two miles out of his way because he had not read carefully enough! Now he had to go all the way back to number 139.

Many students often receive poor marks in their arithmetic tests even though they really understand the work, because they read the questions carelessly. A problem may ask for ¼ % of a sum of money. Some students fail to read the term *percent*, and they find one-fourth of the sum, instead of one-fourth of 1 percent of it. They may know how to do arithmetic, but they do not know how to read the questions. And questions in arithmetic are practically directions.

EXERCISE 1

Make a list of all the directions you meet in one particular day. See how many different kinds of directions you will meet. You may be surprised by the length of your list at the close of the day.

2. METHODS TO USE IN READING DIRECTIONS

I. **Give the directions a quick *first* reading just to get the general idea.** It will help you to decide whether you are interested, whether the directions are too difficult or not, and whether you can obtain the equipment that may be required.

Let us assume that you would like to train a dog to do a few simple tricks, such as obeying commands to sit, to play dead, to beg, to roll over. The dog is very young and playful, and does not even recognize his own name. When you read the directions about training him they begin this way:

> You must be very patient when you begin to train a dog. Teach him only one command at a time. Do not try anything new until the old command has been well learned. Begin with the command "Come." This should be practiced over and over again, but no more than ten minutes at one practice period. Then allow your dog to rest. After an hour you can repeat the practice. Do this five times a day for about a week.

These are not the complete directions. But are you getting the idea that training a dog, even for a simple trick, may take at least a whole week?

Even before you read the directions again, more carefully and more fully, you already realize that it will take a long time and a great deal of patience to train your dog for just a few commands. This first reading gives you a chance to decide whether you will have that patience.

II. **Never take it for granted that you already know any part of the directions and that you can therefore afford to skip them in your reading.**

> **A.** You have a cold and you have been taking medicine right after your meal. Then you get some new medicine. Better read the directions carefully! Part of the directions may read: "These tablets must be chewed, not swallowed whole, and taken at least *one hour before each meal.*" Do not guess at any of the directions. Read them carefully even if you think you know them.
>
> **B.** You are used to pay-station telephones where you deposit your coin first, wait for the dial tone, and then dial your number. There are pay stations in other towns, however, where your coin would be wasted if you deposited it first. Be sure to read the directions. They may say: "Dial your number first. When you hear that you are connected, deposit your coin and you will be able to speak with your party."

What differences did you notice in **B** in the directions for using the dial telephone?

III. **Be sure that you understand fully every step in the directions.** You may have to read with special care for this purpose. If you do not understand the instructions, you may have to obtain the information elsewhere.

> You would like to take some indoor pictures with your new motion-picture camera. The directions read: "Load your camera with ASA 32 speed 8 mm. film for artificial light. Use 500 watt flood lamps for illumination."

Do you have 500 watt flood lamps? Can you borrow them? If you lack proper lighting equipment, you may have to give up the idea of taking indoor pictures. You must have all the equipment specified by the directions.

Do you know what is meant by 8 mm. film? By ASA 32 speed film? If not, you may have to find out by inquiry at the camera shop.

Do you know how to "load" the film in the camera? There may be other directions that explain how this is done. You will have to read those, too.

IV. **It will help you to understand each step better if you can recognize the *reason* for it.**

> **A.** You are repairing a broken dinner plate with a new plastic glue. The directions say: "If any of the glue is spilled on a wooden surface, wipe it off with a damp cloth immediately, while it is still moist."

Why do you think it should be wiped off immediately? Will it be easier to take it off while it is moist than later, when it hardens? Is it possible that some of the glue may soak into the wood if you do not remove it at once?

> **B.** Mary was cutting out material for a blouse. On one pattern piece the directions said: "Place this edge along the fold in the cloth. Cut only around the other edges."

Why was it important to leave that edge without cutting? Can you see that the cloth would then have to be opened along the fold and spread out to a double width? If it were cut along that fold it would come out in two pieces and would be spoiled.

V. If possible, try to form a mental picture of the steps in the directions.

A. How to Plant an Evergreen Tree

1. Set ball in hole to depth of previous planting.
2. Pack loose soil around ball.
3. Cut burlap and push down. Leave it to decay.
4. Water thoroughly and fill in remaining soil.

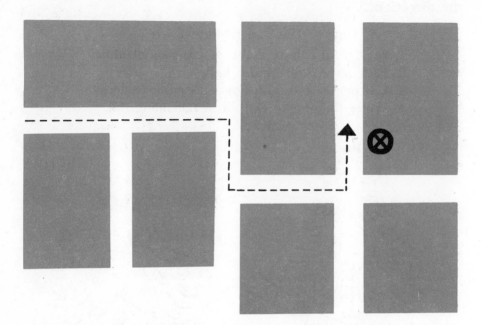

B. "Walk straight ahead for two blocks to the end of this street, turn right for one-half block, then left for one block, and left again. You will see the school on the other side of the street." Here is a picture of what you ought to see in your mind as you read the instructions.

VI. Try to understand why step 1 must be done before step 2, step 2 before step 3, etc. There are good reasons for listing the steps in a certain order.

For making delicious cookies, the directions read as follows:

A. Light the oven and set it at 375°.

B. Sift together the measured flour, baking powder, and salt.

C. Cream the shortening until soft and smooth. Add the sugar and vanilla. Mix thoroughly. Add the egg. Beat until light and fluffy.

D. Gradually add the flour mixture and mix well.

The rest of the directions are omitted for the present.

Can you tell why the oven should be lit at the very beginning? Can you see that the oven is being gradually heated to the right temperature while the mixture is being prepared?

Notice that the flour mixture is prepared before the other mixtures. Why? Can you realize that it must be made ready so that it can be added as soon as mixture C is completed?

VII. **After the careful second reading, step by step, go over the entire set of directions once more.** This time you may be able to remember the steps in the right order. However, you should always have the directions before you while you are performing the steps.

3. SAMPLE SETS OF DIRECTIONS

Besides learning the rules about reading directions, you also need to practice them. The exercises that follow should help to fix these rules in your mind.

EXERCISE 2

As you go through these directions, try at the second reading to form a mental picture of the steps. Imagine that you see yourself carrying out each step, one after the other. Remember the steps in that order.

ROAD DIRECTIONS

Mr. Jones was looking for Hillcrest Road. He stopped and asked for directions at a gasoline station. "Well," said the attendant, "you will have to go back the way you came for about a mile, to the traffic light. Turn left and go about half a mile until you come to the entrance to a park. Continue into the park until you come to a "Stop" sign. Take the road to the right and follow it to the outside of the park. Turn left alongside the park until you come to Main Street. Then go right for a few blocks until you get to Hillcrest Road. It crosses Main Street."

Mr. Jones said "Thank you," then turned to his son John and inquired, "Can you remember the directions?" John thought he could, but when they reached the other side of the park no one could recall which way to turn. They had neglected to form a mental picture of the directions.

A. Copy on your paper the numbers and lines as they are below. Then fill in the blanks from memory.

1. Go back about a mile to the traffic light.
2.
3. Continue into the park until
4.   to the outside of the park.
5.   Main Street.
6. Then go right

B. With the help of the directions as you have written them, see if you can draw a picture of the road to follow.

EXERCISE 3

Read these directions carefully three times. As you read, try to decide why each step must be performed in the order in which it is given. Keep the steps in mind, too, so that you may remember them in proper order.

How to Broil a Steak Over a Camp Fire

1. Get a good fire started, with heavy branches or small logs on top that will not burn up quickly.
2. Find a slim green branch or stick. Whittle away the rough spots and sharpen one end to a point.
3. Get two branches that are forked at one end. Stick them in the ground, one on each side of the fire. The forks should be 6 to 8 inches above the top of the fire.
4. Now cut the steak into small pieces no more than 2 inches across.
5. Push the green stick through them, keeping them close together but with some air space between them.
6. By this time the flames should be steady and low, with some blue flames from the hot "coals."
7. Stick the meat directly into the flames for a moment, turning the stick to sear the meat all around. This seals in the juices.
8. Then place the stick with the meat across the forks and turn it once in a while as the meat broils over the fire.
9. Salt the meat slightly and keep it there long enough to broil it to your taste, whether rare or well done.

Did you go over these directions three times? *Once* to get the general idea, the *second* time to understand each step and its purpose, and the *third* time to keep the steps in mind? Number your paper 1 to 8 and answer the questions below. Cover the directions to avoid looking back at them.

1. Why is it important to get the fire started at the beginning?
2. Why will you need a green branch on which to stick the meat?
3. Why should the meat be cut into small pieces?
4. Why are low blue flames better for broiling than high yellow flames?
5. Why should the meat be seared?
6. What is the step after searing the meat?
7. Why should the meat be turned while it is broiling?
8. How long should it be kept over the fire?

EXERCISE 4

In many sets of directions, the first step will tell you what materials you must have before you begin. Recipes usually begin that way. So do directions for science experiments.

In this experiment there seem to be only four steps. Actually there are many more, but they are presented in paragraph form, not in a long list of separate steps. Watch closely for those steps as you read the four paragraphs here and on page 130.

A SCIENCE EXPERIMENT

1. Have the following materials ready: Iron filings, sulphur powder, magnet, 2 sheets of paper, test tube, a gas burner.

2. Place the iron filings on one sheet of paper and the sulphur powder on the other. Try to pick up some of each with a magnet. What do you observe?
3. Mix the iron filings and the powder and place this mixture on one of the sheets. Bring the magnet close to the mixture. What happens? The sulphur powder will remain on the paper. Observe that mixing the two powders did not change them in any way. They remain two separate substances.
4. Mix the two again and place the mixture in a test tube. Heat the test tube until the mixture is glowing. Remove the test tube from the flame and allow it to cool. Remove the substance from the tube and bring the magnet close to it. Will the magnet attract the substance? What do you think happened to the mixture?

Read the directions again to remind yourself of the following:
a. What materials are needed.
b. How the steps in paragraphs 2, 3, and 4 differed from one another.

Now you are ready to write answers to the questions below. You may look back at the directions if you need to, but try to answer as much as you can from memory.

1. What materials do you need for this experiment?
2. What do you need for the second step? What material do you use for the third step?
3. What material do you need for the last step?
4. Why was it necessary to keep the two substances separate in the second step?
5. Why was the heating done in the last step instead of in the second?
6. In the following statements, if any are right, answer on your paper with R. If any are wrong, answer on your paper with W.
   a. Iron filings and sulphur powder remain separate substances even when they are mixed together.
   b. Iron filings and sulphur powder form a new substance as soon as they are mixed together.
   c. Iron filings and sulphur powder form a new substance only when they are heated together.

4. HOW TO READ DIRECTIONS FOR DOING AN EXERCISE

All through this book you have been practicing ways in which to improve your reading by working out the answers to various exercises. The directions for the exercises may sometimes seem complicated. They demand thorough reading.

Test your own thoroughness by carrying out the directions in Exercise 5. Look through the material itself as you read the directions so that you can see what they mean. Be sure you understand each part before you write your answers.

EXERCISE 5

An Exercise in Directions

A. In this exercise you will find five sentences. Each one contains a word in italics.

Write the numbers 1 to 5 along the left edge of your paper. Write each italicized word alongside its proper number. Below the sentences is a list of definitions. Select the correct definition for each of the words you have written. There are more definitions than words, so you must select your definitions with care. Each definition is designated by a letter. Now fit the correct definition to each word by writing alongside the word the *letter* of the correct definition, not the definition itself.

1. *Disaster* struck the town when the hurricane arrived.
2. To be *diplomatic* you must appear to be friendly even if you do not feel friendly.
3. The *preliminary* chapter was easier than the later parts of the book.
4. The flashlight suddenly *illuminated* the cellar.
5. Things *gravitate* toward the earth.

DEFINITIONS

a. lighted up
b. broke up
c. an event of great destruction
d. first or beginning
e. showing tact and courtesy in relations with other people
f. bringing illness
g. are pulled toward

B. TEST YOURSELF. Answer these questions on your paper without looking back at the instructions.

1. How many words were you asked to define?
2. How many definitions were you given?
3. Where were you to look for the definitions?
4. In your answers, did you have to write words, phrases, or letters?
5. What is the meaning of the word *disaster*?

Brief Summary of Methods for Reading Directions

  I. Your first reading of the directions should be rapid, just to get a general idea about them.

 II. Read them a second time with great care, even those parts that you think are already familiar to you.

III. Make sure to understand each step. You should look up information about any portion that you cannot understand, or inquire about it.

IV. Try to figure out a reason for each step and a reason for its place in the order of the directions.

 V. Try to give yourself a mental picture of each operation.

VI. Finally read the directions a third time. This time concentrate on trying to remember the steps in their correct order.

FINDING THE HIDDEN MEANING

8

When you are on your way to some special place, perhaps to school or to the store on an errand, you usually take the shortest route. Then you are not interested in looking at the houses you pass or at the cars that go by. But if you are taking a walk for pleasure, you may select some other path, one that takes you on side trips, through a park where there are lawns and fountains, or through woods toward a lake. So it is with reading and writing.

When an author wants to give his readers serious information, he writes directly and to the point. He tells you exactly what he means. However, if the author wants to offer you something to read just for pleasure, he is likely to write in a more roundabout way. For example, he may say, "The old man sold his car for a song." This may seem to talk about music, but the author really means that the old man sold his car for very little money.

1. INDIRECT WRITING

Why does the author use this indirect method of writing? Does he wish to mislead you? Not at all. He is sure that you will understand his real meaning, but at the same time he wants to keep you interested. And he knows that readers of stories or plays or poems find them much more enjoyable when they make use of their minds to "read into" the writer's statements. That is why we must understand what the author really means by what he says.

Advantages of Indirect Writing

See what a difference it makes to say things indirectly.

1. The tourists *walked* through the crowds.
2. The tourists *threaded their way* through the crowds.

The first sentence is correct, but it is not very interesting. The second sentence, however, wakes up your mind. It makes you read with more attention. You get a mental picture. You see the tourists as though they were a thread behind a needle, weaving to the right and to the left through the crowds.

You yourself use this method in your own conversation. When you strike out at a baseball game, you may say in disgust, "I laid an egg." Your friends will know what you mean. When you talk of some boy as a "peanut" they understand you to mean only that he is somewhat small in size. Such language is more exciting than the direct way of speaking.

Another of the common methods of indirect writing makes use of the words *like* and *as,* which you will study in this chapter. Every day one hears such expressions as "like lightning" and "smooth as silk." These particular expressions have become timeworn, but new and sparkling ones with *like* and *as* are constantly coming into use.

All the examples thus far were easy. But you are sure to meet many statements in your reading that may not be quite so simple. In spite of this, you will find it fun to see mental pictures as you read. Besides, your understanding will be much richer and deeper than ever before.

In this kind of reading, you not only read the printed words, you also see the thoughts that are not in the printed lines. They will come from your mind.

2. THE CUE WORDS "LIKE" AND "AS"

Writers often make their meaning clear through comparisons. The two things being compared may seem at first glance completely unlike. In comparing them, the writer is saying that they are alike in some one way. In some comparisons, the writer tells you in what way the two things are alike. In others he asks the reader to figure out the likeness—to read between the lines. You can see this difference in these two sentences:

I was so gay that I felt as light as a feather.

My hands were like ice.

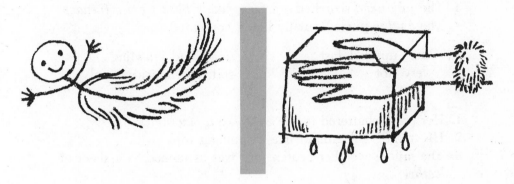

If you read the first sentence literally, it does not make sense. No one ever weighs as little as a feather. But sometimes when a person is gay, he *feels* as though he has no weight. The second sentence is not exactly true either, but it has meaning for the reader.

Clearly, it is important to know when a writer is making an accurate, serious statement and when he is merely making a comparison. The words *as* and *like* are clues to comparisons. When you see them, you know that the writer may be making a comparison.

In the following sentence, you can see the clue word, and the writer tells you in what way the plane seemed like a leaf.

The damaged plane fell gradually, *like* a fluttering leaf.

Did you get a picture of that fall? Did you see the plane looking something like a leaf and falling a little at a time? And did you notice the cue word *like*? The sentence compared *plane* to *leaf* because both were *fluttering*.

135

EXERCISE 1

In each comparison, try to see the two things that are compared, and find in what way they are compared.

Directions: Below each group of sentences there is a list of words and phrases. Choose the one that best explains the comparison in each sentence. The answer for the first sentence is given.

A

1. Far down below us, the automobiles looked like ants crawling along the pavement.
    (small and crawling.)
2. The jet engines shot the *plane* up into the clouds like a *bullet.*
3. The July *wind* scorched our faces like a *blast from a furnace.*
4. The *engine* purred quietly like a contented *cat.*

shot upward fast	small and crawling
very hot	soft, rhythmical sound

B

1. Her *teeth* chattered in the cold like *typewriter keys.*
2. His *mind* went around like a spinning *top.*
3. The sailor's weather-beaten *face* was as tanned as a sheet of *leather.*
4. The *road* looked like a twisting *ribbon* in the moonlight.

curved	brown
had a clicking sound	was whirling

EXERCISE 2

Can you tell when comparisons sound sensible? In this exercise four sentences are started in the left-hand column. In the column at the right, there are phrases to complete the sentences.

Directions: Number your paper 1–4. Choose the phrase that best completes each comparison. Write it.

1. The branches of the tree stretched upward like	a cat just getting up from a nap.
2. His weekly allowance was stretched like	a man's arms extended in prayer.
3. He kept yawning and stretching like	ships that take you to strange lands.
4. Books are like	a rubber band about to break.

EXERCISE 3

Follow the same procedure for the five sentences below.

1. The books were arranged in a neat row like — a real battle taking place before his eyes.
2. The book's description of the battle was like — soldiers on parade.
3. When she was angry, her words were like — her speech had been cut by a knife.
4. She stopped short in the middle of a sentence as though — a hammer on an iron bar.
5. He felt his heart pounding like — icicles freezing in the air.

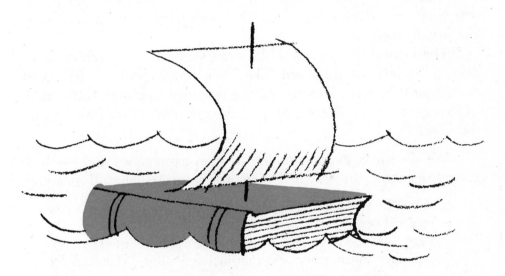

3. SEEING PICTURES IN YOUR MIND

As you combined the sentence parts above, did each whole sentence bring a thought picture to your mind? Suppose we look again at the sentence, "Books are like ships that take you to strange lands." What makes books like ships? Wouldn't it be thrilling to get on a ship and sail to some far-off, mysterious port? Can books take you there? Can you see some books looking like shadowy ships with sails all set, waiting to carry you through their stories to lands more fascinating in imagination than they are in reality? That is the picture you should see as you read the sentence.

EXERCISE 4

Discuss the sentences in Exercises 2 and 3 on pages 136 and 137. For each sentence, show what things are being compared and in what way they are alike. Then describe the picture that the sentence creates in your mind.

4. WHEN "LIKE" OR "AS" IS OMITTED

You have now seen many examples of how authors use words to suggest ideas and pictures to the reader. When you read "The waves plunged after each other like galloping horses," you know that waves are not really like horses. The waves do not have feet, heads, or hides covered with hair. But they are like horses in the way they move. The comparison gives you a mental picture of how the waves moved.

The mental picture would be even sharper and brighter, however, if we left out the word "like." We could speak of the waves as though they were horses, and the sentence might read like this: "The waves were galloping horses, chasing each other furiously up the beach."

We shall look over a number of such expressions and see how interesting they can be when we make sure of their full meaning.

1. "Don't be a *mule*, Tommy," said Mother. "I want you to wear your rubbers."
   (Are mules known to be stubborn? What did Tommy's mother mean when she reprimanded him? What did he say before she spoke?)

2. Nothing could frighten Bob. He had *nerves of steel*.
   (Nerves are associated with one's feelings or courage, and steel refers to something very strong. What kind of courage did Bob have?)

3. Just because he could not have his way, Dick became a surly *bear* for the rest of the day.
   (Bears are supposed to have bad tempers. How do you think Dick was behaving?)

4. Helen was smaller than the other girls, but she faced them with the *heart of a lion*.
   (What kind of courage did she display? What is the clue?)

138

5. The moment the teacher entered the room the class changed into a *beehive of activity.*

(What happened to the class? What were they doing before the teacher arrived? In what way is the class being compared with a beehive?)

6. Bert was a better tennis player, but Hal was a wily *fox* with many surprises in his bag of tricks.

(A fox has the reputation of being cunning and shrewd. What are Hal's chances of winning? Why?)

7. Night is a *black curtain* that shuts away all the light about us.

(Can you get a mental picture of heavy black draperies coming down all around us and causing the darkness of night?)

Do you remember the sentence that began with the words "The waves were galloping horses"? The word "like" was omitted. There is another way of expressing the same idea without using the word "horses."

The waves galloped furiously up the beach in a never-ending chase after each other.

How can we tell from that sentence that the waves are being compared with horses? Waves cannot really gallop, but horses can. The word makes us think of horses, and therefore the sentence creates a picture in our mind of tall waves plunging on so fast that we think of them as though they were horses.

EXERCISE 5

Here are a number of other comparisons. See if you can find in them the exact meaning they intend.

Directions: From the explanations below each sentence, select the one that best fits the italicized words.

1. Smith's vacation was soon over and he was back *in harness* again.

    a. He put himself into a harness.
    b. He is wearing uncomfortable clothing that feels like a harness.
    c. He is doing his usual work again.
    d. He looks something like a horse.

2. When she faced the audience, Susan became nervous and *stumbled over her speech.*

    a. The roll of paper containing the speech dropped to the floor and Susan almost fell over it.

    b. She forgot the words and had to pause several times while trying to remember.

    c. Her tongue became caught in her mouth and it stumbled over the words.

3. Bob was so surprised at the unexpected visitor that he remained *rooted to the spot.*

    a. Bob's character reminds one of a tree with its roots firmly in the ground.

    b. The soles of his shoes had spikes which he dug into the ground like roots.

    c. He was too surprised even to move a muscle.

EXERCISE 6

Study the questions below each sentence. Be prepared to explain your answers in class.

1. As darkness came on, a million stars *blossomed* in the sky.

    a. To what are the stars being compared?

    b. What word gives you the clue?

    c. What was the author thinking of when he made this comparison?

    d. Can you tell whether the author loves flowers?

2. The ranger plodded on stubbornly through the underbrush, while the tempestuous wind *snarled* at him and the driving rain *stung* his face.

    a. To what is the wind being compared? Through what word?

    b. To what is the rain being compared? Through what word?

    c. What kind of sound do you think the wind made?

    d. How would you feel if you were the ranger out in such weather?

3. Dad waited for Danny to explain the disappearance of his best saw and hammer, but the boy *could not seem to find his tongue.*

    a. Was his tongue lost? Where was it all the time?
    b. How does a person feel when he acts as though his tongue were lost?
    c. Why was Danny unable to answer?

4. Our companions on the Scout hike were only twenty feet in front of us, but they had already been *swallowed up by the fog.*

    a. To what is the author comparing the fog? What words tell you?
    b. How much can we see of anything when it is swallowed up by an animal?
    c. How much could be seen of the companions? Why?

5. Immediately upon the sound of the gong a horde of students came *pouring* out of the doors into the school yard.

    a. Students are compared to what? Pitcher? Water?
    b. How fast can a liquid be poured? Very slowly? Very fast?
    c. Did the students come one at a time, or in a steady stream?

6. The marine *inched* his way through the bushes to get a peek at the enemy.

    a. Did he use a ruler to measure his progress?
    b. How far did he go each second? An inch? A foot? A yard? Or doesn't it matter? Slowly or fast?

7. "Fred," said his father, "I'm truly proud of the way you came to my help. You're *a chip off the old block.*"

    a. If the father is being compared to a "block of wood," to what does "chip" refer?
    b. In what way are "block" and a "chip" related to each other?
    c. Father was proud of what the boy did. What else about the boy makes his dad pleased?

5. STRETCHING THE TRUTH

In describing her baby sister a girl may say, "But you ought to see how small she is. She's *no bigger than a penny.*"

Strictly speaking, that statement cannot possibly be true. It is a decided **exaggeration.** Yet there is no intention to deceive in this statement, and surely anyone would understand what was actually meant.

When a person exaggerates for the purpose of getting you to believe an untruth, he tries to make the exaggeration sound honest. However, when his statement is absolutely ridiculous, he is not trying to fool you. The exaggeration is only to make his sentence sound forceful.

You will meet many expressions of exaggeration in the stories you read, and you should be able:

    a. to tell the difference between honest and dishonest exaggeration.

    b. to recognize the true meaning behind the strong language used by the speaker or writer.

EXERCISE 7

What do these italicized expressions really mean? Write the answers on your paper.

1. The little doll was lost and Sally Ann's *heart was broken.* (Was anything broken? How did Sally Ann feel?)
2. He ran off so fast that he must have reached *the other side of the earth.*
3. He reads quickly. He can *speed through a book like a jet plane.*
4. That man has *money to burn.*
5. I've eaten so much I'm *ready to burst apart.*
6. He sold his bicycle *for peanuts.*
7. It's a good idea to pack food in strong tin cans. But when you have to *use a heavy spike and a sledge hammer to get under the lid,* then the idea is not so good.
8. He was so lazy he wasn't *worth a grain of salt.*
9. Susan had *a million excuses* for being late.
10. In order to catch the pass, he darted around the other players *with the speed of an arrow.*
11. Don't let Jim pitch; *he can't hit the side of a barn.*

6. SARCASM

There is something in a person's voice which usually informs you whether he sincerely means what he says, or whether he means precisely the opposite. He may be using language that is friendly and pleasant, yet his tone and manner can tell you that he is angry with you, or that he feels bitter over something that happened. He may be ridiculing you while using words of praise. Language used in this way is called **sarcasm.**

If a friend is holding a nail in position and you strike at it with a hammer and hit his thumb instead, he will glare at you with momentary hatred, but he will probably say, "You're a *real help, you are.* Sure, a REAL HELP!" Of course you know how angry he is, even though his words seem to hide that anger. His voice tells you his true thought.

In a story, however, there is no voice to guide you. You must obtain your clues from the context. Here is an example of how context helps you to understand the sarcasm that is intended.

A traffic officer had just stopped a car that had dashed through a red traffic signal.

"That's a nice big car you're driving, mister," he said. "About how much do you think it weighs?"

"I really don't remember," replied the driver.

"Well, I'm really curious about that. It's on your driver's license. Do you mind looking it up?"

"Not a bit, officer. Here's the license, and there's the figure showing the weight."

By this time, the driver lost the suspicions he had felt at first.

"Hm, I notice you have a fine sounding name, Mister. Nathaniel Peterson. That's a name I'd like to remember, so I'll just write it down on this summons. By the way, when you see the judge tomorrow he'll be pleased with your fine name. And don't forget to tell him about the beautiful big car that you drove so expertly past the red light. Good-by, sir. I hope we'll meet again."

The policeman's language and manner were both pleasant and courteous. Could you see that it was not intended to be pleasant at all? Did you notice any clues that showed this to be sarcasm? "Do you mind if I see the weight of your car *on your driver's license?*"

What did the officer actually want to see? "I would like to re-member your *name*." Why? And on what did he write the name? "By the way, when you see the judge tomorrow—." What was he really telling the driver in that statement?

Here is another example of sarcasm in a story. Read it and watch for the clues.

Dad and Mother were coming home late from the movies, and they met the new baby-sitter as they opened the door. They also met a scene of destruction. Toys were scattered in confu-sion all over the floor, the table was upset, the lamp shade was torn, and feathers from a pillow were still floating about. More than that, the girl who had been "baby-sitting" had her hair all mussed and there was a scratch on her face.

"Oh, dear," sighed Mother, "I hope the children weren't any nuisance to you, Ann."

"Nuisance?" replied Ann. "Oh, no. Not at all. They were darlings. They threw all their toys at me, but that was only their way of making me a present of the toys. When I said I didn't like being hit with toys, they stopped at once and began throw-ing a soft pillow at me instead. When I started to cry, they hugged me lovingly. Of course they nearly broke my ribs and they pulled my hair and scratched my face, but they were the loveliest children I ever tended. And I hope they treat their mother with the same sweet love."

What are Ann's real feelings? Did she enjoy staying with those children? What kind of love does she hope the mother receives from them? In what kind of voice did Ann speak, especially when she called them the *loveliest* children?

Read these two selections aloud at home and practice making your voice sound sarcastic when you come to the parts spoken by the officer and by Ann. It would be interesting to hear several students dramatize the two stories in class the next day.

EXERCISE 8

As you read the next few paragraphs, decide whether the speaker is sarcastic or is speaking in earnest. If he is sarcastic, tell what he really means.

1. "Why, hello, pal!" exclaimed Ben. "Haven't seen you since we enlisted." He playfully whacked Sid across the shoulders.

Sid had his breath knocked out by the blow. Finally, he coughed, sputtered for a moment, and answered, "Oh, hello yourself, Ben. You certainly have a swell way of greeting an old friend. I would like to meet you this way very often, say about every hundred years."

What did Sid mean though he did not say it?

2. Tuffy had just struck out for the second time. "I'm awfully sorry," he told the manager.

"Oh, don't feel that way," the manager answered. "You're really doing the team a big service. You see, this is a hot day, and when you fan the air so often with your bat you create a breeze for the rest of the team. That cools them off and it improves their playing. Just keep on missing the ball and we will all love you for it. Yes, we will really love you."

What did the manager mean though he did not say it?

3. Mrs. Brown and Mrs. Smith had been angry with each other for a month. During that time they used to avoid meeting anywhere. But they met by chance at the church social where the minister began to introduce one to the other. "No introduction is necessary, pastor," said Mrs. Brown. "We know each other very well, don't we, Mrs. Smith?"

145

"Yes, indeed," replied Mrs. Smith. "I know you so well that I can recognize you at a distance. In fact I enjoy recognizing you at a great distance."

What was Mrs. Smith really saying to Mrs. Brown?

Helps in Making Inferences

Writers often make statements that do not mean exactly what the words say. The reader must get the meaning by inference. It is interesting and exciting to make inferences. They help you see things in a new way, and they give you mental images as you read. In your reading you must watch for:

1. *Like* and *as*, used to compare two things that are not alike:

   His mind was like a spinning top.

2. Comparisons without *like* or *as*:

   Where we live, the birds are a five A.M. alarm clock.

3. *Exaggeration*:

   The money burned a hole in his pocket.

4. *Sarcasm*:

   I just love to trip over your foot.

MAKING USE OF CONTENTS AND INDEX

9

You have heard the expression, "You can't tell a book by its cover." This is true, but you do not have to read an entire book to find out what it contains. The author of the book usually supplies you with a **Table of Contents,** not far from the front cover.

The table of contents is a list of the titles of sections, of chapters, or of stories, poems, or articles. The list also tells you the page on which the selection begins.

In a literature book, for example, the page number may be all the help you will need because you have only to know where the selection begins. In a science or social-studies text, however, you need more help. You need to know exactly where in a chapter to find the information you seek. Therefore, the author adds another kind of list to help you. This is usually placed near the back cover of the book. It is the **Index,** which is a directory to each topic of information in the book.

1. USING THE CONTENTS AND THE INDEX

Many students fail to use the index because it does not look as simple as a table of contents. It does take a little more skill to use it, but once you have mastered that skill you will find the index very helpful.

It is important to know when the index will be more useful to you than the table of contents. Sometimes you must use both to find your information.

The table of contents lists only the main parts of the book. The topics are very broad or very large. In a history book, for example, the table of contents would list such topics as "The Revolutionary War" or "How the West Was Settled." To locate information about small topics, such as "The Boston Tea Party" or "Nathan Hale," you would have to turn to the index.

Here you will see samples of both kinds of lists. They are taken from the same textbook. By reading them carefully, you will see how each one may be helpful to you in your reading.

In the Table of Contents

1. Titles are listed in the order in which they appear in the book.
2. The page number tells you where the chapter or selection begins.
3. The titles refer to large topics of information.

In the Index

1. Topics are listed in alphabetical order.
2. There may be several page numbers after a topic to tell you all the places where a topic is discussed.
3. If the topic is a large one, it is divided into smaller topics, called sub-topics.

Find the answers to these questions in the Index given on page 148:

Why does *Indians* come before *Inventions*?

In how many different places is Andrew Jackson discussed?

How many sub-topics are listed under *Inventions*?

2. ARRANGEMENT OF THE INDEX

In preparing his index, the author uses a number of devices which serve as a kind of code. Once you have become familiar with this code, you will find the index easier to use.

Sodium, 224–226, 229, 241

Soil: erosion of, 158–160; how plants get food from, 242–243; conservation of, 250

You will notice that:

1. The main topic is printed in some way that makes it stand out in the list. In the example it is capitalized. In some indexes it may be in larger or darker type, or in italics.

2. A dash is used between page numbers to indicate that the discussion of the topic covers several pages in one part of the book. In other words, "224–226" means that a discussion of sodium will be found on pages 224, 225, and 226. Another reference is made to sodium on page 229, and still another on page 241.

3. Punctuation marks are used to help you. When several sub-topics are given, a *colon* is sometimes placed after the main topic. A *comma* separates the topic from the page numbers. A *semi-colon* is used to separate each sub-topic from the next one.

EXERCISE 1

To be sure you understand the index code, answer the questions following the index items at the top of the next page.

Snow, 205, 213, 216

Sound: of human voice, 440; of musical instruments, 442; quality of, 443; recording of, 463–468; speed of, 426, 438

Spiders, 326–327

Storm: dust, 89; sound and distance of, 420; wind force in, 301

QUESTIONS

1. What is the last sub-topic about storms?
2. On how many pages will you look for information about spiders?
3. How many sub-topics are listed under *storm?*
4. In how many different places is snow discussed?
5. What topic is discussed on page 438?

3. KNOWING WHAT TO LOOK FOR

When you look for a friend's name in the telephone directory, you know that the list is arranged with last names first. If you want to find James Darby, you look first for *Darby*, not *James*. In the index, also, the most important word of a phrase, or a title, or a topic is listed first. Names of battles, for instance, are probably listed in this way:

> Bunker Hill, Battle of
> Saratoga, Battle of
> Yorktown, Battle of

The Key Word

In any topic, there usually is one word that is more important than the others. This is the one you will find listed in the index. Suppose you wish to learn about the formation of clouds. You would look it up under the letter "c" for *clouds*, not "f" for *formation*. The word *clouds*, therefore, is the **key word,** the one we hope to find in the index.

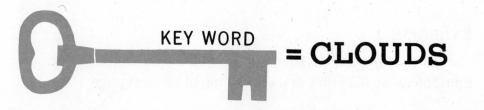

KEY WORD = CLOUDS

EXERCISE 2

List the numbers 1 to 10 on your paper. Beside each write the word which you consider the key word in the corresponding topic below.

1. the growth of democracy
2. the colonial use of candles
3. the smashing of the atom
4. aluminum in industry
5. Thomas Edison's contributions
6. the origin of fire
7. Alexander Graham Bell
8. the American Navy
9. the telescope as a hobby
10. instruments of the orchestra

More Than One Key Word

When there is more than one key word in the topic or question, you may wonder which one to use. All of them may be helpful.

Suppose that your question is, "In which of the colonies did the Quakers settle?" It may be hard to tell whether to select *colonies* or *Quakers* as your key word. Each seems like a good choice. In the index, you may find many page references under *colonies*. One of the sub-topics may be a reference to Quakers. However, if you look up *Quakers,* you may also find several references to *colonies.* You can see, then, that *both* key words may be helpful. This is why a good index will contain many sub-topics and many page references.

EXERCISE 3

In this exercise read quickly over each question to decide on the key words. Then use the sample index below to locate the pages where you will find your information. Remember that one of your key words may be listed as a sub-topic under another topic.

Directions: List the numbers 1 to 8 on your paper and write the proper key words beside each one. Then, from the index, enter the page or pages where the information may be found. Use the following form as your guide. Do not write in this book.

Sentence	Key words	Pages
1	California, gold rush	335–338
2		
3		

QUESTIONS

1. How did the gold rush change life in California?
2. What were schools like in the New England colonies?
3. Why were plantations needed for the growing of cotton?
4. When was slavery first introduced in America?
5. What part did the stagecoach play in the growth of western transportation?
6. When was oil first discovered in Pennsylvania?
7. What was one of the old missions in Texas?
8. What effect did McCormick's reaper have on agriculture?

4. USING A SIMILAR TERM

When the key word which you have selected appears in the index as a topic or a sub-topic, it is a simple matter to go on from there. However, you may not find the key word even though you are quite certain that the information you seek is in the book.

This does not mean that the index is not a good one. It would be impossible for an author to know and to list in the index exactly the words that your teacher or you have been thinking about for the topics.

He may use a word that has a meaning similar to the one you have in mind, or he may list his topics in a more general way. You may, for instance, be looking for the word *trade*. The author may have used the word *commerce*, which means the same. Information about *schools* may be listed under *education*. Facts about *stars* may be listed under *astronomy*. It is important, therefore, to know different words under which your topic may be listed.

EXERCISE 4

Match each word in Column **A** with a word of similar meaning in Column **B**. Write both words.

A	B
engines	1. petroleum
canals	2. voting
farming	3. atmosphere
laws	4. agriculture
money	5. sports
suffrage	6. currency
hygiene	7. solar system
air	8. waterways
sun	9. locomotives
oil	10. government
	11. health
	12. forests

5. TURNING TO A MORE GENERAL WORD

There is still another skill that will be helpful in using an index. Sometimes the index list may not contain either your key word or a similar word. This is the time to use your own general information and to think of some word or topic that is related to the key word. For example, if you cannot find "Types of roses," you should try "Flowers," since roses are one kind of flower. If you cannot find "chairs," try "furniture," since chairs are one kind of furniture. If you cannot find "jet engines," try "airplanes" or "aviation."

EXERCISE 5

If you have some skill in skimming, you will not mind looking in several different places until you find the reference you are searching for.

This exercise will help you develop skill in relating key words to more general terms. The list above the box is composed of general words. The key words are listed inside the box.

Directions: Copy the box on your paper, including the key words in Column **A**. For each key word find two general words related to it. Write them under **B** and **C** in your box.

(Select from this list)

hides	homes	satellite
textiles	cloth	forests
medicine	leather	moon
lumbering	metals	camera
hygiene	floods	minerals
photography	winds	shelter
weather	disease	weight

A	B	C
1. shoes	1. hides	1. leather
2. pictures that move	2.	2.
3. orbit	3.	3.
4. hurricane	4.	4.
5. diet	5.	5.
6. rayon	6.	6.
7. vaccine	7.	7.
8. igloo	8.	8.
9. wood	9.	9.
10. copper	10.	10.

EXERCISE 6

Decide on the key word in each question at the top of page 155. Then look in the Index List for one topic that is *related* to each key word. No key words appear in the Index List.

Directions: Number your paper 1–10. Write your key word for each question. Write the topic related to it.

1. How did factories cause the growth of large cities?
2. What is the principle of reflection?
3. How did early man color his garments?
4. How does our Constitution provide for justice?
5. How did the ancient Egyptians defend themselves in battle?
6. What people were sun-worshippers?
7. Who made the waltz rhythm popular in Europe?
8. How did Queen Victoria dress?
9. Why do we have "leap" year?
10. In what ways are seeds scattered?

INDEX LIST

art	dairying	musicians
agriculture	dyes	oceans
atmosphere	earth	paper
Bible	horses	rainfall
calendar	inventions	religion
canals	light	schools
costumes	plants	weapons
courts	manufacturing	

6. OTHER FACTS ABOUT INDEXES

As you become more familiar with the use of the index, you will discover that it is helpful in other ways besides those we have already discussed.

In the following sample you will notice that the word "map" is included after a page number. Most indexes have some way of indicating to you that a map, a chart, or a diagram appears on a certain page.

> grapes, 52, 93, 108, 153; in Europe, 102 (map); see *vineyards*
> Holland; see *Netherlands*

You will observe also that after the references to *grapes* you are told to see *vineyards*. This is called a **cross-reference** and means that you will find further or more complete information under the topic to which you are referred. You will notice that the cross-reference for Holland is *Netherlands*.

Another thing you should know about indexes is that they are not always found near the end of a book. In some books, such as the *World Almanac* or a "book of facts," you will find the index at the beginning in place of a table of contents. A newspaper index or a directory index may also appear at the beginning.

In an **encyclopedia,** where the information fills a number of volumes, you may find that one volume contains an index to all the information in the others. Look for this kind of index the next time you visit your library.

Some books contain more than one index. A book of poems may contain an index of subjects or topics, an index of authors, and a third index of the first lines of poems. All of these are helpful.

7. RULES FOR USING INDEXES

1. Read your question or problem carefully to understand what kind of information you will need. Will it be geography? history? science? music?

2. Be sure you are using the right book. Remember that the index of a book refers only to the material within that book. A book on Europe will probably not contain information about Tibet.

If you cannot tell which "subject" book to use, or if you do not think the topic will be found in the books you can get, use an encyclopedia.

3. Select the key words in the question.

4. Try to decide which of the key words is a main topic. The others may be found as sub-topics.

5. Skim over the index to find the key word. If it is not there, try a synonym or a related topic.

6. Make note of the page or pages where the information may be found. Then look for the information you need. It may be only a phrase or a short sentence somewhere near the bottom of the page. Or it may begin at the middle of one page and run over to the next one.

7. Do not waste time reading anything else on the page. You should merely skim along as rapidly as possible until you come to the required information. Then slow down and read that information carefully.

EXERCISE 7

Test yourself on skimming and slowing down by finding the answers to the questions above the following paragraphs. Be sure to save time by skimming until you find what you need. Then read very thoroughly to answer the questions accurately.

Take up one question at a time, and answer it before going on to the next one. You will not need to use the exact words of the paragraphs for your answers.

QUESTIONS

1. Briefly describe a spelldown.
2. Describe the appearance of the pupils' benches.
3. What was the length of the school day?
4. Where did the teacher live?
5. How did he obtain his meals?

A PIONEER SCHOOL

On the outside the schoolhouse looked like any other cabin. It had one room, a wood stove, a door, and windows. Inside the schoolhouse there were benches on two sides of the room for the little children. These benches were made of logs that had been smoothed off. The benches had no backs. On another side of the room was a long shelf. There was a bench in front of it for the older children. When they needed to write, they turned and used the shelf. The teacher sat in the center of the room.

The school day was long. Sometimes it started at seven in the morning. The children went home at six in the evening. Nearly every day the children stood up and had a spelldown. If a child could not spell a word, he sat down. The last one standing won the spelldown.

Each night the teacher stayed at the home of a different pupil. The fathers and mothers gave him his meals and a place to stay, and in this way they partly paid him.

EXERCISE 8

Directions: Here is a final test of your skills in using an index. Number your paper 1–10. For each question, write the page numbers from the index that show where you will find the answer.

1. When were steamboats first used for ocean travel?
2. What is the exact wording of the Pledge of Allegiance?

157

3. What makes aluminum such a useful metal?
4. Copy a chart of the solar system.
5. How may injuries be received from electricity?
6. What problems of space travel must still be solved?
7. What do most Belgians work at to earn their living?
8. What methods are used to save our topsoil?
9. What changes in ways of living were brought about by the use of automobiles?
10. What are the provisions of the 16th amendment?

INDEX

PHRASE IDEA WORD PHRASE WORD
WORD PHRASE WORD
PHRASE IDEA
PHRASE IDEA
PHRASE IDEA

MORE ABOUT STREAMLINED READING 10

In the previous section on skimming you learned how to look for words or phrases. You were not concerned with anything else. Your eye and your mind hurried over the other words and thoughts in the text. You were actually skipping over everything until your eye found the words you were seeking.

Now we shall try another kind of skimming. This will not be quite so rapid as the kind of skimming you learned in Chapter 5, because this time you will be looking for thoughts, not just words or phrases.

The skill of skimming for ideas is an easy one to gain and a valuable one to have. It will be very helpful to you in preparing your class assignments and in all your serious reading.

159

1. SKIMMING FOR THOUGHTS

In Chapter 5 you probably had very little difficulty finding the place where your information might be. That is because the sentences contained many of the words you had selected as the key words of the questions. You must keep in mind that the information you are seeking may be expressed in entirely different words. If, for instance, you are asked, "What kind of sound awakened the campers?" you may find that the word *sound* is not used in the story or article. You may, however, find "a scream," "the beating of drums," or "a shrill whistle," and you will recognize the expression at once as a sound. If you are asked to find the distance between two towns, you may not find the word *distance*. Instead you may find the *idea* of distance expressed in a number of miles.

EXERCISE 1

In the next exercise, see how quickly you can recognize a related idea. Select the phrase in Column **B** which will complete the sentence begun in Column **A**. Write the complete sentences on your paper.

A	B
1. The villagers were *dressed*	a. raise large crops
2. The strange object was *shaped*	b. is a popular way of speaking and writing
3. The speed *limit* on the highway was	c. into two main parts
4. The *direction* they took was	d. in colorful native costumes
5. The *government* of the country had always been	e. had lived in the town for 50 years
6. *Farmers* in the Middle West	f. are beginning to find jobs in factories
7. The English *language*	g. toward the mountains in the north
8. The older *inhabitants*	h. set at 50 miles an hour
9. The country was *divided*	i. a rule by kings
10. More and more *workers*	j. like a huge saucer

Another point to remember in using key words is that the author may use a synonym or phrase which is similar in meaning yet is not the same as the one you selected from the question. Your teacher may ask you to find why the Danish people have become successful. The paragraph which will answer your question may begin, "There are several reasons why the Danes have *prospered*." (The word *prospered* has a meaning similar to *have become successful*.)

EXERCISE 2

Try the following exercise to see how quickly you can match similar meanings. In Column **A** is a list of phrases. In Column **B** you will find the same idea expressed in a topic or title in a different way. Key words in each phrase will help you to work with more speed.

Directions: Number your paper 1–10. For each topic under **A** find a matching phrase under **B.** Write the letter that precedes this phrase.

A	B
1. A lesson in government	a. How the Buffalo Vanished
2. Lives of great men	b. Why a Volcano Blows Its Top
3. A lonely place to live	c. Flights of Our Feathered Friends
4. A celebration of the discovery of oil	d. A Town in the Middle of Nowhere
5. The eruption of a mountain	e. Birthplace of the Circus
6. The disappearance of an animal	f. How a Bill Becomes a Law
7. The migration of birds	g. Biographies of American Leaders
8. The place where an entertainment originated	h. Cape Cod Ideal for Fall Vacation
9. A town where a sport is popular	i. Oil Has an Anniversary
10. A good place to go in the autumn	j. The Game of Hockey in Quebec

2. LOCATING ANSWERS IN A LONGER SELECTION

You are ready now to test your skill in skimming over a longer selection to find the answers to your questions in the shortest time possible. Remember to use key words.

In this first attempt at skimming a longer selection, your progress may be slow. However, you will find that your speed will increase as you work with additional exercises.

EXERCISE 3

Directions: On your paper list the letters *a* to *j* in a column. Alongside each letter write the number of the paragraph which contains the answer to the question. Then write the answer. It will help you if you read the whole selection quickly first. Then find the answers to the questions one at a time.

QUESTIONS

a. What is the Latin American name for a cowboy?
b. What common sport was the invention of the Indians of Mexico?
c. What kind of actions cause the crowd to cheer the bullfighter?
d. What was the first *el pato* like?
e. What American game is something like *jai-alai?*
f. Which Latin-American game is fast and dangerous?
g. What game was first played on the plains of Argentina?
h. Why are some seats more expensive at a bullfight?
i. What equipment is used by a *jai-alai* player?
j. When does the crowd applaud the bull?

LATIN AMERICAN SPORTS

1. Our Latin American neighbors are sports lovers just as we are. You may know that the rubber ball was an invention of the Indians who lived in Mexico centuries ago. They played a kind of basketball with teams and cheering crowds.

2. Today our own games of football, baseball, and soccer are enjoyed in many parts of Latin America. Polo, skiing, and tennis are also popular. However, the sports which Latin Americans seem to enjoy most are ones not so familiar to us. One of these is jai-alai (HY-a-LY), which resembles our game of handball. The player fastens a long curved basket to his arm and uses this to catch the ball and throw it. It is a fast and dangerous game.

3. In Argentina, the cowboys invented a rough game, *el pato,* which is played on horseback. In the beginning, a cooked duck (el pato) was actually sewed up in a piece of rawhide to make a ball. Four cowboys, called gauchos in Argentina, raced about on horseback trying to get possession of the ball. The game often turned into a long, wild race over the plains. The modern game of *el pato* is played with a leather ball which also has leather loops fastened to it.

162

4. The favorite sport of most Latin Americans is the bull-fight. This sport came from Spain. It takes place in an arena in the afternoon. The price of the ticket depends upon whether one wishes to sit in the sun or in the shade. The shady side, of course, is more comfortable and more expensive. The music, parades, and brilliant costumes make this a colorful sport. The most exciting moment is the one when the bull rushes into the arena. As the bullfighter makes a quick, graceful play with his cape, the crowd cheers. Although the man is the hero of the crowd, the bull is also cheered when he puts up a good fight.

EXERCISE 4

First, read through the entire selection. Then read the first question below. To find the answer, skim over the paragraphs, using key words, until you come to the answer. Write it on your paper. Proceed with the other questions one at a time.

THE LAST FRONTIER

1. When Daniel Boone fought his way across the mountains into the western wilderness, he said he was looking for "elbow room." It was getting a little crowded in the east. Perhaps Daniel Boone was so adventurous that he only wanted to see what was on the other side of the mountain; but the pioneers who followed him were looking for places to settle and work. As they pushed the frontier farther and farther away, they found plenty of room and good reasons for settling on the land.

2. Today we still have one last frontier, but it is not likely that settlers will rush there to claim the land. The great white continent of Antarctica is not a good place to live.

3. The huge land of the Antarctic is twice as large as our United States. It has high mountains and deep rivers, but they provide no forests or swift-flowing streams. They are buried under thousands of feet of ice. During the short "summer" season, icebergs drift from the rivers into the sea to join the great ice sheet that surrounds the continent.

4. Living there is made even more rugged by the severe low temperatures and the blizzards which often whip up to a speed of 150 miles an hour. The extreme cold and fierce winds and rugged surface make this huge land a dangerous place for mankind even to explore.

5. Scientists, however, are very much interested in Antarctica, although not as a place for new housing developments.

They believe that it may be made to serve us in several other important ways. First, since much of our weather has its beginning in this region of the world, a knowledge of the conditions there will be useful for weather forecasts. Second, scientists are certain that this land is one of Nature's treasure boxes of valuable minerals which man may soon open with his mining skill.

6. A third use will be in the matter of transportation. Since man has learned to fly, the future of air transportation in the Southern Hemisphere will be aided by a further study of this part of the world. Some day the air over Antarctica may become the scene of the heaviest air traffic in the world.

QUESTIONS

a. Why did the pioneers of the West push back the frontier?
b. How does Antarctica compare in size with the United States?
c. Which word describes the kind of life that scientists face in Antarctica?
d. How many reasons are given for this continent's usefulness?
e. Which people are chiefly interested in the Antarctic?
f. How fast do the winds sometimes blow?
g. Why is this region considered a frontier?
h. What has its origin in this part of the world?

3. SKIMMING FOR THE GENERAL IDEA

You have now learned about three kinds of skimming:

1. Looking for a word or words in a list
2. Looking for a word or words in sentences or paragraphs
3. Looking through a selection for a thought where the language is different from the words of the question

You have learned through experience that the first is the most rapid kind of skimming, and the third is the least rapid.

There is still another important kind of skimming. This kind will be the slowest of all, but it is still skimming and is faster than other kinds of reading.

Suppose you wish to get a quick, general idea of a selection without giving much attention to the details. Or suppose you wish to know very quickly whether that selection will be useful or interesting to you.

You are not trying to find the answers to any questions. You are not trying to obtain information about any topic. You simply want to know, in a very general way, what the selection is about.

This requires a new way of skimming. Instead of reading all the words of the selection, you make an effort, in spite of your hurry, to spot certain words that can give you some hints to the meaning. Your eyes deliberately skip the other words.

How can you tell which are the important hints? There is no exact method. Usually you concentrate on the longer words and skip many simple and common words that you meet in all your reading. You soon learn to pick words that seem to carry the ideas in the selection, and your mind fills in enough to permit you to skim ahead in the same way. You should actually read only about three or four words on a line, sometimes only two, sometimes as many as five.

EXERCISE 5

In the following article those special words are printed in heavy type to show which words might be selected. Read the article through once, reading all the words. Then read it a second time, but this time read only the words in heavy type. You will find that you can read much faster by concentrating on those special words, and you will understand enough of the thought to obtain the general idea of the whole selection.

See if you can go through the second reading *within a minute.* Perhaps your teacher will time you.

THE GIANTS OF THE FORESTS

Man has **used** many **ways** to try to **trace life** on **earth** back to the **beginning. Much** of the dead **past** is still a **mystery** but there is **one living family** which can **trace** its **ancestry** directly **back** to the **age** of the **dinosaurs.** This is the **Big Tree family** in **California.** Its **oldest member** is **thousands** of **years** old.

This old **Sequoia tree** is **known** as the **Grizzly Giant.** It is still **strong** and shows **no signs** of **old age. It never requires medical** treatment or tree **surgery** and it has **no enemies. Fire** will **not hurt** its **bark,** which is two feet **thick.** The **tannin** in the

165

bark **kills insects** which can **harm** other trees. Even **man** is **no** longer an **enemy** of the old tree.

When these **giants** of the forest were **discovered** in **1852, lumbermen** made some **efforts** to **cut** them down. They soon **found,** however, that the great **trees** were **too big** to be handled. They often **splintered** when they **crashed** to the ground because of their great **weight.** Later **National Parks** were **made** of the areas around the trees to **protect** them, and they will continue to live on and on.

Even **bigger** than the Grizzly Giant is the **General Sherman Sequoia.** It is the **largest growing thing** in the **world** and stands **278 feet** tall. Its **waistline** measures **105 feet.** It has been **admired** by **millions** of people. There is **another Sequoia** that has had a **tunnel** built through it.

The Redwoods, another family of western giants, **prefer** a **warmer** climate than the Sequoias and **live closer** to the **seacoast. One** of them is even **taller** than the **General Sherman,** though **not** as massive. The **wood** from the **redwoods** is very **useful** and **valuable,** and some trees **may be cut** for lumber.

EXERCISE 6

See if you can answer these questions without looking at the selection again.

1. Which of these topics gives you the best general idea about the selection?
   a. The Grizzly Giant is thousands of years old.
   b. The General Sherman is the biggest tree in the world.
   c. The Sequoias and Redwoods are the largest and oldest trees in the forests of this country.
   d. The Big Tree family is thousands of years old.
2. Which two of these statements are correct?
   a. Lumbermen often cut down these trees.
   b. National Parks around these areas protect trees from destruction by men.
   c. The trees are too big to be handled by lumbermen.
   d. Trees are protected by nature from being cut down by lumbermen.
3. What protects the trees from fire and insects?
   a. The tannin in their bark kills insects.
   b. The wind and rain will put out any fire.
   c. The bark is so thick that fire cannot harm it.

4. What are the names of two of the very biggest trees?

5. There is a tunnel built

      a. through the forest

      b. through one of the trees

      c. underneath the forest

4. USING HINTING WORDS

Is it possible to derive any understanding of a selection from the use of important "hinting" words alone? Here is a chance to test that idea.

EXERCISE 7

This exercise will show you how much meaning you can get by concentrating on important words. In the selection below, only the important words are given. Skim quickly over the selection. Work for speed.

Directions: Number your paper 1–8. Write the word or words that complete each of the sentences on page 168. Do not write in this book.

    _____ coyote _____ always _____ considered _____ villain _____ western plains. _____ recent years, _____ moved east _____ become _____ problem _____ Adirondacks _____ New York State. No one _____ sure_____ _____ coyote _____ travel _____ far _____, but hunters, cattlemen _____ poultry keepers _____ hate _____ animal as _____ westerners _____.

    _____ coyote _____ larger _____ fox _____ more crafty. _____ eat _____ anything _____ sheep, calves, chickens _____ mice. _____ everything _____ available. _____ will eat berries, grasshoppers _____ June bugs. _____ hard _____ trap _____ will not rush _____ bait. _____ Conservation Department _____ worried _____ coyotes _____ increasing _____ number.

    _____ no one _____ reported _____ coyote _____ harmed _____ human _____. Perhaps _____ coward, or perhaps _____ too smart _____ close _____ man. _____ places, _____ bounty _____ $25 _____ paid _____ killing _____ coyote.

1. The coyote is described as a _____?_____ .
2. _____?_____ is now troubled by coyotes.
3. Men who deal with _____?_____ hate the coyotes.
4. A reward of _____?_____ is often paid for killing a coyote.
5. A coyote will eat _____?_____ .
6. In this article he is compared to the _____?_____ .
7. The _____?_____ Department is worried about the increasing number of coyotes.
8. Coyotes are not known to attack _____?_____ .

EXERCISE 8

Now try your own skill at skimming a complete selection to get a quick impression of the author's ideas. Try to look only at the words that seem important. Answer the questions *without reading the article a second time*. Remember that you are reading for speed. Wait for the teacher's signal before beginning to read the selection. At the end of exactly one minute you will receive another signal, this time to stop reading and begin your answers without looking back.

Directions: Number your paper 1–6. Write the letter standing before the phrase that completes each sentence correctly in the test on page 169.

The heart of every true American quickens when he sings the national anthem or when Old Glory passes by. But to really feel the spirit of freedom on which our nation is built, an American must visit the place where liberty was born. He must walk in the streets of our early capital, old Philadelphia, Ben Franklin's city.

Philadelphia is a big and busy city these days, but the visitor will find signs everywhere to lead him to "Historical Shrines." He has only to turn into Independence Square to feel that he is living in colonial days. There stands Independence Hall in quiet dignity, restored to its original state. One might sit on the bench opposite this Birthplace of Independence and imagine that he can see tall, red-haired Tom Jefferson striding by.

Visitors stand in quiet wonder in this great shrine where men once met to decide the fate of a nation. It was here that the Declaration of Independence was read, discussed, and finally approved. It was here that the Constitution became the law of our land. And it is here that the visitor may still see the famous Liberty Bell.

It was on July 8, 1776 that the bell rang out to call the citizens of the town together for a public reading of the Declaration of Independence. It rang on other occasions, too, but a crack in its surface ended its service after 1835. Anyone is free now to walk up to the old bell, where it rests on heavy beams, to touch it, snap a picture of it and read the words around its top. Although it no longer rings, the bell serves to inspire all those who read these words: "Proclaim Liberty throughout all the Land Unto all the Inhabitants Thereof."

TEST

1. You get the impression after a quick reading that the author of this article is

    a. patriotic
    b. a sightseer
    c. critical

2. In general this is an article about

    a. one of our largest cities
    b. the birthplace of freedom
    c. early America

3. In discussing the Liberty Bell the author is chiefly interested in

    a. its appearance today
    b. its value as a symbol of freedom
    c. the way it became cracked

4. Two great Americans mentioned are:

    a. Lincoln and Washington
    b. Roosevelt and Eisenhower
    c. Franklin and Jefferson

5. The inspiring quotation the author uses appears

    a. over Independence Hall
    b. in the Declaration of Independence
    c. on the Liberty Bell

6. The Liberty Bell may be seen in

    a. Philadelphia Court House
    b. Independence Hall
    c. The Betsy Ross House

Summary

In this chapter and in "Streamlined Reading," you have learned about four types of skimming, from the easiest, which requires little skill, to the most complicated type which takes much more skill. You should give yourself many opportunities to practice all these kinds of skimming, with various lists, with newspapers, and with material from your textbooks. These types include:

1. Looking up a word or words in a list
2. Locating a word or a phrase on a page of printed content
3. Locating an answer when its wording is different from the wording of the question or topic
4. Skimming to obtain the general thought

DISCOVERING RELATED IDEAS 11

Suppose you have just begun to read a selection. You may read one thought in the first sentence. You may read another thought in the second sentence, and another in a third sentence. Or you may read two thoughts in one sentence.

None of these thoughts are strangers to each other. They are all **related.** But in what way are they related? Are they friends or enemies? Do they agree or disagree? Do they report events that happened together or separately? You cannot understand these thoughts unless you can see how they are related to each other.

It often takes just one little word to supply the clue to that relationship. If that word is missing, you will feel that something is wrong. Here is an example.

It was a bitter cold night. The old man wore a light jacket, and his head and hands were bare.

You may wonder why two such different ideas are placed together in the same paragraph. If one small word were added, it would show you why.

It was a bitter cold night, *but* the old man wore a light jacket and his head and hands were bare.

The word *but* shows that the two thoughts are different. They are contrasted to each other. There are other clue words, too, which show that thoughts are related by contrast.

1. OPPOSITES, OR DIFFERENCES

There are a number of expressions which tell us that two thoughts are pulling in different directions. "But" is one of them. There are many more, and you will see some of them in these sentences about the old man.

Even though it was a bitter cold night, the old man wore a light jacket and his head and hands were bare.

In spite of the bitter cold night, the old man wore a light jacket and his head and hands were bare.

It was a bitter cold night; *yet* the old man wore a light jacket and his head and hands were bare.

It was a bitter cold night. The old man, *however,* wore a light jacket and his head and hands were bare.

It was a bitter cold night. *Nevertheless,* the old man wore a light jacket and his head and hands were bare.

You can see why these words are so important when we read. They really help to make the meaning clear.

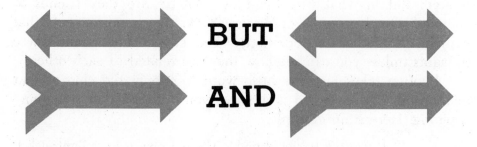

BUT

AND

EXERCISE 1

Read each sentence carefully. From the three choices that follow select the one that most nearly expresses the idea of the sentence.

1. *Although* most of his working hours were spent in the laboratory, he managed to find some time each day for his children.

    a. He gave as much time to his children as to his work.
    b. It was too difficult to give any time to his children.
    c. He gave a little time daily to his children.

2. When they reached New York, they had only a few dollars left. *Nevertheless,* they decided to take a sight-seeing trip around the city.

    a. They came to New York fully prepared to go sight-seeing.
    b. They could barely afford the sight-seeing trip.
    c. They were not able to take the sight-seeing trip.

3. When Beethoven was still a young man he began to grow deaf, and soon he could not hear any of his music. *Yet* he created some of our most beautiful compositions.

    a. His was an unusual accomplishment.
    b. It was natural for him to be a great composer.
    c. His deafness prevented him from writing good music.

4. The hardships endured by this group of people on that "covered wagon" trip were almost unbelievable. *In spite of* those hardships, they reached their goal without losing one of their number.

    a. One would expect them all to reach their goal.
    b. One would not expect them all to reach their goal.
    c. Such trips were always made successfully.

5. *Despite* his feelings for his sister's friends, he was a polite and generous host.

    a. He liked his sister's friends.
    b. It was easy for him to be a good host.
    c. He disliked his sister's friends.

The following selections are taken from *Rip Van Winkle,* a story by Washington Irving. The author gives you two opposite ideas for each paragraph, but he signals the change with clue words such as you have used in the previous exercise.

Directions: Read each paragraph carefully. Be ready to answer the questions in class.

1. Rip was a descendant of the Van Winkles who figured so gallantly in the good old days of Peter Stuyvesant and accompanied him to the siege of Fort Christmas. He inherited, *however,* but little of the fighting spirit of his ancestors.

(Rip's ancestors were gallant fighting men. How can you tell that Rip was not?)

2. If left to himself, he would have whistled away all his days in perfect contentment, *but* his wife kept dinning in his ears lectures about his idleness, his carelessness, and the ruin he was bringing his family.

(Would Rip have been happy with his lazy life? What kept him from enjoying his laziness? How does the author tell you this?)

3. What seemed especially odd to Rip was that, *although* these little men were evidently amusing themselves, they had the gravest faces and the most mysterious silences.

(Why did their appearance seem strange to Rip as compared with their actions?)

4. Rip paused for an instant, *but* he thought the noise was the muttering of one of those passing thundershowers and he went on his way.

(Why did Rip pause? Why did he go on his way? What two different thoughts must have entered Rip's mind?)

5. True it is, in all points of spirit befitting an honorable dog, he was as courageous an animal as ever scoured the woods, *but* what courage can withstand the ever-doing and all-besetting terrors of a woman's tongue?

(What are the two opposite or contrasting ideas?)

2. WHEN THE OPPOSITE IS NOT STATED

In the five sentences, page 174, one thing is stated to be the opposite of another. Many sentences containing the words *but, however, yet*, and so on, do not exactly state the two things that are opposite. The writer gives only a clue. He gives one side of the opposition. The reader must supply the other. Here is an example:

> Columbus thought he had reached the East Indies, *but* he was wrong.

The word *but* is a clue that something different or opposite to the first statement is coming. However, *he was wrong* is not really the opposite. The true opposite is ". . . but he had only reached the islands lying off South America."

Sometimes it is the part of the sentence before the clue word that needs to be restated.

> Mr. Johnson was rich and famous. *Yet* he was an unhappy man.

First thought: He was rich and famous. (means "He should have been happy.")
Second thought (opposite): He was unhappy.

> It rained and snowed all day long, *although* the weatherman had predicted fair weather.

First thought: It rained and snowed all day long.
Second thought: The weatherman had predicted fair weather.

EXERCISE 3

On your paper write the clue word for each sentence or pair of sentences. Then rewrite one of the two thoughts, changing the wording to make it sound opposite to the other.

1. He insisted that he was right even after we pointed out to him all his mistakes.
2. It takes a great deal of scientific knowledge and money and time and preparation to launch a space rocket. In spite of all the problems, there have been numerous successful launchings.

175

3. The driver stubbornly insisted that the traffic light was green when he passed it. Nevertheless there were witnesses' to the accident who claimed he either was mistaken or was lying.
4. Fred decided to start out on that stormy day regardless of all the warnings he received from his family and friends.
5. He did not have enough popularity for election as president of the G. O. However, he could speak well, he could direct meetings, and he could plan important activities for us.

3. CLUES THAT MORE INFORMATION IS COMING

A new sentence or new thought may add to the previous statement and support it instead of opposing it, like this:

> Tommy was the best player on the team; *in addition,* he was the top student in his class.

The moment you read the clue "in addition," you knew that you were going to find more praise about Tommy. The second thought gave more strength, more importance, to the first.

There are a number of other clue words that serve the same purpose, such as *besides, furthermore, moreover.* They tie thoughts together. They keep them closely related.

EXERCISE 4

Explain how the second thought in each pair below adds to the effect of the first. Name the clue word. The first pair will be explained for you.

1. Joan likes to drink orange juice; *besides,* it is good for her health. (a. Joan likes orange juice. b. It is good for her to like it.)
2. The boy promised to return all the money he had lost. Furthermore, he said it would be delivered to the owner the very next day.
3. Two chairs were damaged when the store delivered the furniture. Moreover, one small cabinet was missing.
4. Dick Dorman received a medal for swimming, as well as honorable mention for his running in the 100-yard race.
5. I insisted on getting an answer, and I also demanded that it should not dodge the question.

4. TIME RELATIONSHIP

Careless readers are like careless travelers who must turn around and go back because they missed a small signpost and so went in the wrong direction.

In order to understand a story you must know what happened first, next, and so on. Authors, however, do not always tell their stories by saying: "This happened, then that, then this." They use many different signal words. Some of them are familiar to you, but you may meet others in your reading.

Authors often switch events, too. The second event may occur first in time, or the other way around. Unless you are alert for the signals, a story may soon become puzzling to you. It is important to notice the clue words, or signals, that show time and that tell which event followed another. Notice them in these sentences and see how the thoughts are related in time.

1. *Not until* the last bullet was used, did they surrender the fort.

("Not until" tells you that the men in the fort did not surrender easily. They fought until not a bullet was left. Only then did they surrender.)

2. *The instant* he leaped from his horse, he saw the Indian raise his bow and arrow.

(The clue word lets you know that the leap from the horse and noticing the Indian occurred together.)

3. The highway was made by workers who improved the trail the soldiers had *already* made.

(Notice how the time word *already* tells you that the soldiers had made the trail before workers began to build the highway.)

4. The sun had *long* set in the west *before* they reached the settlement.

(Can you tell from the words "long before" that it was evening and not daytime when the people got to the settlement?)

5. New trouble broke out *shortly after* the peace treaty was signed.

(The word *shortly* adds new meaning to the word *after*. It tells us that it was *soon* after, not a long time later. Which happened first, the trouble or the treaty?)

EXERCISE 5

After each passage below, two events are listed. Decide which event occurred first. Find the time signal which tells you the time order of the events.

1. At round-up time, the new-born calves were branded with the mark of their owner. Soon afterwards, the owner selected the cattle which were to be sent on the long drive to the market.

   a. Branding the calves
   b. Selecting the cattle

2. Their differences of opinion resulted in a quarrel. Thereafter they avoided each other as much as possible.

   a. The quarrel
   b. Avoiding each other

3. It was only when all the guests had left that Johnny decided to play his guitar.

   a. Johnny decided to play
   b. Guests left

4. The boy listened to his father telling about the skyscraper he was helping to build. Then and there he decided he was going to be a steel worker.

   a. Listening to his father
   b. Deciding to be a steel worker

5. As soon as Aladdin begins to rub the lamp the genie appears in a bright cloud.

   a. The genie appears
   b. Aladdin rubs the lamp

5. TIME ORDER IN LONGER SELECTIONS

In writing a long narrative selection, an author may not tell the events in the exact order in which they happened. If he changes the time order, he will give the reader signals. Note how the writer of the following news report tells you the order in which things happened.

> The explosion shook the area at three o'clock. Firemen were *still* quenching the flames caused by the crash which had occurred a half hour *earlier*.

The time signals show that events occurred in this order:

1. the crash
2. the flames
3. quenching the flames
4. the explosion

In the following selection the events are not reported in their order of happening. The time signals are italicized.

> It was not until the Rosetta stone was found *in the 1800's* that Europeans could read the writings of the Egyptians. They had found the records of the Egyptians *centuries before* but were unable to read them. The Egyptians had invented a kind of writing *thousands of years ago* by using symbols to stand for syllables. The Rosetta stone had the same words carved on it in three languages. This made it possible to read the Egyptian writing.

Careful reading will show you that the events happened in this way:

1. Egyptians invented a kind of writing
   (*thousands* of years ago)
2. Egyptian records found
   (*hundreds* of years ago)
3. Finding of the Rosetta stone
   (*in the 1800's*)

EXERCISE 6

Look for time signals as you read this passage. Decide the order in which the events actually occurred.

> At this spot on the west bank of the Hudson River, Aaron Burr raised his pistol one morning in 1804 and shot Alexander Hamilton through the heart. The quarrel that led to the duel had occurred in a political campaign a few months earlier. The two men had been rivals in law practice from the day the Revolutionary War ended. Then in 1800, Hamilton had helped to keep Burr from winning the Presidency.

Directions: On your paper list the events below in the order in which they occurred.

    a. Burr shot Hamilton.
    b. Hamilton and Burr were rival lawyers.
    c. The quarrel occurred in a political campaign.
    d. Hamilton helped to keep Burr from winning the Presidency.

6. PLACE RELATIONS

It is important to know *where* things happen as well as *when* they happen, in order to understand what we read. An author may use **place signals** for this purpose. Sometimes, however, he may omit the signals and let you decide for yourself.

In the following sentences, the place signals appear in italics.

1. They mounted their horses and headed *in the direction from which they had come.*

(Did they continue ahead, or did they ride *back*?)

2. The crowd of waiting people became quiet as a number of men approached them at a run. A *little distance behind them* ran the trumpeter.

(Can you see a mental picture of the crowd waiting, then the men arriving, then the trumpeter? Who was closest to the crowd?)

3. The tower is mirrored in the still lake *at its base.*

(What expression tells you that the tower and the lake are close to each other?)

4. The children longed to know what was *beyond the horizon.*

("Beyond" means a *distance away from* or *past*. The horizon is as far as you can see. How far was the place the children wanted to know about?)

5. *From the plane* the crater of the volcano looked like a dark spot in the desert.

(Was the plane high or low? How can you tell?)

EXERCISE 7

How good a detective are you? By noting the details and place signals, can you tell where these people are in the following passages?

Directions: List the numbers 1 to 10 on your paper. Select the best answer, and write its letter alongside the number for the sentence.

181

1. When we were more than three miles high we began to level off.

The people were

   a. in a plane
   b. on a high mountain road
   c. on a bridge

2. I tripped over a root and fell flat on my face on the trail.

The accident occurred

   a. in the playground
   b. in the woods
   c. on a country road

3. We crept close to the edge and saw a giant carpet of velvety green spread out far below us.

The observers were

   a. in a castle
   b. in a plane
   c. on a mountain top or cliff

4. The night had come quickly, and stars were twinkling overhead. We could hear the mighty throb of the engine far down below the deck.

The people were

   a. on a ship
   b. in the jungle
   c. in a trailer

5. The first time I met Bill Larkin he was standing on a ladder, waist high in water, peering through the window of his helmet.

Bill was

   a. a soldier at an army camp
   b. a deep-sea diver about to leave the ship
   c. at a swimming pool

6. As we rounded the curve, I could see the full moon turning the steel rails into silver ribbons.

We were

   a. on a ship
   b. on a train
   c. in a wagon

7. Coming down the slope between the tall pines were two wooly cubs, and their mother, I think, and cameras began to click.

The bears were

   a. in the zoo
   b. in a national park
   c. in the jungle

8. We went out early that morning after the storm to look for driftwood.

We were

   a. on a ranch
   b. at the beach
   c. on a farm

9. Wearing his pitcher's glove, Johnny, aged ten, sat all by himself in the left-field bleachers, hoping the batter would whack a homer and the coveted sphere would come his way.

Johnny was

   a. at the movies
   b. at a baseball game
   c. at a tennis match

10. Bill and I bounced along with some speed but with little comfort, and my legs soon grew weary of pedaling grandfather's old red tandem.

We were

   a. on a tandem bicycle
   b. in a horse and .buggy
   c. on a merry-go-round

7. CAUSE AND EFFECT

In your science work, you learn to ask, "Why does this or that happen? What is the reason? What is the cause?" In a great deal of your reading, the author will show you why something happened by using the word *because*. He will say, "This happened (the effect) because of that (the cause)." The clue word *because* makes it very simple for you. But as your reading material becomes more difficult, the writer will expect you to understand *why* something happens, or *why* people act or speak as they do, even when the clue word is omitted. For example:

> The mountain was all rock and its walls were nearly straight up. It was considered to be one of the hardest climbs in the world.

A careless reader might read each sentence as a separate idea and fail to see that they are related, that one fact is the **result** or **effect** of the other.

Cause: Mountain was all rock and nearly straight up
Effect: One of the hardest climbs in the world

It would be much easier to understand how the thoughts were related if they included a clue word, like this:

> The mountain was considered to be one of the hardest climbs in the world *because* it was all rock and its walls were nearly straight up.

Here are two facts taken from an old Greek legend:

> King Aegeus threw himself into the sea and was killed.
> The king had seen a ship returning with a black sail, the signal that his son was dead.

At first, these two statements may seem to be separate ideas about the king, but they actually belong together. One fact was the cause of the other, as you can see when the statement is rewritten.

> King Aegeus threw himself into the sea *because* he had seen a ship returning with a black sail, the signal that his son was dead.

In each of the following examples, the two facts will be marked (a) and (b). Decide which is the cause and which is the effect.

1. (a) John was the last boy in the line of graduates because (b) he was the tallest boy in his class.
2. (a) Because Walter Reed and other scientists experimented to find the cause of yellow fever, (b) we know now that one kind of mosquito carries yellow fever.
3. (a) In 1588, Spain lost her power on the sea because (b) her great fleet was defeated by the English ships.

EXERCISE 9

Perhaps you noticed in Exercise 8 that the "cause" fact always followed the word "because." In the following exercise there is no clue word to help you distinguish between cause and effect. The facts themselves should provide that information.

Directions: Divide your paper into two parts. Over one write the heading *Cause*. Over the other write *Effect*. Number 1–5. For each pair of sentences below, decide which is cause and which is effect. Write the letter for each statement in the right column.

1. a. The traders built their posts near the biggest Indian camps.
   b. The trappers did not have to travel far to sell their furs to the traders.
2. a. One of the most expensive gems in the world is the diamond.
   b. The diamond is beautiful, lasting, and useful.
3. a. As the pilot glided down toward the field, he suddenly pulled his plane up again toward the sky.
   b. The pilot realized that the field was too small for landing his plane.
4. a. The Weather Bureau warned that a hurricane was on the way.
   b. The people who lived along the beach rushed to fasten their boats more securely to the docks.
5. a. Years ago people made their own clothing and produced their own food.
   b. Years ago people did not depend on each other as they do now.

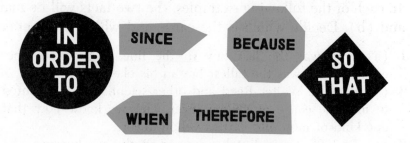

8. EXPRESSIONS THAT MAY BE USED IN PLACE OF "BECAUSE"

Authors often use other expressions than "because," and we must learn to recognize those as signals, too. In the following sentences you will find some of these words or phrases.

1. The captain agreed to let the boat remain in the harbor *so that* the passengers could go ashore for a look at the town.

(Here the words *so that* will help to tell us why the captain kept his ship in the harbor. They lead us to the effect.)

2. Canada has a long, hard northern winter; *therefore* autumn, when she must provide for the months ahead, is her busiest season.

(Here the word *therefore* is used to signal the effect of the long winter in Canada.)

3. There are many monasteries in Tibet, *since* the people are very religious.

(Here the word *since* is used to signal the reason or cause *why* there are many monasteries in Tibet.)

4. *When* the low, moaning sound reached his ears, the trapper crept cautiously toward his gun.

(Here the word *when* signals the reason *why* the trapper acted cautiously.)

5. She lifted the lamp a little higher *in order to* see the face of her unknown visitor.

(Here the words *in order to* let you know that a reason for her act is about to be given.)

6. There was a great increase in traffic during the holiday. *Consequently,* cars that should have been going through the tunnel were lined up at the entrance for a half-mile.

(Here the word *consequently* is used to signal the result of the holiday traffic.)

EXERCISE 10

You now have had some experience with several ways in which an author indicates the cause, and the effect of that cause. In the following exercise, the blank needs a word or phrase selected from the list of signal words given below.

Directions: Number your paper 1–8. Write the signal word or phrase that best fits each sentence. Do not write in this book.

since	consequently
when	so that
in order to	therefore
because	

1. The giraffe is so tall that it is difficult for him to reach down to eat from the ground. _____ he likes to eat the top leaves of the tall trees.
2. _____ men began to travel farther and farther across the sea, they needed new and faster ways of moving their ships.
3. _____ get their inspiration from Nature, artists often set up their easels in the park or at the seashore.
4. The fathers of the boys hired a small truck _____ they could move the piano to the club house.
5. _____ he has been saving money from early boyhood, Jack has almost enough for his first year at college.
6. The crowd began to cheer _____ they realized that the child had been rescued safely from the well into which he had fallen.
7. When many people came to work in the cities there was not room enough for a house for each family; _____ tall apartment buildings were necessary to provide homes for many families.
8. Robin Hood lived in the forest as an outlaw _____ he could escape the sheriff's men.

9. FINDING CAUSE AND EFFECT IN LONGER SELECTIONS

In longer selections you will find that authors may supply clue words in some places and leave them out in others. In addition, the statements about cause and effect may be separated from each other. That may make it somewhat harder to see the relation between them.

The selection below will be a guide for you in the exercise that follows it.

> A constant danger in the mines is the cave-in. A man who works in the mines develops the habit of listening for faint, creaking sounds which may be a serious warning.
>
> Not long ago, a miner who was sitting in a movie theater suddenly jumped out of his seat, shouted a warning, and ran for the nearest exit.

QUESTIONS

1. Why does a miner develop the habit of listening sharply? (Faint noises may be a warning of the start of a cave-in.)
2. Why do you think the miner leaped from his seat? (The selection does not say, but you infer (or guess) that he heard the same faint, creaking sounds which indicate the beginning of a cave-in at a mine.)
3. Can you predict what probably happened in the theater after that? (Predictions require *good guessing*. We may infer that the miner's judgment was correct and that the cave-in occurred soon after. *How soon?* Very soon, because the miner *ran* for the nearest exit. He certainly expected the crash to come quickly.)

4. It will now be interesting for you to follow another trend of thought which will bring out another set of cause-effect relationships. Could the miner, who may not have been in a mine for some years, have only imagined that he heard the creaking sound? Might he have been escorted out of the theater by a policeman? Might some quick-witted person have jumped to the stage and quieted the audience by assuring them there was no danger?

All the questions above are tied in the cause-effect relationships. The answers you have worked out will put you on the right track to answer the questions in the next exercise.

Read this selection and answer the questions that follow. Re-read the selection if you wish. Then be ready to discuss the answers.

THE RUSH FOR GOLD

After the discovery of gold in California, a great many men decided to travel there and get rich quickly. There were three different routes they could follow in making their way to that state.

The overland trip by covered wagon was a hardship. The gold seekers were impatient to get started, so that many of them left with poor equipment and without enough provisions. There were rivers and streams to cross, the heat of the plains was hard to bear, and the cold of the mountains had to be met. Meanwhile their provisions gave out and their equipment broke down, and as a result the trip took a great deal longer than they had hoped.

A second route was by way of Panama. There was only a short strip to cross there, but there was no canal in those days. Therefore the journey had to be made through the jungle to the Pacific. It was hard to get passage on a ship from there to California, because the vessels which made the trip were not meant for passengers. Yet many men who were in a hurry chose this way since it was the fastest, if they could find a ship that would take them.

The safest route was altogether too slow for the impatient gold seekers. This was the very long passage all the way by water around the tip of South America and north to California. The men who took this route brought merchandise to the west and sold it to the settlers for high prices. Therefore they became rich even though they did not dig for gold.

1. Why did many gold seekers find the overland route the hardest?
2. Why were so many men poorly prepared for the overland trip?
3. Why did many choose to go through the jungle of Panama?
4. Why wasn't the trip from Panama the best way?
5. Why didn't all gold seekers choose the safest way?
6. Why weren't those who went the long way in a hurry to find gold?

EXERCISE 12

Read the following selection and then look over the questions that come after it. You are to match each *effect* in the first column with its proper *cause* in the second column. On your paper join the cause with the effect to make a complete sentence. You may turn back to any part of the selection for help in obtaining your answers.

THE SOUND STAGE

The huge sound stages, with their heavy concrete walls, look dark and lifeless from the outside. However, they are the center of all studio activities, as most of the filming takes place here.

When pictures are taken out of doors, it is sometimes difficult to control the lighting of scenes and to register the voices of actors. Outdoor noises often interfere with those which are being recorded for the movie. Sudden changes in the weather may disturb the plans for lighting. Sound stages are, therefore, used for nearly all outdoor scenes as well as indoor scenes.

Within these soundproof buildings, actors' voices can be recorded easily because outside noises are completely shut out. There are no windows which rattle in the wind or through which noises from the lot may enter. There are only a few doors, and these are heavily padded. Red lights over the outside doors indicate when a movie is being shot and are a warning so that no one will enter.

Any type of weather which the scene requires can be produced in a sound stage. Water running through pipes can be controlled to produce a heavy or a very light rain. Fog can be created by turning air on dry ice. Huge fans are used when light breezes or heavy windstorms are needed. Giant arc lights are used to produce the effect of extreme heat for tropical scenes. The lights can be dimmed for moderate sunshine. Colored and frosted lights can be used to give the appearance of a moon-lit night. Lightweight cloth, wire screens, and odd, wiggly shapes can be placed in front of the lights to manufacture shadows or to throw gay, spooky, or even frightening effects on a scene.

A studio lot may have twenty or more sound stages. The sound stages are large, and street scenes and mountain and lake scenes can be set up without difficulty. The large number of sound stages permits the filming of a great many scenes at the same time. Carpenters, electricians, and other workers may be busy setting up or dismantling scenes in some of the sound stages. In others, actors may be at work on a "take," as the movie people call the photographing of a picture.

In one sound stage, a variety of scenes may be arranged at one time. A certain movie may call for a number of outdoor scenes as well as many indoor sets. You may see a street scene, a farmyard, or a park, and the interior of a living room, an office, or a hospital room, all assembled in different sections of one sound stage. Sometimes the complete building may be used for a single scene in which two or three hundred actors are before the camera at once.

Effect

1. Sound stages look gloomy from the outside because . . .

2. Sound stages are the center of the movie-making industry because . . .

3. Voices are difficult to record outdoors because . . .

4. Plans for outdoor lighting must often be changed because . . .

5. Red lights sometimes shine on the sound-stage door because . . .

6. Scenes that look like outdoors can be set up easily because . . .

7. A moonlight scene can be made indoors because . . .

8. A storm can be made indoors because . . .

9. Many scenes can be made at one time because . . .

10. Hundreds of actors can be working at the same time because . . .

Cause

A. large fans can be used.

B. outdoor noises interfere.

C. there are many sound stages on one studio lot.

D. they have heavy concrete walls.

E. the sound stages are so large.

F. special lights can give that effect.

G. each sound stage is large enough for many scenes.

H. most of the filming is done there.

I. people must be warned not to enter.

J. there are so many changes of weather and light outdoors.

What to Remember About This Chapter

Even though two statements are written as two separate sentences, it is frequently necessary to understand how they are related to each other in meaning. Sometimes there are clues to help you. Sometimes you have to rely on your reasoning power.

The ideas the two statements express may be **opposite to each other.** You can instantly recognize this by such clues as "but," "nevertheless," "despite," etc.

The second thought may **add an important meaning** to the first thought. In that case you will probably find clues like "in addition to," "furthermore," etc.

The thoughts may be related by **time:** "before," "after," "whenever," "the moment that— " "ever since," etc.

The thoughts may be related by their **place or position:** "in front," "behind," "at the bottom," "over," etc.

Finally, one thought may be the **cause** or the **effect** of the other.

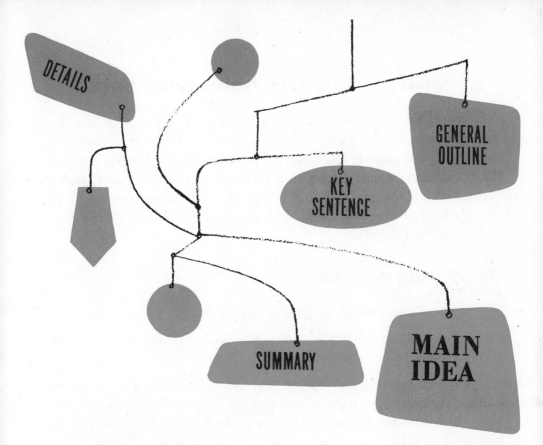

THE PLAN
BEHIND
THE PARAGRAPH

12

Before an author writes a paragraph he usually plans it in his mind. He knows what he wants to say. He must decide on the best way to say it. Will it be best for him to give a list of examples? Should the material be told in time order, like a story?

You will understand the paragraph better if you can see the author's plan as you read. If you can recognize the plan, you will be able to read the paragraph with greater speed and more confidence. You will know what to expect. It's like waiting to catch a ball. If you know, ahead of the throw, whether it will be slow or fast, high or straight, your muscles will be set to catch it. But if you do not know what to expect, your hands will probably be stung by the ball or you might even miss it.

1. PREDICTING THE PLAN FROM ADVANCE HINTS

When the main thought of a paragraph appears in the first sentence, you have a clue at once as to what the rest of the paragraph will tell you. If the main thought is placed farther down in the paragraph, it may take you a moment or two to find it. But no matter where the main thought appears, it is important to find it quickly so that you will be able to see how the details in the paragraph are tied together.

Plan A. Listing the Details

Suppose the paragraph begins this way:

> Many unexpected difficulties had to be overcome after the canal was completed.

You can tell that the author will give you a list of various difficulties. It does not matter in what order they are given. Your mind is set to watch for them, and you will feel easier because you are prepared for what is coming.

Some other key sentences follow:

1. *A number of legends* are told about the mistletoe.

This paragraph will, of course, present a short list of those legends.

2. *Most of* the holidays we celebrate today began with ancient customs.

Again, you will expect a list, or a number of examples. This time they will be about holidays and how they began with ancient customs. Such words as *many, much, a number of, several,* and *most* tell that examples will follow. These words are clues, but they do not always appear in paragraphs that list examples. Look for clues of a different kind in the next group of key sentences.

3. The little earthworm is really *a great help to the farmer.*

The clue here is "a great help to the farmer." How can the author support this statement? He will have to offer several *examples* to show how the work of the earthworm helps the farmer. Therefore you will expect a list of those examples.

4. The Aztecs were *much more advanced* in their civilization than the Indians who lived farther north in America.

How can the paragraph show that the Aztecs were much more advanced? A list is to be expected.

5. If you are planning a debate in your class, follow *these rules*.

What list would you expect to find following this statement?

6. When De Lesseps, a French engineer, began the construction of the Suez Canal in Egypt, he ran into *paralyzing problems*.

What will be listed in this paragraph?

7. A smashed automobile wheel is not necessarily "junk."

What should you expect here? Surely you will ask yourself, "Why not?" The answer to that question will probably be a list of ways in which the wheel can still be used.

8. The Battle of Midway will go down in history as *one of the most important* naval battles in the world.

The reader is not satisfied with this statement alone. He wants to know why it was so important. He will therefore expect the author to give a list of reasons.

Plan B. The List May Have a Definite Order

There is another kind of paragraph that also presents the reader with a list. In this kind, however, the list must be in correct order: first one event, then another, after that still another, and so on, until the story or explanation is complete. Somewhere in the key sentence there will be a clue to inform you that the items will take place in a certain order.

Here is one such key sentence. The rest of the paragraph will follow that order.

> *The mosquito goes through a number of stages* in its growth. It *begins* as an egg. *Then* after four days it becomes a larva. Twelve days *later* it will be seen as a pupa. Within five days *after that* it appears as a full-grown mosquito.

The word *stages* is the important clue in the key sentence. The signal words *begins, then, later,* and *after that* help further to show you the passage of time. But even the first sentence makes clear that the events will occur in a certain order.

This type of paragraph really answers the question, What happened? or How does it happen?

Let us examine some additional key sentences and see what to expect.

1. Lighting for our homes has gone through an interesting *history of changes.*

The very word "history" promises that this paragraph will list the changes in time order.

2. Through *one* improvement *after another* the automobile has become more nearly perfect.

Can you guess from the clue "one after another" that the improvements will be listed in time order?

3. Railroad trains have made tremendous progress during the years *since their beginning,* about 1825.

What would you expect in this paragraph?

4. As each event became *more and more* mysterious, we became more and more frightened.

Can you see the need for a step-by-step account of those events?

Plan C. Paragraphs That Tell How

Read carefully the paragraph below about motion pictures. Try to discover how it differs from the types of paragraph you studied in Plan A and Plan B. Notice the way the writer makes the paragraph "tell how."

> Motion pictures are really a succession of still pictures. If you should stare at a picture and then close your eyes suddenly, you would notice that you can still see it for a small fraction of a second. Then the image fades. The picture itself disappeared from view, but your vision of it persists. If you could be shown a second picture before the image of the first one faded, the first one would merge into the second. If the first picture showed a man with his arm at his side and the second with his arm slightly raised, it would appear to you as if he were actually raising his arm. Slight changes like these are shown on the motion picture screen at every picture or "frame," but the frames keep changing at an extremely rapid rate, sixteen in each second. To the observer, the people or objects in the pictures seem to be moving.

You should now notice that this is not just a list of details, as was the case in all the paragraphs that were given before. There is not a single detail that, by itself, proves or supports the main thought. But taken all together they carry it out properly. You cannot prove the main thought of such a paragraph by any *one* of the details. It takes the whole paragraph to do that.

Now see if you can predict what should follow in the paragraph for each key sentence below.

1. The Bessemer *process* made it possible to change ordinary iron into tough steel.

The word "process" means *method*. The paragraph should list the steps for carrying out this method of turning iron into steel.

2. Through the use of the X ray some curious objects were once discovered inside a statue.

You should expect the author to tell you the story, from beginning to end, of why the X ray was used, how it was used, and what was found inside the statue. If you read such a paragraph with these questions in mind, it will become clear to you at once.

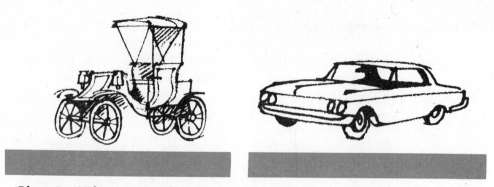

Plan D. When Two Things Are Compared

The following outline will show you how a paragraph is planned and built to show a comparison.

Key sentence

The automobiles of 1902 were like toys compared with the modern car.

One popular early automobile

1. Looked like open carriage, made of wood
2. Weighed 1200 pounds
3. Seated only two persons
4. Ran on bicycle-type wheels
5. Had 12-horsepower engine
6. Had a top speed of about 10 miles per hour

Modern automobile

1. Has streamlined design, made of metal
2. Weighs 5000 pounds
3. Can seat more people
4. Runs on metal wheels, with air-filled tires eight inches wide
5. Has 300-horsepower engine
6. Has a top speed much over 100 miles per hour

You will recognize that even though the key sentence used the word *compare*, the paragraph actually described the differences. The word *compare* may refer either to likeness or to difference. You should notice also that a paragraph based on this outline would have two parts. The first part would deal only with early cars; the second part would deal only with modern cars.

Let us now examine several other key sentences for their clues.

1. The work of the cowboy today is *much different from* the work he did in the days of the old West.

You should be able, from that sentence, to predict that the paragraph will describe the work of both the early cowboy and today's cowboy, and show some of the ways in which they are different. You yourself could probably make many good guesses about those differences.

2. When early man discovered the bow and arrow, his method of hunting went through a *complete change*.

This paragraph says nothing about comparison or differences, but the word *change* means "different from the old way." Therefore the paragraph undoubtedly will describe both the old methods of hunting and the new way, and show how very different they were.

3. How have our ways of living been *changed* by the use of scientific methods?

You have already met key sentences that are questions. Now again you meet the word *change*. What two things would you expect to find compared?

4. We now have *better* sanitary conditions *than* we used to have.

Here is a new phrase, *better than*, that also tells us we are going to find a comparison. What two conditions are going to be compared? Will they be described as being alike or being different?

5. People of today are able to obtain many *more* kinds of food *than* did their ancestors of a century ago.

The words *more than* are your clue. If we eat more now, then people must have eaten less a century ago. The paragraph will probably compare the large variety of food that people eat now with the small variety they used to eat.

What comparison should you expect to follow the sentence below?

6. The great development of machinery in modern times has brought disadvantages as well as advantages.

Now we come to a more difficult paragraph opening.

199

7. A century ago people in cities used to buy water for home use from a water wagon that traveled about through the streets. Today we have a piping system that brings pure water right into the faucets in your home.

This kind of beginning is especially important because it takes two sentences to give the main thought. You should recognize here that the author is going to show the difference between (1) buying water a century ago, and (2) obtaining pure water today. Can you guess that the water of the early days was not so pure?

EXERCISE 1

In class discussion, explain the comparisons in the next group of key sentences.

1. In many ways the Canadian people are very much like the people of the United States.
2. The small, compact car has advantages over the larger models.
3. Accidents may occur at home as well as on the street.

EXERCISE 2

The sentences below are the opening sentences of paragraphs. Study each sentence carefully. Look for clue words. Decide what kind of details you would expect to find. Decide whether the paragraph will list details, give details in time order, or make comparisons.

Directions: Number your paper 1–10. Under each number write *a, b, c* on a separate line. After *a* write the clue word or words. After *b* write the kind of details. After *c* write *list, time order,* or *comparison* to show the plan of the paragraph.

1. Passenger planes now make a great many nonstop flights to various parts of the world.
2. Seals can easily be trained to perform a variety of different tricks.
3. Mountain climbers frequently run into unexpected hardships.
4. To make a tasty omelet, here is a new method you should try.
5. The Battle of Bunker Hill turned into a surprising victory for the Continental Army.

6. Soldier ants on a march through the jungle act very much like a trained army.
7. Life is much more comfortable today than it used to be.
8. You have to follow directions very accurately in building model planes.
9. The modern automobile has created great dangers as well as great conveniences.
10. The gradual change from ocean water to clouds, to rain, and back to ocean water is a complicated process.

Taking Stock of What You Have Learned: Summary of the Paragraph Plan

The Main Thought and Where It May Be Found

1. Though paragraphs contain a number of details, usually they all help to tell you one thought.
2. That one thought is the *main thought.*
3. That thought is often found in the *key sentence,* but at other times it is suggested by the paragraph as a whole.
4. The key sentence may occur in any part of the paragraph.
5. The main thought may be part of the first sentence.
6. It may be given in both the first sentence and the last sentence, though expressed differently.
7. It may be a sentence anywhere between those two.

Making a Short Outline of the Paragraph

1. The key sentence can be written as a **short phrase.**
2. Each **supporting detail** may also be a short phrase.
3. Each detail can be entered in outline form:
   Topic:
   Details
       A.
       B.
       C.
4. In this form the paragraph can be understood and remembered more easily, and reviewed more rapidly.

Predicting What the Paragraph Will Say

1. The key sentence can give a clue to what will follow.
2. Some paragraphs present a **list of details** of what the key sentence is about.
3. Certain **clue words** are helpful: *many, much, some, several,* etc.
4. Some paragraphs present a **list in time order** of stages or steps. They tell or explain how something happens or happened.
5. Some paragraphs tell **how something is done.** The details are also in time order.
6. Some paragraphs **compare** two things to show likenesses or differences.
7. By giving advance hints, key sentences help you
   a. to know what kind of details to expect
   b. to understand the sentences better
   c. to read the sentences more rapidly

The Importance of Practice

Everyone knows that it takes practice to become skillful. In order to develop skills in reading paragraphs, you will need to practice with all the types of paragraphs you have learned about so far. Some practice in reviewing the material in this book will be helpful, although practice in reading and outlining paragraphs from your textbooks will be more valuable.

2. MAKING MENTAL OUTLINES OF PARAGRAPHS

Now that you have learned about writing outlines from paragraphs, you are probably ready to make mental outlines without actually writing them out. With a little effort, you will be able to do them in your head while you are reading. This will require reading with more care than usual, but you will be able to remember most of the paragraph. It will be fairly easy to answer questions about it.

The sample material below will show you how to make mental outlines. First read the sentence at the left; then read the brief form of it at the right.

WHAT YOU READ	WHAT YOU SHOULD THINK
Many cities in the United States use surface water such as streams and rivers to supply their needs.	*Key sentence:* Cities use surface water to supply needs. (Paragraph will explain how)
Some cities purchase land around distant streams in the mountains to obtain pure water. New York, Los Angeles, and Denver are among the cities that do this.	*First step:* Land bought around mountain streams. (*Examples:* New York, Los Angeles, Denver)
There they build dams to block the stream and create a large lake or reservoir.	*Second step:* Dams built.
This water is delivered to the city in great pipes 18 feet in diameter.	*Last step:* Water brought to cities in large pipes.

EXERCISE 3

How much can you remember of the paragraph as a result of mentally outlining it?

Directions: Cover both the paragraph and the outline. On your paper write the numbers 1 to 9 in a column. For each numbered sentence below, write *R* for right, *W* for wrong, or *N* if the paragraph contains nothing about the statement.

1. Many cities use surface water, such as streams and rivers, for their supply.
2. River water is always pure.
3. Water from distant mountain streams is pure.
4. A reservoir can be made by putting a dam across the stream.
5. The dam is also used as a bridge.
6. New York, Denver, and Los Angeles get their water from mountain streams.
7. The reservoir water is brought to the city in pipes.
8. It is also delivered by freight trains.
9. The pipes used are about one foot wide.

EXERCISE 4

The three paragraphs that follow, lettered **A** to **C**, form one selection, but you will read only one paragraph at a time. This exercise will give you practice in outlining mentally as you read. Follow the directions after each paragraph. You may be asked to make a paragraph outline. Read each paragraph carefully, but cover it up immediately after reading it.

SCIENCE IMPROVES OUR WAYS OF LIVING

A. Up to 200 years ago there was little chance of growing old enough to become middle aged. Most people died before they were thirty years old. One out of every four babies died before it was a year old. Those who lived beyond that age frequently became ill with some serious disease before the age of twelve. Smallpox, measles, whooping cough, diphtheria, and scarlet fever killed many of them. After that age there was the risk of catching yellow fever, malaria, cholera, and typhoid. Any one of those could be a fatal disease. Life was, indeed, very uncertain in those days.

Directions: Number your paper 1–8. Write *R* for right, *W* for wrong, or *N* if the paragraph gives no information.

1. Only 3 out of 4 babies had a chance to live more than one year.
2. Many children developed serious diseases before the age of twelve.
3. Those diseases could always be cured.
4. Among the serious diseases were scarlet fever, diphtheria, and smallpox.

5. Smallpox can be prevented by vaccination.

6. Most people lived until well past thirty years.

7. Even measles and whooping cough could sometimes be fatal.

8. People were not likely to live long in those days.

    B. Today many babies are born in hospitals, where they are protected against infections. With the help of science, disease is under control today for almost all of our population. Young people are given advance treatment to protect them against smallpox, diphtheria, and typhoid fever. People are no longer under the great risk of dying before the age of thirty. Today a person can expect to live to be seventy years old.

Directions: Give definite answers on your paper to these questions.

    a. Where is the main thought?

    b. What has made it possible to control many diseases today?

    c. Why are newborn babies safer than they used to be?

    d. What is the average age to which a person can expect to live?

    e. How do we prevent young people from getting smallpox and diphtheria?

    C. It is difficult to imagine the miserable and unsanitary conditions of our larger cities just a century ago. The streets were narrow and unpaved. They had no drainage system, and mud and dirt would collect after every rain. Besides, garbage and other refuse were ordinarily thrown into the street. Sewage was allowed to soak down into the earth. As a result, disease germs in the waste from human bodies would gradually drain down into the wells from which people obtained their drinking water.

Directions: Write the answers to these questions.

    a. Where is the main thought?

    b. What three reasons are given for the unsanitary conditions in cities of a century ago?

    c. Would you consider the last sentence to be a reason or a conclusion?

3. WHEN PARAGRAPHS ARE BROKEN

Paragraphs are easy to understand when they are short and when the key sentence is the first one in the paragraph. They are not too hard to figure out even when they are longer and the key sentence is within the paragraph. Sometimes, however, material containing only one main thought may be spread out to look like two or more paragraphs. Let us call this the **broken paragraph.**

Reasons for broken paragraphs

When the author finds that a paragraph is becoming too long, he will sometimes break it into two parts to make it seem simpler for the reader.

Eskimo sled dogs, usually called huskies, are never treated by their masters as pets. They do all the work of transportation over the snow and ice of the frozen northland. The loads they pull are sometimes over 2000 pounds in weight. The dogs are hitched to the sleds in teams of from four to twelve dogs. But the weight they pull is heavy and the ground they go over is hard on their feet.

They may have to pull this load as far as twenty miles in a day. This is tiring work and the dogs become greatly fatigued. Yet no sympathy is wasted on them. Any dog who neglects to pull his share of the load feels the instant lash of the master's whip. In addition, the lead dog will leap at him and slash his shoulder with one quick snap.

Topic: Huskies are never treated as pets.
  A. They do all the transportation over snow and ice.
  B. Pull loads weighing over 2000 pounds
  C. Hitched in teams of 4 to 12 dogs
  D. Load is heavy and ground is hard on feet
  E. May have to pull 20 miles in day
  F. Work very tiring, dogs become fatigued
  G. No sympathy wasted on them
  H. Dog that neglects share of work gets lashed
  I. Besides, lead dog gashes him with quick snap

You can see that all these sentences together would make a long paragraph. That is why they were written as two paragraphs. The outline shows that every sentence in both paragraphs gives details about the main idea: *Huskies are never treated as pets.*

EXERCISE 5

There are three pairs of paragraphs in this exercise. See if you can tell, for each pair, whether they belong under one main thought or under two. Then write the paragraphs, in short outline form, on your paper. If they should be written as one paragraph, use the form shown in the account of the huskies on page 206. If they should be written as two, write your outline in the form shown here.

I. Topic
   Details A.
          B.
          Etc.
II. Topic
    Details A.
           Etc.

1. ICEBERGS

No matter how large an iceberg may seem to be, the part that you cannot see is even larger—in fact, many times larger. That part of the iceberg is under water and out of sight. Only about one ninth of it is visible above water. Yet even the visible portion may be tremendous in size. Many of these icebergs are almost a city block long and seem to be three or four stories high.

Can you imagine how large the underwater portion must be? It may spread out to a width of perhaps five blocks and a depth of twenty stories or more. Altogether the iceberg of average size may be about the height of a skyscraper building. There are a few icebergs that extend for nearly a mile along the surface of the ocean. We can only guess how great their depth must be. It is difficult to realize the great mass of an iceberg from the small portion that we actually see.

2. THE STORY OF THE TURNPIKE

Several centuries ago the custom was started of collecting a *toll* (or tax) at some place along a road. If the road was a good one, the traveler would be willing to pay the toll instead of driving along some very rough road. At the point where the toll was collected, a long pole studded with spikes (or *pikes*) was stretched across the road. The stagecoach or wagon was forced to stop at the pole until the toll was paid. Then the pole would be turned up and the driver could pass on. This pole was called a *turnpike*.

Today we still have many roads where tolls are collected for the privilege of driving through. However, in the course of time, conditions have changed. The pole across the road is rarely used. Instead automobiles are stopped at a booth and the driver pays the toll. Besides, when we use the word "turnpike" we no longer think of the pole. Instead, it is the *road itself* that is now called the *turnpike*. Most people have completely forgotten the original meaning of the word.

3. Hurricanes

The most dreaded of all storms are the hurricanes. They are responsible for greater destruction and more loss of lives than any other kind of storm. A hurricane is a great circle of wind 400 or 500 miles wide. It keeps spinning around at a furious speed, especially at the outer edge of its circle.

With a fierce wind speed of 300 miles an hour or more, it can shatter buildings, toss automobiles about like leaves, sink large ships at sea, and then pass on leaving a mass of ruin behind. It sucks a billion tons of water out of the ocean and pours it down again on helpless cities and farms. Rivers become swollen and flood the nearby towns and villages. Houses are torn from their foundations and sent floating down a newly created sea. Then it may take years before the homes are rebuilt and the vast damage repaired.

4. PARAGRAPHS IN DIALOGUE

You have just learned of one reason for breaking a paragraph into parts. There is also another reason. When you read anything with conversation, you can see that a new paragraph is begun whenever another person speaks. Those paragraphs are likely to be very short. Sometimes as many as five or six of them are all about one topic. In print, however, they will look like separate paragraphs. Paragraphs of this kind occur very frequently in stories, and it may require thought and attention to understand which of them belong together in carrying out one main thought.

Read the following conversation between two men preparing for a westward journey in a covered wagon.

"Sam," said Cyrus as he entered the barn, "what kind of wood are you using to build our wagon?"

"Good, tough oak," answered Sam. "I know the wagon will have to take a great many hard bumps, and I want it to be ready for them."

"How about the wheels?" asked Cyrus.

"Oh, I'm making them strong, too. Have no fear."

"It isn't the strength I'm worried about, Sam, but the size. Do you realize that we will have to wade through many streams?"

"Well, is there any change I ought to make, Cyrus?"

"Yes, indeed, Sam. Build those wheels at least five feet high. Even then we'll be lucky if the wagon stays above water at every crossing."

"Well! I never thought of that, Cyrus, and I'm mighty glad you warned me about it. Our wagon must be made ready for any kind of rugged travel on our trip."

In spite of the fact that this conversation took eight paragraphs, they all referred to only one main thought. You met that thought in the very last sentence of the conversation: "The wagon must be made ready for every kind of rugged travel."

There were really only four details mentioned, even though there was considerable talking back and forth between the men.

a. Good, tough oak was used.
b. The wagon must be able to withstand many hard bumps.
c. Wheels must be built five feet high.
d. They will then be likely to keep the wagon body above water at river crossings.

EXERCISE 6

Now read the rest of the conversation. Can you find the main thought in these paragraphs?

"I just learned about something else our wagon job will need, Sam," continued Cyrus. "Some of the men are building their wagon flooring in a strange shape."

"What do you mean? Just what can be strange about the floor of a wagon?"

"I was watching Ben Thorpe's work this morning. He explained it all to me. The floor has to be deep in the middle. Then it curves up at the sides and also at the front and back."

"That sounds crazy, Cyrus," exclaimed Sam. "The floor should be level and smooth. What is Thorpe thinking about, anyway?"

"Well, Sam, he reminded me that some rivers will be altogether too deep for wading through. A wagon with a regular floor might float, but still it might float too low and ruin all our supplies."

"Oh, now I get your point, Cyrus. This other kind of floor is really something like a boat, isn't it? That way it will ride on top of the water and keep all our things dry. It's a good thing we get all this information before we build our wagon the wrong way."

Directions: Copy this form on your paper. Use it to write the main thought and details in the dialogue.

Main thought: ——————————
   Details: A. ——————————
             B. ——————————
             C. ——————————

5. SUMMARY OF VARIOUS TYPES OF PARAGRAPHS

When you read fiction you may want to read quickly to find out what is happening in the story. When you read informational material, however, it is necessary to keep looking for the main thought in each paragraph.

This may slow your reading to some extent, but it will greatly increase your understanding. It will even improve your speed of understanding because you will know what to expect and you will be reading with a sharp mind.

In *A* and *B* which follow you will find reminders of what you have learned about the paragraph thus far and what you should look for in the many kinds of paragraphs you will meet in your reading.

A. Where the Main Thought Might Be Found

1. The key sentence at the beginning
2. The key sentence at the end
3. The key sentence at the beginning and repeated at the end
4. Main thought in part of the key sentence
5. The key sentence somewhere within the paragraph
6. Main thought in two or more parts of a broken paragraph
7. One main thought in a group of conversation paragraphs

B. How to Predict What the Paragraph Will Say

1. Clues that foretell a list of details (many, much, several, etc.)
2. Clues that foretell a list in time order or steps (how something happens or happened)
3. Clues that foretell how something is done (explaining or giving directions)
4. Clues that foretell comparison between two things

6. SUMMARIZING THE PARAGRAPH

What Question Does the Paragraph Answer?

It will help you in your reading to know how to change the thought of a paragraph into a question. This lesson will prepare you to work out such questions. We shall begin with a few key sentences without full paragraphs. We do this because the key sentence is the one that is most valuable in providing the clue to the question.

Let us see how the following sentence can be made into a question.

> Samuel Morse met many discouraging disappointments before his invention of the telegraph was finally accepted by the world.

First, what is the important word or expression in that sentence? We can tell what it is when we predict what the rest of the paragraph will be about. It will have to list some of those disappointments, of course. Our question will have to ask about the disappointments. Notice how the question is made.

Original sentence: Samuel Morse met many discouraging *disappointments* before his invention of the telegraph was finally accepted by the world.

Question form: **What** discouraging *disappointments* did Samuel Morse meet before his invention of the telegraph was accepted by the world? (Notice the use of the question word *what*.)

Shorter form: What disappointments did Samuel Morse meet before his invention of the telegraph was accepted? (This omitted "discouraging" and "by the world.")

Very short form: What disappointments did Samuel Morse meet? (Many words are omitted in this very short form.)

What is one question word. There are others that you will need. Which one to select depends, of course, on the kind of question you ask. Below is a useful list of "question" words.

Question Words

who	how	what kind of
whom	when	in what way
what	where	how many
which	why	how much

describe ⎫ These are not really "question" words, but
tell about⎭ they serve the same purpose.

How can you change the sentence below to a question? What word or words can you use?

> As soon as the telegraph was found to be successful, America and Europe began to use it very extensively.

What can you predict about the paragraph that will follow this sentence? It should be clear that it will tell about how America and Europe used this invention very extensively. It will *not* tell about the success of the telegraph.

Now we can examine the change from sentence to question.

The original sentence reads: As soon as the telegraph was found to be successful, America and Europe began to use it very extensively.

With unimportant part omitted: America and Europe began to use the telegraph very *extensively.*

Question form: In what way did America and Europe begin to use the telegraph extensively?

Shorter form: In what way did America and Europe use the telegraph?

EXERCISE 7

Three topic sentences are given below. For each one, discuss what the rest of the paragraph would say. Then change the sentence into a question. Make the question as short as possible, dropping unneeded words.

1. In 1858 Cyrus Field *developed a method* for sending telegrams across the Atlantic Ocean.

(Try beginning "What was Field's method . . ." Try also beginning "Describe Field's method . . .")

2. The telephone, invented by Alexander Graham Bell in 1867, quickly became a much more popular method of communication.

(Begin your question with "Why" or "In what way.")

3. The wireless telegraph, however, the invention of Marconi, was the most thrilling method of sending messages the world had ever known up to then.

How Should the Paragraph Question Be Answered?

It would certainly seem foolish to answer the paragraph question by turning it back again into the key sentence. For instance:

Question: What disappointments did Samuel Morse meet?
Poor answer: He met many discouraging disappointments.

The question is actually answered by the whole paragraph, not by the key sentence. That sentence said "He met many discouraging disappointments." The rest of the paragraph is expected to tell what those disappointments were and what made them discouraging. The complete answer should give this information.

However, it is hardly ever necessary to repeat the whole paragraph. There is a way of **summarizing the paragraph.** This means giving its thoughts in one long sentence, or perhaps two. The summary should certainly contain *some* of the details, in this case some of Morse's disappointments.

Therefore we have to learn how to select details that are really important and work them, somehow, into one sentence, or perhaps two.

Study the whole paragraph about the telegraph in outline form below. This is the form you would probably compose in your mind if you were reading the actual paragraph in complete sentences.

Topic: Morse met discouraging disappointments before his telegraph was accepted.

Details: A. Gave many demonstrations to business men, but they were not interested.
B. Tried desperately to show Congress how important it was to the country to receive quick messages from a distance.
C. For over four years kept trying without any success.
D. Meanwhile lost all his money and became discouraged and seriously ill.
E. Near death when Congress, at last, appropriated a large sum for the first telegraph line.
F. Success immediate and telegraph popular at once.

As you read down through the details you see that **a, b, c,** and **d** describe his disappointments. It should be possible to combine those into one sentence, perhaps like this:

For four discouraging years Morse tried desperately to interest business men and Congress, until his money was gone and he was seriously ill.

Then we can combine **e** and **f:**

Then when he was near death, Congress finally approved his request and the telegraph became an instant success.

Now we are ready to see whether the question seems to be answered.

Question: What disappointments did Samuel Morse meet before his telegraph was accepted?

Answer: For four discouraging years he tried desperately to interest business men and Congress, until his money was gone and he was seriously ill. He was already near death when Congress finally approved his request and the telegraph became an instant success.

EXERCISE 8

Following the example of a paragraph summary above, make your own summaries of the next group of paragraphs. You may first write an outline, if you wish, or you may compose it mentally. The summary should contain not more than two sentences. Number your answers to match the paragraphs.

1. As soon as the telegraph was found to be successful, America and Europe began to use it very extensively. It was so much faster than the mail that it was in great demand everywhere. Private companies began a rapid program of building telegraph lines. Within ten years every important city and town was connected to the whole nation by 100,000 miles of telegraph wire. In Europe it was the governments that built the lines, though they did not equal the speed of the American companies.

2. In 1858 Cyrus Field developed a new method of sending telegrams across the ocean. If a message could travel by wire 3000 miles across our nation, why not across 2000 miles of ocean? Naturally the wire would have to be laid along the ocean floor. It would have to be a thick cable containing many wires. That would permit many messages to go through together. The cable would have to be very strong and tough. It would have to resist rust from the salt water of the ocean. There were other problems that had to be solved too. But at last, in 1858, there was a cable that connected all the American lines with the European lines.

3. The telephone, invented by Alexander Graham Bell in 1867, became a much more popular method of communication. There was something delightful about having a conversation with someone who was 1000 miles away, yet whose voice came to you as though he were right alongside you. Besides, you did not have to wait four days for an answer as in the case of a letter. Even a telegram would require two days for a reply. Now you could hear each other instantly. No wonder everybody began to

clamor for a telephone! Today practically every family in the nation has the marvelous convenience of a telephone right at home.

4. The wireless telegraph, however, the invention of Guglielmo Marconi in 1902, was the most thrilling method of sending a message the world had known up to that time. It seemed to everyone to be some kind of magic. Electric sparks were produced at the top of a high tower and powerful waves were sent out in all directions through the air. Far out at sea the messages of those sparks could be read by any ship that had a little receiving station. In the same way a ship could send such messages that could reach other distant ships. Imagine how exciting it was when a sinking ship sent out its first S.O.S. message and two other ships, though many miles away, received the message and dashed to the rescue.

Summary

In this book you have learned many things about paragraphs:

How to *read* them with understanding
How to *recognize* the main thought, wherever it appears
How to *note* the way in which details support the main thought
How to *predict* what a paragraph will tell
How to *outline* paragraphs
How to *compose* the question that the paragraph will answer
How to *summarize* the paragraph

CONTEXT CLUES
TO MEANING   13

In Chapter 3 you learned that you can often discover the meaning of a new word through the help of nearby words and thoughts. You learned of two ways by which this can be done. Sometimes the other words around it give you the explanation you need, or perhaps even an actual definition. You met sentences like these:

   1. In George Washington's time, the *mortality*, or *number of deaths*, from smallpox was very high.
   2. Johnny would always *procrastinate*, that is, he would always *put off* for tomorrow what he ought to do today.

   In such sentences, the writer uses clue words such as *or* and *that is* to show that he is defining the unfamiliar word. In other sentences, the meaning may be shown by a phrase or statement that is the opposite of the unfamiliar word. For example:

> The President hoped for *bipartisan* support, but only the Republican Senators came to his aid.

In this sentence the clue word is *but*. It shows that an opposing idea is coming up. You can see then that "only the Republican Senators" is the opposite of bipartisan. You may rightly judge that *bipartisan* refers to "two parties."

1. USING YOUR REASON

Another kind of context clue is one that requires some reasoning. The writer expects you to use the information he has given you to figure out the meaning of the new word. If we read that the beggar was so *famished* that he was satisfied to eat crumbs, we can recognize that famished means *hungry* or *starving*.

EXERCISE 1

In the following sentences decide on the meaning of the italicized word from the context by reasoning. Select your answer from the three choices. Write the answers on your paper and number them to match the sentences.

1. His sleeves were so short that his arms *protruded* from them.

Protruded means:
   a. stuck out   b. hidden   c. were protected

2. A police patrol *preceded* the visitor's car in order to clear the path of all danger ahead.

Preceded means:
   a. followed   b. went before   c. traveled with

3. The ringing of the fire gong brought our meeting to an *abrupt* close.

Abrupt means:
   a. surprising   b. quiet   c. sudden

4. He *disdained* their offer of friendship, for he was far too proud and haughty to associate with men who wore shabby clothes.

Disdained means:
   a. accepted
   b. looked with contempt upon
   c. liked

5. The judge scolded the parents for their *negligence* in letting the child wander off into the woods.

Negligence means:
   a. carelessness   **b.** pleasure   **c.** poverty

Where to Look for the Clue

When there is no clue to a word in the sentence in which the word is used, the alert reader may find one in another part of the paragraph. It may be in a sentence which follows the one with the word.

> **1.** His interest in baseball never *waned*. At the age of eighty, he could öften be seen in the grandstand enjoying the game with the enthusiasm of a youngster.

(Does the second sentence explain the meaning of *waned* for you?)

> **2.** I *assumed* that the white building just ahead of us was the inn. When we reached it a moment later, I realized my mistake.

How can you tell that *assume* means *to suppose*?)

The clue may be in the earlier part of the paragraph, before the sentence containing the new word.

> The bloodhound is claimed by many to be the best breed of dog for police work. This claim, however, is *disputed* by those who have used boxers and German shepherds with great success.

(What does *disputed* mean? Where is the clue to its meaning?)

There may be several clues in the paragraph to help you determine the meaning of a word. In the next paragraph you will be able to figure out the meaning of *jubilant* in this way. Try it!

> Everyone was on hand to welcome the train. There were banners flying, music playing, and people cheering. No wonder they were *jubilant*! The team had brought home the championship pennant.

(If you know the meaning of *jubilant*, but cannot think of a good synonym, consult your dictionary.)

EXERCISE 2

See how quickly you can find the meanings of the italicized words in the following paragraphs. What clues helped you?

1. The mother looked at her wiggling youngster. "Sit still, child," she *admonished*. "Your dress will be mussed. How many times do I have to tell you about it?"

2. The traveler attracted a good deal of attention as he entered the hall. It was filled with gay and well-dressed lords and ladies, but his appearance was very *woebegone* indeed. His head was bowed and his cloak dragged on the floor; his face was bearded and dirty; his shoulders were hunched and his hood had fallen over his eyes.

3. It was the most exciting moment of the game. Jim was at bat, ready to give them the home run they were shouting for. The pitch came—but the cheers turned to groans as Jim, struck by the ball, slumped to the ground. He was instantly surrounded by players and doctors. The fans sat and waited. Then they saw Jim rise to his feet and pick up his bat. The crowd applauded and the game was *resumed*.

4. The steam engine invented by Watt was fixed to one spot to lift coal from the mines. It was a long time before anyone thought of making an engine that could move from place to place, pulling a load of coal along with it. Instead, several *stationary* engines were placed along the roads at short distances from each other, and the loads were pulled by cable from one engine to the next.

5. The people of this region make a *meager* living. Most of them grow a few crops on their small farms, doing all the labor by hand. They raise some sheep and weave the wool into coarse cloth.

This method of using the context will be of great help to you in cases where the dictionary is not very helpful, cases when the words are from a foreign language.

Note how the context helps you in the following example.

1. In the game of jai-alai, the player wears a long, curved wicker basket attached to a leather glove. The object of the game is to catch the ball in this *cesta* and hurl it against the wall.

(The dictionary will probably not list *cesta,* since it is a Spanish word. Can you define it?)

2. The tourist was badly frightened when an evil-looking Frenchman grasped him by the collar and made a threatening gesture. Fortunately at that moment a *gendarme* appeared and ran up to help. At sight of the blue uniform the Frenchman ran away.

(*Gendarme* is a French word. Can you tell its meaning?)

3. For his unusual bravery on the battlefield and for his courage in fighting on, though seriously wounded, he was awarded the *croix de guerre* (pronounced *krwah de gair.*)

(What do you think the award was?)

2. REVIEW TEST

You have met many new words in this section on finding meaning through context. Some of these words were explained to you. Others appeared in the exercises. You probably remember a number of them, but it is natural that you should have forgotten some others.

All these exercises were intended to develop your skill in recognizing the meanings of new words, even words that you have not yet seen. Whenever you meet such words in your daily reading, make an effort to find some context clues to their meaning.

However, this section and all the exercises in it had another purpose. As you learn new words, your vocabulary becomes enriched. You can express yourself more freely, more clearly, and more interestingly. In addition, your reading and understanding will be greatly improved.

This review is being presented to remind you of some new words you have met in this book. The sentence context will again aid you in getting the meanings if you do not remember them.

EXERCISE 3

Directions: Number your paper 1 to 26. Write in your own words the definition or meaning of the italicized word in each sentence. If you understand the word but cannot think of a way to express the definition, write another sentence in which the word is used properly. Be ready to discuss your answers.

1. After two days without food they were so *famished* that they were ready to chew on leather.
2. Tommy was very eager to go swimming, but Ben was *reluctant*. The water was still too cold.
3. The earth spins around on itself like a top, but this *rotation* is very slow.
4. The ambassador from a foreign country was pretending that he was very friendly toward us. Was it *diplomatic* of our Senator to remind him that he was not quite honest?
5. Cyclones, hurricanes, and tornadoes always leave ruined homes, loss of life, and other *disaster* behind them.
6. Little Irene was always *inquisitive* whenever packages were brought into the house. She could not rest until she saw what each one contained.

7. A jury will usually doubt the *veracity* of a witness who has a reputation for not telling the truth.
8. The *preliminary* preparations were tiresome, but the fish caught later in the morning made them seem worth while.
9. The candle provided very poor *illumination* of the cave.
10. It is not enough to get your arithmetic problems nearly right. They must be *precisely* right.
11. The spy tried to hide the rifle, but the barrel was noticed when it *protruded* from underneath the cloak.
12. In buying china cups you must avoid choosing any that are *fragile*. Cups that break easily are too expensive.
13. The soldiers sprawling over their bunks jumped up *abruptly* when the major entered.
14. We could hardly hear the radio announcer because of the *tumult* in the stadium.
15. It takes amazing *agility* to be a circus performer on the trapeze and "fly through the air with the greatest of ease."
16. The crowd kept pushing toward the wounded man on the sidewalk until the officer ordered them to *disperse*.
17. On arrival at camp, the boys displayed *voracious* appetites, asking for second and third helpings of everything.
18. The workmen's *boisterous* laughter disturbed the quiet of the doctor's study.
19. Most of North Africa is *arid;* that is, there is little moisture, and there are few plants or trees.
20. Charlie was shy and afraid to speak up; on the other hand, his brother Fred was so *aggressive* that the other boys were afraid of him.
21. Mary thought she might need a new dress for the party, but she finally decided her blue one would be *adequate*.
22. The old man was *parsimonious* indeed. He never threw anything away, no matter how worthless it might be. He never spent a cent unless he absolutely had to.
23. The captain said, "I would be *remiss* in my duties if I did not explain the risks you will take."
24. Strangers probably thought Jason was *eccentric*. He did some queer things sometimes, but we understood his reasons.
25. Phil has a fine collection of stamps, postcards, and postmarks from all over the world. His friends sometimes call him "Phil the *philatelist*."
26. The store received hundreds of *queries* about the advertisement, and they answered every one of them by letter.

Review of Context Clues to Meaning

Quite often when you meet a strange new word, the context will give you clues to its meaning. These clues will not give you the full meaning of the word but enough of the meaning so that you can make sense of the sentence. Here are some points to remember about context clues.

1. The word may be clearly explained in the sentence in which it appears.

> The Phoenicians gained a **monopoly**—that is, *complete control*—of the trade in tin.

2. A short definition or explanation of the word may appear in the same sentence or nearby.

> **a.** The **equator** is *an imaginary line* around the earth midway between the poles.
> **b.** The ancient Egyptians could even predict the **eclipse** of the moon. That is *the time when the earth's shadow* would pass across the full moon.

3. Sometimes the context makes the meaning clear almost immediately. Even if there were a blank instead of the strange word, you would understand what was intended.

> **a.** It was a **sumptuous** meal, *almost a feast.*
> **b.** Through his field glasses he could **discern** a machine gun in the shadow of the tree.

4. The clue to the strange word may appear several sentences earlier or later. Keep the word in mind as you read or reread, and the meaning may be made clear.

5. Sometimes, especially when signals like *no* or *but* or *although* are noticed in the sentence, a word or a phrase with the opposite meaning will give you the clue to the meaning.

> *Although* the mountain goat looks *clumsy,* he is really very **nimble.**

6. There are times when, instead of one clue, a number of facts will be found that help, all together, to give you an understanding of the new word.

7. Do not depend entirely on context clues. Always refer to a good dictionary for exact meanings.

3. AN OPPORTUNITY TO USE THESE CLUES

Up to this point you have been finding the meaning of new words in sentences or paragraphs. Now you are better able to seek out meanings by yourself. You are prepared to meet new words in a long selection and to put your new skills to work.

In the selection that follows, you will notice many words in italics. Most of these may be unknown to you, but you should no longer feel discouraged by that fact. There will be various clues in the context to guide you in figuring out their meanings.

Do not rush on in your reading the moment you think you understand the word. Go back over the sentence again. Does the meaning you discovered sound sensible in place of the new word? If so, you can be sure you are right and you can read on with more confidence.

Do not expect complete success. This use of context clues is still new to you, and it will take much more practice to make perfect use of them. Besides, there will be occasions when there will not be any clues, and you will then recognize the need for consulting the dictionary. You will find it helpful to discuss your answers in class and compare your meanings with those selected by your classmates.

EXERCISE 4

On your paper list the italicized words in the following selection. Write after each word the meaning you were able to obtain from the context. Jot down the clue words that, in your opinion, gave you help. Be ready to discuss your meanings with the class when you are called upon.

How Writing Was Developed

1. In the *prehistoric* days, that *primitive* age when there was neither civilization nor written history, men were entirely *illiterate*. Although they had not yet reached the stage of writing, nevertheless they were *capable* of *transcribing* their experiences on stone or parchment. They made a very early discovery of how to *transmit* their thoughts to others.

2. The earliest form of writing was *pictorial* writing. Even savages could describe events by drawing pictures about them. This form of writing was used by the American Indians. For example, ☀ would mean *one day*, because it showed the

path of the sun through the sky from morning until evening. ☀ ☀ would *denote* two days. The picture of two arrows in opposite directions ← → was read as war, the *symbol* for peace was a broken arrow —— → and the pipe of peace ✓ *indicated* a treaty of peace. *Wigwams* were shown by crude drawings of tents X X

3. With pictures such as these it was possible to *record* a story on skin and send it back to the chief of the tribe to be *interpreted*. This picture story (shown below) was understood to mean "We traveled for two days until we crossed the mountains where we saw the wigwams of our enemies. There we made war, fighting many battles until they begged for peace. Then we made a treaty with them."

4. Pictures, however, are a very *crude* form of writing, too simple to express anything very exactly. After all, they are only *representations* of objects, and we cannot easily express such words as "hope," "loyalty," or "courage" by pictures of objects. Yet there was an earlier period in the story of mankind, more than 4000 years before the *era* of Indian writing, when the Egyptians found a much *superior* method of *conveying* their thoughts in written form.

5. They, too, had begun through the *employment* of pictures. With the *progress* of time, however, they began to use pictures to represent sounds instead of objects. This introduced an entirely new *procedure* into writing, and this made it possible for later men to develop our present kind of writing or printing with letters spelled into words.

6. The Egyptian sound-writing scheme was called "hieroglyphics." You may sometimes see this same *device* in children's books of puzzles. You read the pictures by *articulating* the sounds to yourself and then, from the sounds, you can uncover the words that were intended. Read the picture sentence below. What do the sounds of the pictures say?

7. The Egyptians developed this system to combine sound-pictures into longer and more complicated words. The meaning of the pictures was *ignored.* Only the sounds were remembered and *utilized* in the new words. For example, *belief* could be *derived* from the pictures of a bee and a leaf. Try to think of other combinations of sound-pictures.

4. PUTTING YOUR RICHER VOCABULARY TO USE

Substituting One Word for Many

Having a larger vocabulary makes you a much richer person— richer in thought and understanding, and richer in the power to express yourself intelligently and interestingly. You have been adding greatly to the storehouse of words you can read and understand. You have been extending it in two ways:

1. by your power to recognize word meaning from its structure
2. by your power to seek out word meaning from context

There is still a third way to improve your vocabulary, and that is by making frequent use, in your conversation and in your writing, of the new words you keep learning. When you learn a new word and you do nothing with it, you soon forget it. But if you will only use it in your speech just three times, the same day or the next day, that word will remain in your possession forever!

Carry a small "Vocabulary Notebook" or keep a place for new words in your large notebook. Add to your list each new word with its definition.

EXERCISE 5

You will meet in these sentences a number of phrases in italics. It will be your task to select a single word that means as much as the whole phrase. You will receive some help from the list of words following the sentences.

Directions: Number your paper 1–10. Beside each number write the phrase that appears in italics in the sentence. Then select an appropriate word from the choices below the sentences and write it next to the phrase.

Example: 1. *main idea*—point

1. I do not understand the *main idea* of your joke.
2. Her fingers were very *active and skillful* as she played the piano.
3. For many months the young man *paid much attention* to Mary Ann to win her favor.
4. He read about his skillful football plays in a *long strip of news* in the paper.
5. He flipped on a switch and the whole theater was *lit up*.
6. Alice agreed to come along but she *would have preferred not* to go.
7. The young woman was *very careful about every detail* in her clothes.
8. The vase had to be handled carefully because it *could be broken at the slightest jar*.
9. His wound was *so serious that it resulted in his death*.
10. The moon *turns on its axis* once a month.

reluctant	rotates	illuminated	beautiful
fatal	fastidious	nimble	column
fragile	point	courted	tender

EXERCISE 6

Directions: From the list of words following the sentences choose one to replace each italicized phrase.

1. The pearl was *manufactured from a combination of chemicals.*
2. I believe completely in the *truth of all his statements.*
3. Jai-alai players use a *glove that ends in a curved basket.*
4. After a moment of interruption he *began again* to speak.
5. At sight of the police squad the mob *scattered in all directions.*
6. When she learned of her high mark she was *happy and excited.*
7. The *French policeman* came to his aid.
8. The *noise and excitement* in the street disturbed the whole neighborhood.
9. The natives *could neither read nor write.*
10. The tiger ate *with a fierce, enormous appetite.*

jubilant	dispersed	veracity	illiterate
cesta	gendarme	home-made	tumult
voraciously	resumed	ran	synthetic

5. NEW WORDS FOR OLD ONES

When we read the sentence, "The girl walked across the street," we don't learn much about the girl or how she walked. We cannot tell whether the girl was happy or sad, whether she was proud or shy, whether she was in a hurry or was not going anywhere in particular. The sentence sounds dull because the word *walked* is just an ordinary word. It does not give us a clear picture.

Now let us read the following sentences and notice the change when we read other words in place of *walked.* They tell us something more interesting and more definite.

"The girl *skipped* across the street" means also that she felt gay.

"The girl *limped* across the street" means also that she was lame or had hurt her leg.

"The girl *hurried* across the street" means also that she was in a hurry or was excited.

"The girl *strolled* across the street" means also that she was taking her time.

"The girl *strode* across the street" means also that she felt proud or strong.

Such words are valuable to you, for they enrich your language when you speak or write. But it is important for your reading that you should understand them. Each one gives a different meaning to the sentence and creates a different mental picture for you.

If you read "The wolves walked around the tent" you can hardly see any picture in your mind. But if the sentence reads "The wolves *prowled* around the tent" you can almost see exactly what they are doing—sneaking, alert for possible gun shots, yet waiting for a chance to rush in.

"The mouse *ran* into its hole" is not very descriptive, but "The mouse *scampered* into its hole" gives you a sharp picture of a rushing, scurrying little flash of gray fur.

A ten-ton truck can simply "*go* down the street," but it could "*lumber* down the street."

A lively pony can simply "*run* across the pasture," but it could "*canter* across the pasture."

EXERCISE 7

In each sentence below, a synonym is used in place of *walked*. A synonym is a word similar in meaning to another word. Each italicized word tells of a particular kind of walking. It also tells something about the girl.

Directions: Read each sentence carefully. Be ready to explain what the italicized word tells you about the girl and about how she walked across the street.

1. The girl *struggled* across the street.
2. The girl *tiptoed* across the street.
3. The girl *danced* across the street.
4. The girl *flew* across the street.
5. The girl *trudged* across the street.
6. The girl *crept* across the street.
7. The girl *staggered* across the street.
8. The girl *toddled* across the street.
9. The girl *marched* across the street.
10. The girl *tramped* across the street.

EXERCISE 8

Synonyms are words similar in meaning. They are not exactly the same. Therefore they cannot be substituted for each other recklessly. A synonym can be used only when it fits the meaning of the context.

Directions: Read each sentence carefully. For each sentence select from the list below the right synonym for the word *said.* The sentence context clues will help you.

> ordered   coaxed   repeated   whispered
> growled   shouted   explained   thundered

1. "I am reminding you again," he *said,* "to be careful when crossing the road."
2. "Close ranks," the sergeant *said,* "and stand at attention."
3. "This is the way you should work the example," *said* the teacher.
4. "Hurrah!" they *said.* "We won! We won!"
5. "Please try to hear me," *said* the captain. "They are in the next room, and I don't dare talk louder."
6. "Look—you," he *said,* "can't you do anything right?"
7. "Come on, boys," he *said,* "let's get the grass cut."
8. "Out of my way!" *said* the giant, as he strode down the valley.

EXERCISE 9

Try this exercise to discover how many synonyms you already know from your reading or speaking. In every group of four words there will be three synonyms, and one other word that will be out of place in that group. See if you can select the three synonyms in every group. Write them on your paper.

1. watch	2. foolish	3. extract	4. commotion	5. sob
peek	unusual	expect	noise	weep
seem	silly	await	shouting	cry
peer	ridiculous	watch for	noose	shout

6. answer	7. news	8. learn	9. obtain	10. mend
question	report	teach	receive	bold
reply	paper	explain	get	fix
respond	information	educate	grant	repair

6. WORD ORIGINS: HOW DID WORDS GET THEIR MEANING?

Many of the words in our language gained their present meaning in an unusual way. Once you read the story of the strange beginnings of these words, you will find their present meanings easy to remember. Ten of these interesting words follow:

1. *sandwich.* This word comes from the name of a man, the Earl of Sandwich. He loved card playing so much that he would not leave his game even for meals. Therefore he instructed his servants to bring his meals to him in such a form that he could continue to play without interruption. His cook cleverly placed portions of meat between two slices of bread so that the food could be picked up by hand. This method soon became popular. The food served this way was soon called *Sandwich food,* and finally it became known as *sandwiches.*

2. *lunatic.* There was a belief that people exposed too long to the light of the moon (or *luna*) would become mad, or moonstruck, or *lunatic.* Now the word means a person who is insane or extremely foolish.

3. *calculate.* In the very early days before reading and writing, there were few people who could even write figures. They did all their figuring with the help of little stones (or *calculi*) usually strung on a wire or cord. Therefore working arithmetic problems came to be called "calculating."

4. *candidate.* When a Roman wished to campaign for office, he put on a white robe to inform people of the purity of his intentions. The Roman word for white is *candidus.* Originally, therefore, *candidate* meant *clothed in white.* Today a candidate in Rome wears clothing of any color he chooses, and of course this is true in our country.

5. *ballot.* Secret voting was done in early England by dropping *little balls* or *ballots* into a box. Today we have forgotten about the little balls, and we use either printed forms or voting machines. We still call the printed forms "ballots."

6. *preposterous.* The word means *ridiculous,* but originally it meant *before* (from *pre*) and *after* (from *post*). That impossible combination of "before-after" was naturally ridiculous, and so we come to the present meaning of the word.

7. *salary.* Roman soldiers used to be paid their wages in an allowance of *salt* (or *sal*). The allowance was called *salarium,* from which we get the word "salary." But we would not be willing to accept our salary in salt today. What is meant by "He's not worth his salt"?

8. *Bedlam* means "confusion." At one time there was an insane asylum in London called *Bethlehem.* People then were somewhat careless in their pronunciation, and soon they began calling it *Bethlem,* then *Betlem,* and finally it became *Bedlem,* or *Bedlam.* It no longer means a madhouse, but it does refer to the confusion and disorder that you might expect in the old-fashioned aslyum for the insane.

9. *Neighbor* comes from two old German words, *neah* (meaning *nigh* or *near*) and *bor* (farmer). Therefore a "neighbor" was a *nearby farmer.* He does not have to be a farmer any more. *Neighbor* can also be traced to early English. It meant a "nigh-dweller."

10. *Alphabet* is from the first two letters of the Greek alphabet (*alpha* and *beta*). When a child today says he knows his "A B C's" he is using the same kind of name as the Greeks did when they spoke of their *"alpha-beta."*

233

1. You can add greatly to your vocabulary by looking up word origins in the dictionary. It can be a fascinating game. You might, for example, look up the following words:

tawdry	prevaricate
supercilious	precipice
pedagogue	companion
taxicab	marmalade
sacrifice	magazine

2. After you have investigated the words suggested above, see whether you can find some interesting word origins yourself. Use a dictionary and other reference books. Report your findings to the class.

3. Try to illustrate a word origin for the bulletin board. Consider drawing a cartoon of a word or some sort of design to make the origin clear.

4. Use a dictionary to make a list of common words in English that had their origin in a foreign language such as French, German, Italian—or in an ancient language such as Latin or Greek.

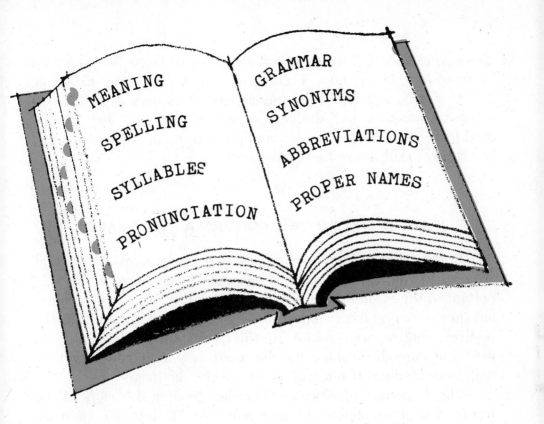

USING
THE DICTIONARY

The dictionary can be of help to you in many wonderful and interesting ways. In addition to giving you the meanings of words it also gives you their pronunciation, their spelling, and synonyms that can be used in their stead. It even offers you sentences to show you how the words are used. It contains all sorts of names of people and places and includes information about them. Suffixes, prefixes, and abbreviations are also listed. For most of the words the dictionary gives a brief history of how each word came into our language and what it meant originally.

These aids and still others are provided by the dictionary. But you must know how to look up the information you want. It takes skill to use the dictionary with ease and speed. Dictionaries may be compared to cameras. A small dictionary, with only about

15,000 words, is like an inexpensive camera that can be used only for snapshots in sunlight. The larger dictionaries, with 40,000 or 70,000 words, and the great unabridged dictionary with 500,000 words or more, are like the very expensive cameras. They can be used for a great many purposes, and produce many kinds of results, but it takes skill to use them effectively.

1. WHEN SHOULD YOU CONSULT A DICTIONARY?

In the midst of your reading, you will come across words that are new to you. Do not ignore these words; they may be very important to the meaning of what you are reading. First, try to figure out their meaning from context clues. Second, look for clues in the prefixes, suffixes, and stems. In this way you may be able to work out enough meaning for the word to permit you to get on with your reading. If not, you must use the dictionary.

The dictionary gives more than one meaning for many of the words. You must choose the meaning that fits into the sentence you are reading. When you go to the dictionary, you must consider the whole sentence in which the word occurs.

2. LOCATING THE WORD IN THE DICTIONARY

How to Find the Word

Before you can select a definition you must first find the word. You can become so skillful in this search that you can locate any word in a few moments. Many students take so much unnecessary time in turning over page after page that they become discouraged. But if you give yourself a little time to practice this skill, you will be fully repaid.

First, of course, you must be sure that you know the alphabet, not only forward, but backward, at least for a few letters at a time. The words in a dictionary are arranged in strict alphabetical order and are called *entry words*. The words beginning with S come after the words beginning with R.

If you were looking for the word *monopolize* and you opened the dictionary to the *Q* group, would you turn forward or backward to find your word? How many "groups" would you have to skip? When you have found *monopolize*, and then want to find *halcyon*, in which direction will you turn? A few pages, or many?

Opening to Nearly the Right Page

Your first step toward saving time is to open to that part of the dictionary which is close to the page you want. To do that you should imagine the dictionary divided into four quarters. In the first quarter are found the groups of words beginning with A, B, C, and D. The initial letters for the entire book are in the following parts of the book:

> In the first quarter, A through D
> In the second quarter, E through L
> In the third quarter, M through R
> In the fourth quarter, S through Z

To find the word *mirage*, for example, open the book to about the half-way mark. If the page contains the *M* words, you do not have to turn far. If the page contains the *L* words, turn over a batch of pages to the right.

To find the word *therapy*, open the book about midway between the middle and the end. You will probably find yourself at the letter S. Then *T* (for *therapy*) will be found in the next group.

To find the word *gauntlet* try to open the book at a place a little after the first quarter. If you meet an *H* page, turn backward to *G*. If you meet an *E* page, turn forward to *G*.

EXERCISE 1

In which quarter of the book will you find the words listed below? Copy the words on your paper and write the quarter beside each word: I for first quarter, II for second quarter, etc.

community	shaft
notify	handicap
bombard	massacre
stumble	lagoon
violent	density

What Alphabetical Order Means

You know that in naming the alphabet, you start with A and end with Z. All the other letters occur in a fixed order. This is the order of the alphabet, or *alphabetical order*.

The beginning letter of a word determines where the word is listed in the dictionary. The words *on* and *honor* begin with the same sound, but they do not appear together in the dictionary because their first letters are different.

What decides the order of all the words beginning with the same letter? Their order is determined by their other letters. We start with the second letter. The word *absolute* comes before *account* because *b* comes before *c* in the alphabet. If the first two letters are the same, we go on to the third letter. Thus *account* comes before *across* because *c* comes before *r*. We follow this same process to the fourth letter or as far as necessary. The words in these two columns are in alphabetical order:

afar	affection
affair	affective
affect	affirm
affectation	affix
affected	afflict

EXERCISE 2

All the words at the top of the next page begin with the same letter. Use the second letter as your guide and rewrite the words of each list in the correct alphabetical order.

I	II	III	IV
pledge	crow	thought	ghost
pulled	candy	teach	gear
park	cease	train	glow
pray	clatter	tally	garret
pour	chatter	twang	grab

EXERCISE 3

Rewrite the words of each list in the correct alphabetical order. Watch the letters to determine the order of the words.

I	II	III	IV
graduate	granulate	Greenland	household
grade	grant	Greenwich	housekeeper
gradual	grantor	greenish	housewife
grain	granite	greening	house
graceful	grange	greenery	housefly

The Guide Words

After you turn to nearly the right page to find a word, your next move is to turn to the exact page. For this purpose the dictionary offers you an important aid. At the top of every page there are two **guide** words in heavy black print. The first one, at the left, repeats the first entry word at the beginning of the page. The second one, at the right, repeats the last entry word at the end of the page. By looking at the guide words you can tell whether the word you are looking for belongs somewhere between those words (that is, on that page) or whether it belongs on an earlier page or a later one.

If the guide words are *harmony* and *harvest*, will *harp*oon appear on that page? The first three letters are alike, and the fourth letter, *p*, comes after *m* of *harmony* but before *v* of *harvest*.

harmony   harpoon   harvest

Therefore *harpoon* belongs somewhere between those two guide words, and it will be found on that page. If you are looking for *hardly*, it will be on an earlier page. The first three letters are still alike, but the fourth letter, *d*, of *hardly*, comes before the *m* of the first guide word, *harmony*.

EXERCISE 4

There are three lists below, each headed by a pair of guide words. Decide which words in each list would be found on the same page as the guide words. Make three columns on your paper, placing the guide words above them. Write the words from the list that would be found with them.

(1)	(2)	(3)
corral cottage	**humorous hurt**	**stagger stanch**
corner	hurry	stampede
correct	hurtle	stagnant
cotton	huge	staff
cork	hunch	stake
corridor	hut	stand
cordial	hump	stamp
corset	humid	stage
course	hurl	stammer
cote	hustle	starch
countess	hunter	stalwart

EXERCISE 5

This exercise will help you decide whether a word belongs on the page with the guide words. It will also give you practice in telling whether the word belongs before or after that page.

Directions: On your paper copy only the numbers of the words. After each number write your decision about the place of the word. If it belongs on the page, make a check mark (✓). If it belongs before the page, write *b;* if it belongs after the page, write *a.*

thick think	**shape shave**
1. these	9. shanty
2. thistle	10. shatter
3. thicken	11. shawl
4. third	12. sharpen
5. thine	13. shame
6. thing	14. shark
7. therefore	15. sheath
8. thimble	16. shapely

EXERCISE 6

In this exercise you are to locate the page on which each word in the first column may be found. The page numbers are shown alongside the guide words. Match each word in the first column with the appropriate guide words, and you will find the correct page. On your paper write the words and the number of the page on which each can be found.

	Page	Guide Words
campaign	130	calico .... callow
captivate	131	calm .... camel
calipers	132	cameo ...... campus
canyon	133	canal .... candor
caloric	134	cane .... canopy
cardinal	135	canteen ..... capability
cannon	136	capacious ... capitulate
capillary	137	capitulation .. carabao
carbonic	138	caracul ..... carcinoma
candidate	139	cardiac ...... carillon

Finding Derived Forms

Would you be surprised to learn that the dictionary does not list all forms of the words we use?

If you were to look up the word *books,* you would not find it. But you *can* find *book.* Usually the dictionary does not list words formed simply by adding *s,* or *es,* or *ed,* or *ing.* The dictionary expects you to know the original word. That word will be found in the list of entries. Therefore, instead of looking for *recovering,* find the word *recover.*

Even when the spelling is changed because of the ending, you should still look up the original word. The word *plan* + *ed* becomes *planned.* The entry word to find is *plan.* On the same line, in heavier print, just before the definition, you will find *planned* and *planning,* to show you the spelling change that is made. If the dictionary is a large one, you may find the word *planned,* too, in the list of entries, but without any definition. Instead, it will say "see *plan.*"

In the same way, look up *see* instead of *saw* or *seen,* and *ox* instead of *oxen,* and *mouse* instead of *mice,* and so on.

Compound Words and Certain Phrases

Compound words can also be found in the list of entries. Some are written as one word, such as: *applesauce, moonbeam, headache.* Some are written as separate words or hyphenated words, such as: *dining room, high school, short cut, tip-off.* Certain phrases that are often used may also be found in the dictionary, but the entry word will usually be the first word in the phrase. In the explanation following the entry word *far*, the dictionary may include such phrases as *far and near, far and wide, so far so good.* In the entry after the word *first*, you may find *first and last, at first, from the first.*

Abbreviations

All abbreviations that are in common use may be located in any of the larger dictionaries. All the letters in the abbreviation are treated as though they were part of one word. Therefore the abbreviation *e. g.* may follow the word *effusive* and come before the word *egad*. The definitions are extremely brief, just enough to give the intention of the abbreviation. Thus after *R.R.*, you find *railroad*. After *etc.*, you find *and so forth*.

EXERCISE 7

Copy the following abbreviations on your paper, find them in the dictionary, and then write their meanings.

1. Mr.	6. i.e.	11. St.
2. M.D.	7. A.D.	12. Rd.
3. Rev.	8. B.C.	13. Sr.
4. Prof.	9. R.S.V.P.	14. Jr.
5. e.g.	10. S.S.	15. N.E.

Suffixes

Words with suffix endings may also be found as entry words in some dictionaries. However, if your dictionary does not list the word with a suffix, you should look for the form of the word with the suffix removed. For example, if you cannot locate *dangerous* in the list, look for *danger*. If you cannot find *clownish*, look for *clown*.

3. WHICH DEFINITION FITS THE THOUGHT?

The most important information which the dictionary gives you is the **meaning** of words. No matter what strange or unknown word you may meet, you will find its definition in a dictionary unless the word has very recently come into general use. If it is a highly technical word, used only by specialists in some field of science, you may have to consult an **unabridged** dictionary. But the word will be there. If it is a familiar word, but used in a way that seems strange to you, you will find that one of its definitions will be the one you are looking for.

Most of the words in our language have more than one meaning. Some words have as many as fifteen definitions or more. In looking for a definition you cannot simply choose the first one you find. Your problem is not over when you locate a word. You must now locate the appropriate definition. Which one will you select?

Your choice must depend on the way the word is used in the sentence, or in the context around the sentence. Notice these definitions for the word *guard*.

> **guard,** 1. to keep safe; to watch over; to protect. 2. to prevent from getting out. 3. to take precautions against. 4. a person or group that does the guarding. 5. any object or appliance that protects against injury or loss. 6. a player whose position on the team is mainly for defense. 7. a person who opens and closes the doors on a train.

This is not the entire group of definitions for *guard*, but it will serve our purpose. Now let us consider some sentences containing that word and see which definition above will match the different uses of the word. The number of the proper definition is indicated in parentheses after each sentence.

a. A low wall was all that *guarded* the cars from slipping over the edge into the canyon. (1)

b. A steel fence with a powerful electric charge *guarded* the prisoners in the exercise yard. (2)

c. He *guarded* against a mistake by writing a stroke for each correct answer. (3)

d. The *guard* at the palace gate was on duty all night. (4)

e. A metal *guard* in front of the circular saw keeps you from getting your fingers cut. (5)

f. Wilson played *guard* on the basketball team. (6)

g. The *guard* opened the gate and we all crowded into the train. (7)

Those definitions were rather close in meaning, yet it was necessary to choose the definition carefully for each sentence. There are other words whose various meanings are quite different from each other. We shall examine four definitions for the word *flag*.

> **flag,** *n.* 1. a section of cloth showing a. pattern or a pattern with colors that indicate some country or other geographical unit, or a club or other kind of group. 2. a stone used in making a path; a flagstone.
> *–v.* 1. to stop by using a flag as a signal: *The agent flagged the train.* 2. to get tired, to grow weak.

What to notice. There are four definitions here. After the entry, *flag*, you see the abbreviation *n.* The letter *n* means that the definitions that follow it will define *flag* as a noun (a name word). The first definition, marked 1, defines the word as it is most commonly used. The second, marked 2, defines *flag* as "a flat slab of stone."

Next you see the abbreviation *v.* This stands for *verb.* The two definitions that follow it are also numbered 1 and 2. They define *flag* when it is used as a verb (an action word). In number 1, *flag* means "to stop." In number 2, *flag* means "to get tired."

In all larger dictionaries, instead of *v.* for the verb you will find *v.i.* or *v.t.* Those combinations still mean *verb.* They refer to two kinds of verbs, which need not be explained here.

EXERCISE 8

Write the letters **a** to **d** in a column. Beside each letter write the definition of the word *flag* that applies to each sentence. Write *n* or *v* to tell whether the word is used as a noun or a verb.

a. The freight train, after a long delay for repairs, had barely started again when the brakeman *flagged* it to a stop.

b. The path remained muddy and forsaken until the farmer rebuilt it and covered it with white, smooth *flags*.

c. New American *flags* decorated the main avenue of New Delhi when the President of the United States visited India.

d. The boy started to read his novel with great excitement, but after an hour his interest began to *flag*.

EXERCISE 9

In this exercise, you will work with a list of words with their definitions. Below them, you will find sentences in which one word is italicized. By referring to the definitions, you can find the meaning of the italicized word that fits the sentence.

1. Keep in mind the general sense of the whole sentence.

2. Try to decide whether the given word is a noun or a verb or an adjective (*adj.*). Adjectives are describing words.

3. First skim through the definitions of your word to locate the abbreviation (*n., v.,* or *adj.*) that points out the part of speech you need for the word.

4. Then skim through the definitions within the group for that part of speech.

5. Select the definition that makes sense when you use it in place of the required word.

Directions: Copy on your paper the italicized words in the sentences on page 246. Find the definition of the word that fits the sentence. Write that definition after the word.

DEFINITIONS

bark, *n.* 1. the tough, outside covering of a tree. 2. the short, sharp sound that a dog makes. 3. a ship, usually with three masts. –*v.* 1. to make a sound like a bark. 2. to shout sharply or gruffly.

beam, *n.* 1. a large, long piece of timber or metal. 2. a ray of light. 3. distance across the width of a ship. –*v.* 1. to shine or send out rays of light. 2. to smile very happily.

compact, *n.* agreement. –*adj.* packed firmly together.

custom, *n.* 1. usual habit or action. 2. business given by a customer. –*adj.* made to order for an individual.

defile, *n.* a narrow passage or valley. –*v.* to make filthy or dirty.

245

a. The captain displayed his impatience as he *barked* his orders to the crew.

b. Some hoodlums had *defiled* the monument by smearing paint over its base.

c. Mary *beamed* with joy as she listened to the praises of her friends and relatives.

d. The gentleman insisted that he would wear only *custom-made* shirts.

e. William Penn made a *compact* with the Indians which was never broken by either side.

f. The ship was very wide in the *beam* so that it was safe even in rough waters.

g. The soldiers marched in a single column through the *defile*.

h. The material was folded into a *compact* package.

i. The giant trees of California are protected by *bark* that is nearly a foot thick.

j. It was the *custom* in that town to celebrate a wedding for three days.

k. Our dog always *barks* at the mailman.

l. The house was built with a steel *beam* across the cellar.

EXERCISE 10

Directions: After you have decided on the definitions for the italicized words in the sentences that follow, rewrite the sentences, but substitute the definition for the required word. You may have to make some slight changes so that the sentences will sound right. The first one has been done for you.

Number the sentences in your answers.

DEFINITIONS

hamper, *v.* to hold back; to hinder. *—n.* a large basket.

hand, *n.* 1. the end part of the arm. 2. something resembling a hand in appearance or use: *The hands of a clock.* 3. a hired worker who uses his hands. 4. a share in doing something: *Lend me a hand.* 5. a round of applause. 6. cards held by a player. *—v.* to give something with the hand.

late, *adj.* 1. happening after the usual or proper time. 2. recently dead: *the late president of the company.*

prior, *adj.* coming before or earlier. *—n.* head of a monastery.

tumultuous, *adj.* 1. very noisy, disorderly, or violent. 2. rough and stormy.

1. The *late* Mr. Jones was one of the most charitable men in our town.
   (*Rewritten:* Mr. Jones, *who died recently,* was one of the most charitable men in our town.)
2. The cruiser was badly battered by the *tumultuous* waves.
3. The *prior* governed his monastery with gentleness and devotion.
4. The farmer took on several new *hands* to help harvest the crop of wheat.
5. Mother prepared a large picnic lunch and Father carried it out to the car in our new *hamper.*
6. The meeting of the strikers soon became highly *tumultuous.*
7. The man had been discharged from his *prior* employment.
8. Mrs. Russell was annoyed when her husband returned *late* for dinner.
9. The actors were overjoyed at receiving a big *hand* on their opening night.
10. He tried desperately to control his pitching, but a gnawing pain in his wrist *hampered* him at every throw.

4. FINDING INFORMATION ABOUT NAMES

The dictionary is an excellent book for obtaining information about certain persons and places. Well-known names from the Bible, from fiction, from legends, and from history are to be found there. The explanation will tell why the name is important. Geographical names are also included, with some information about location, size, and population wherever those facts are important.

EXERCISE 11

You should now be able to locate names, like words, very quickly. As soon as you find them in the dictionary, see how fast you can find answers to the following questions. Write the answers on your paper and number them. Remember to use the last name for locating persons.

1. What is the town of *Hamelin* famous for?
2. What important service to the world was contributed by *Alfred Nobel*?
3. For what is *Mount Olympus* best known?
4. When did the *French Revolution* begin?
5. What discovery was made by *Galileo*?
6. What discovery was made by *Alexander Fleming*?
7. Who was *Stradivarius*? What is he known for?
8. On what date was the *Armistice* declared for *World War I*?
9. Where is *Guadalcanal*? Why is it important in history?
10. What is the *Hippocratic oath*?

5. MAKING SURE OF THE PRONUNCIATION

The dictionary is an authority for all the information it contains. The larger the dictionary, the greater the amount and kinds of information. In the unabridged dictionaries there may be special sections devoted to abbreviations, foreign words and phrases, geographical terms, historical events, and other types of information, usually in the back pages.

In the front part of the book you may find rules for spelling, pronunciation, separating words, pronunciation of letters in foreign languages, and so on. Check the dictionaries you use at home and at school to see whether they contain these rules. Most people turn to the dictionary to find the *spelling*, the *meaning*, or the *pronunciation* of a word.

Pronunciation of a word usually appears in parenthesis right after the word. The word is respelled to show how it is sounded. This is known as **phonetic spelling.** You will see marks over some of the letters. They are called **diacritical marks,** and their job is to show how letters are sounded.

Example: photograph (fō′tᵊ-grăf′)

248

Diacritical marks vary from one dictionary to another. However, every dictionary has a **pronouncing key.** You will find this key at the beginning of the dictionary. In most dictionaries you will also find it at the bottom of each double-page spread. To be sure of the pronunciation of a word, you must use this key.

How Letter Sounds Are Shown

The letters of our alphabet may be divided into two groups— vowels and consonants. The vowels are *a, e, i, o, u,* and sometimes *y* and *w.* All other letters, with *y* and *w,* are consonants.

Most of the consonants give little trouble. There are a few, however, that have more than one sound. Also, there is more than one way of spelling certain consonant sounds. The dictionary key provides a way around these problems.

1. The letter *c* is sometimes pronounced as *k* (as in *cat*), and sometimes as *s* (as in *cent*). This is how the dictionary will show them:

   cat (kat)   cent (sent)

2. The letter *g* is sometimes hard (as in *get*) and sometimes soft, or like *j* as in *gem.* This is how the dictionary will show them:

   get (get)   gem (jem)

3. The letter *s* has two sounds, *s* and *z.* This is how the dictionary shows them:

   glass (glas)   has (haz)

4. The sound of *sh* may be spelled differently in different words. The dictionary shows the *pronunciation* of all by *sh.*

   sure (shur)
   ocean (oshin)
   machine (masheen)
   action (akshin)

5. The sound of *s,* as in *pleasure,* is shown by *zh.*

   pleasure (plezhur)
   garage (garazh)
   azure (azhur)

The vowels give us much more trouble than consonants because there are so many sounds for each vowel. The long sound, the name of the vowel, is shown by the macron ($-$), a straight line placed above it. The short sound may be shown by the breve ($\smile$), or by the vowel printed by itself. Other vowel sounds are shown by the following marks: ä, â. The key always gives you a familiar word to show what these marks mean.

ă   This is the short sound. In some dictionaries it is shown as in the word făt. In other dictionaries it may be shown without the breve, as in *fat*. You will find this sound in *bat, cat, mat.*

ā   This is the long sound. The key word is *ape*. You will find this sound in *bake, rain, break, bail,* and *obey.*

â   The key word for this sound is *bare*. This will be your key word for the vowels in such words as *fair, there, their, bear.*

ä   The key word is *car*. This is your key word for *far, heart.*

e   as in *ten.* This is the short sound.

ē   as in *even.* This is the long sound, found in *we, free, bean, receive, people, key, machine.*

i   as in *is*

ī   as in *bite*

o   as in *lot;* also in *bother, bonny*

ō   as in *go;* also in *boat, bone, toe, grow, soul, sew*

ô   as in *horn;* also in *saw, caught, ball, alter*

oo as in *look;* also in *foot, would, full*

ōō as in *too;* also in *tool, boom, move, shoe, through, threw*

oi as in *oil;* also in *boy, boil*

ou as in *out;* also in *how, crowd, found*

u   as in *cup*

u̇   as in *put*

ü   as in *rule*

ū   as in *use;* also in *music, beauty, few, view, you*

û   as in *fur;* also in *her, fern, work, hurt, shirk*

You will discover that many English words contain silent letters—letters that are not pronounced. The dictionary pronunciation of a word contains no silent letters. Thus *came* is given as kām. The word *bead* is given as bēd since the *a* is silent.

6. SYLLABLES AND THE ACCENT

There are words that have only one syllable. Others have two syllables, three syllables, and even four or five. A word of two syllables is sounded in two parts, for example *re tail* (rē′tāl). A word like *enlightenment* has four syllables; that is, it is divided into four parts. In each syllable there is one vowel sound.

In some dictionaries the separate syllables are shown by space between the syllables. In some dictionaries they are separated by dots, like this: EN·LIGHT·EN·MENT. Below you see examples of a word divided into syllables, a compound word that is written as *separate* words, and a compound word that requires hyphens. Do not confuse these three.

en rich   is a single word with two syllables
high school   is a compound word written as two words
brother-in-law   is a compound word written with hyphens between the separate words

It is important to know which syllable to accent, and the dictionary gives you that information, too. The accent may be indicated by a slanted line, like this: *hab′it.*

For most of the words that you use, you are already familiar with the correct accent. You always say rePEAT, not REpeat; or WALnut, not walNUT; or perCENT, not PERcent. In the dictionary, the pronunciation would be shown as follows:

RE·PEAT   (ri-pēt′)
WAL·NUT   (wôl′nut)
PER·CENT   (per-sent′)

Do you always accent the proper syllable? Watch for the accent marks in the list of words below. Have you been pronouncing these words correctly?

mu nic′i pal   (not muniCIpal)
the′a ter   (not theAter)
or′ches tra   (not orCHEStra)
in quir′y   (not INquiry)
mis′chiev ous   (not misCHIEVous)
com′pa ra ble   (not comPARable)
in′fam ous   (not inFAMous)
ex′qui site   (not exQUIZit)

251

Among the words with several syllables, there are many that have two accents. In these words, one accent is heavier than the other. In some dictionaries, the lighter accent is shown by two slant lines, as in *gasoline*, which is shown as *gas"l·ēn"*. In other dictionaries, the heavy accent is shown by a heavy dark line and the lighter accent by a light line: *gas"l·ēn'*.

EXERCISE 12

Say the words below to yourself and take note of how many syllables you use in pronouncing them. If there are four or more syllables, the word may need both a heavy and a light accent.

Where you are not sure of the syllables or the accents, consult your dictionary at once. Then be prepared to pronounce the word with the right accent. If it has two accents, be ready to tell on which syllables they fall.

For additional practice, write the words in syllables and mark the accents.

direct	helicopter	examination	evaporate
meteor	impair	replaceable	interruption
maximum	impartial	irreplaceable	invaluable
inclement	political	interrogative	reputable
implement	stimulate	mechanism	incubator
minimum	magnetize	interdependence	incubation

7. SOME SPECIAL CONSONANT SOUNDS

It is necessary to repeat that the pronunciation spelling shown in the dictionary contains only those letters that give you the correct sounds. They may look completely different from the actual spelling of the word. For example, *quick* may appear there as (kwik), and *picture* as (pik'cher).

Following are a few special consonant sounds.

1. The *ch* sound, as in chop.   2. *f* as in fan

nature	(nā'cher)	muff	(muf)
picture	(pik'cher)	rough	(ruf)
righteous	(rī'chis)	phase	(fāz)

3. *j* as in jam

magic	(ma′jik)
graduate	(graj′o͞o·it)
hedge	(hej)

4. *qu* as in quick

quick	(kwik)
choir	(kwīr)

5. *sh* as in she

mansion	(man′shin)
facial	(fā′shil)
nation	(nā′shin)
sure	(shoor)

6. *ŋ* .as in sing

running	(run′iŋ)

EXERCISE 13

In the following phrases and sentences the words in parentheses are spelled phonetically. Decide what those words are saying, and then turn them into the correct spelling. Write them in a list on your paper and number them to match the phrases or sentences.

1. He liked to read books of (fik′shin).
2. Jack the (jī′int) killer
3. To (laf) at a joke
4. It was only a (frāz), not a sentence.
5. To ask a (kwes′chin)
6. (Rōz′iz) smell sweet.
7. (Sōl′jerz) at war
8. He (dojd) the punch.
9. A boat on the (ō′shin)
10. He is my (kuz′n).

8. PHONETIC SPELLING OF VOWELS

The Schwa

This is a schwa: ə. It looks like an **e** turned upside down. The schwa represents a vowel sound that is probably used more often than any other sound in our language. It stands for the vowel that you pass over very lightly in pronunciation. No matter what vowels are used with the schwa in the spelling, you sound them all in much the same way. You slur them, you hurry over them, you say them very softly, and you cannot be sure whether you are saying an *i*, or *e*, or *a*, or any other vowel. It does not matter.

Say these words to yourself. Notice how the schwa is sounded.

again (ə-gen')   cabinet (kab'ə-nit)
occur (ə-kur')   success (sək-ses')

EXERCISE 14

In a good dictionary look up the words listed below. Find the key word for the vowels that are underlined. Write in a column on your paper the words listed here, with their numbers. Beside each word write the key word that is correct for the vowel or vowels in that word. Then say the vowel softly, to make the pronunciation clear to yourself.

(NOTE: Wherever two pronunciations are given, use the first.)

1. sarcoma
2. sarcophagus
3. sausage
4. sauté
5. sauterne
6. scour
7. scourge
8. scrod
9. scrofula
10. scroll

11. scurrilous
12. scurry
13. scurvy
14. seamy
15. séance
16. sear
17. search
18. student
19. studied
20. studio

MAKING
INFERENCES 15

In Chapter 8, you learned how to "find the hidden meaning." Your mind would see thoughts that were suggested by what the words said. Your mind was reading more than your eyes saw. You were **making inferences.** That is what you did when you read exaggerated statements and sarcastic statements. That kind of reading is particularly necessary in fiction and other forms of literature. It may be needed in informational material, too, though not so often.

You already know why authors write in this manner. They do it to make the reading more exciting, more pleasing. At the same time, they want to make sure you receive the hidden thoughts. They leave clues for you, all kinds of clues. As a reader you are also an amateur detective, for you must make inferences from these clues and arrive at the hidden meanings.

1. FINDING CLUES

Below are two sentences about a man. In one of them the author describes the man fully. You can easily picture him. In the other, the author does not mention a single word about his character. Nevertheless, there are clues in the second sentence that permit you to recognize his character easily. You will see that both sentences tell the same thing about him.

>1. Uncle Harry was a jolly man, full of laughter and funny stories.
>2. There was never a dull moment when Uncle Harry came to visit us.

Now read the following sentence and see how much you can tell about the character of the woman, and even about her appearance, although the author does not mention either.

>At the very sight of her, the children would instantly stop their merry chatter and freeze into silence until she was out of sight again.

What was there about her that made the children stop their happy conversation? What did they see in her face? Were her lips smiling or was her mouth drawn into a tight line? Did they like her or fear her? Why? Do you think she had ever spoken to them? What kinds of things do you suppose she had said to them? What clue suggested your answers?

An author expects you to make inferences from the clues he gives you. Were you surprised at the number of inferences you were able to make about the woman? This kind of reading will stir your emotions and make the characters come alive for you. Perhaps, while you are learning and practicing, your reading will slow down for a moment every time you make an inference. Very soon, however, these inferences will come to your mind in a flash, and every story you read will then become much more enjoyable.

EXERCISE 1

Look for inferences that will answer the questions after each sentence or short paragraph in this exercise. Select the best answer. Be prepared to justify your answer in class discussion.

1. The men in the crew met many hardships on their long trip into the Arctic, and they were worried and discouraged. But whenever the admiral appeared, their burden seemed easier and their hopes were lifted.

What kind of person is the admiral? (Jolly? Kind? Wise and capable? Dignified?) What clue helped you?

2. Molly threw her coat over a chair, flew past her astonished parents to her own room, slammed the door, and flung herself face down on the bed.

How does Molly feel? (Very tired? Bitterly disappointed? Frightened? Angry at her parents?) What kind of event might have happened to her?

3. The captain looked over the men gathered before him. "There'll be no mutiny on my ship!" he announced, in a voice that was soft and deep but with a ring of grim determination.

Describe his character. (Stern and feared by the men? Peaceful? Pleasant? Has good judgment?)
Why had the men gathered there? What clues gave you these inferences?

4. She spoke as if her tongue had been dipped in acid.

How did she feel? (In pain? Sorry? Angry and mean? Pleased and peaceful?)
How did the people feel about the way she spoke? To what is her tongue being compared?

5. Even a tiny speck of dust on his carefully pressed uniform would receive his immediate attention.

Describe his appearance as completely as you can imagine. (Carefully dressed in every particular? Had no dirt spots on his clothing? Wore a masquerade costume?)
What kind of person is he?

6. "You certainly did a wonderful job," commented Father, viewing the spilled paint.

What does Father really mean? Is this statement exaggeration or sarcasm? What clue helped you?

2. INFERENCES ABOUT WHAT MAY HAPPEN

If you read with your mind, or "between the lines," you can learn much about a story from its very beginning. Sometimes the clue will be seen in the opening sentence. In most cases you can make an excellent inference about the kind of story it will be from something within the first two paragraphs.

> 1. When I left home that morning to become a water-boy, I never dreamed how much the world of sawdust was going to affect my life.

The "world of sawdust" is the circus. You can readily see that this story will tell of gradual changes from water-boy to some very important positions in the circus. It may be as a star performer, or perhaps as the manager. But the first sentence lets you know what to expect when you read on.

> 2. Just as the train pulled in, a man came running up, his hat pulled low over his eyes, his collar turned up, his brief case clutched tightly, and his eyes glancing furtively about him.

What will this story be about? We do not have enough clues for all the details. But the man's appearance and manner announce to us that there is something mysterious and fearful, perhaps a murder or a spy hunt, from which he is running away. Therefore we may expect a crime story or a spy story.

3. The ghost that walked into our house last month has created so much fuss ever since that I am sorry I woke up the family that night. I should have gone right back to sleep and allowed the ghost to keep right on walking.

This will be a ghost story, of course. But it will also be an amusing story. What clue helps you here? The beginning of a story provides a hint about the kind of story that will follow. It also introduces the persons in the story and gives hints about the time, the place where the story occurs, and what is happening.

The Four W's

The following paragraph is just the beginning of a story. Within these few sentences you will read some facts about **who, what, when,** and **where.** See how much you can discover.

Ralph paused for a moment before he wound up for the pitch. There was something about the new hitter now facing him that Ralph did not like. As he swung the bat over the plate, he seemed too experienced and confident, and perhaps too old for a Little Leaguer. Where had the Clinton team found him? Ordinarily, it would not have mattered to Ralph. But this was an important game for Milford, and Ralph knew that Milford's chance of entering the district tournament was at stake.

Umpire Artie called out, "What's the matter, Ralph? Why don't you throw?"

"I'm just wondering if that batter is a regular player," replied Ralph somewhat doubtfully. Immediately shouts of protest arose and tempers flared all over the field.

Who: *Ralph,* a pitcher on the boy's team at Milford. The *new batter* (we do not know much about him yet). The *two teams* and the *umpire*

When: During the baseball season

Where: The baseball field in either Clinton or Milford, both small towns

What: The new batter may possibly be a "ringer" brought into the game illegally to help the Clinton team. We shall probably find out whether Ralph will have enough courage and spirit to pitch a good game, and win for his team in spite of the odds against him.

Here are the beginning paragraphs for two other stories. For each one write on your paper the answers to the four questions: *Who? Where? When? What?*

1. "Frank!" shouted Mrs. Mitchell, "I've called you three times. You come down this minute or you'll be too late for breakfast."

"Coming, Ma," he answered, and a moment later he appeared on the stairway. Mrs. Mitchell gasped when she saw him, but Dotty merely grinned.

"I kept wondering what made you stay in the bathroom so long," exclaimed his mother. "But I never expected you, all by yourself, to comb your hair so slick and to wear a regular shirt and a tie. *And a tie!* Are you sick, Frank?"

"I can tell you what it's about," volunteered Dotty. "He met that new girl with the golden curls, and he's ga-ga about her."

"I am not. Don't you listen to her, Ma. She's just like all little sisters, always saying something to tease me." And Frank glared at Dotty, hoping that his fierce look would scare her into silence.

"Ha, ha! Think you can frighten me, do you? And that isn't all, Ma. He walked her all the way home yesterday and carried her books, too."

Watch for the answers to the questions: *Who? What? When? Where?*

2. Dr. Storey was reading up on a case he had treated that morning and had lost track of the passing time. The ring at the door reminded him to look at his watch, and then he wondered who could be coming to consult him at two in the morning. He opened the door and admitted two men, one of them half carrying, half dragging the other, who apparently had been injured. Dr. Storey helped bring him to the examining table. There he ripped open the man's shirt and saw the wound in his shoulder.

"He's been shot," said the doctor. "I'll give him some immediate treatment for the emergency, but I'll have to call the police before I do any more than that."

"You'll give him the best treatment you ever gave anyone," snarled the other man, "and you'll keep your trap shut, too."

3. USING INFERENCE TO UNDERSTAND JOKES

You can enjoy a joke only if you understand it. Yet the most important part of many jokes, the part that gives you the laugh, is deliberately omitted. It is left to your imagination to fill in. Therefore, to understand jokes, you must use your mind to guess at something the author actually leaves out.

Let us see what a joke includes, and what it omits.

> *Nervous passenger:* I can't bear to watch you driving so fast around corners. It makes me nervous.
>
> *Driver:* Keep your eyes closed, madame. I'd be scared, too, if I looked.

What was omitted from this little story? What happens if the driver closes his eyes? Less danger? Or much more? The driver's advice is ridiculous; it is so ridiculous that we know it is impossible.

But if a joke is explained this way it is no longer a joke. The explanation of the missing part must come *to your own mind*, while you are reading the joke. It will be worth while for you to supply the missing portion in the jokes that follow, even though they may be partly spoiled for you. Learning how to read jokes will help you enjoy other jokes more fully.

EXERCISE 3

The following stories are amusing because something is left unsaid. Explain what is missing.

> **1.** An officer was finding fault with the camp cook, who was stirring something in a big soup kettle. "I've been getting complaints about your cooking," shouted the officer. "Just let me taste the soup." The cook quietly gave him a spoon and the officer took a taste. He spat it out at once. "Why, that tastes like dish water," he yelled. "Yes, sir," replied the cook. "That's what it is."

Did the officer know what it was at first? Would you expect that the cook would tell him? But did the cook tell him? He did not, and that is what caused the officer's mistake. Why wasn't this explained to the reader in the middle of the story? If it had been, you would not feel the surprise and humor that came at the end of the story. The story becomes a joke only because of that omission.

2. During the war, a shipyard worker was teaching a new lady riveter what to do.

"I'll hold the rivet," he said, "and when I nod my head, you hit it with the sledge hammer."

She did.

He saw stars for two weeks!

What was omitted?

3. A man telephoned to a doctor asking him to rush over at once. His son had swallowed a fountain pen.

"I'll come at once," said the doctor. "But what are you doing in the meantime?"

"I'm all right," the man replied. "I'm using a pencil."

What was omitted?

4. First man: What happened to your face? It's all cut.
Second man: A fellow threw a tomato at me.
First man: But a tomato can't cut your face.
Second man: Oh, he forgot to take it out of the can.

What was omitted?

4. PUTTING FACTS TOGETHER TO MAKE INFERENCES

The section on jokes was presented partly for your enjoyment, but the real purpose was to show the importance of thoughts that are deliberately omitted. You learned how to recognize those omissions and how to supply them in your thoughts.

Suppose a story tells of a prisoner who has just finished a long term in jail. He is about to leave and the warden hands him five dollars, the legal parting gift for a prisoner. This is all the money he has. Yet he takes a taxi to the town, pays the driver one dollar, and then gives him another dollar as a tip. He stops for a shine, and gives the bootblack fifty cents.

What inferences can you make from these facts? How can you use them together, plus your own previous general knowledge, to obtain new meanings? Can you see that spending so much just for tips is rather strange for a man who possesses only five dollars? Does this look sensible? Then try to imagine why he did it. Consider the four possibilities at the top of the next page.

1. He might be merely stupid. That would be one inference.
2. He might have been accustomed to spending money freely before he became a prisoner. But would he forget that this would leave him only $2.50?
3. He might not need any of the five dollars at all. Possibly he is a wealthy man, and he is going home where he need not worry about money.
4. Or possibly he is still a criminal at heart, and he is going to meet some of his partners in crime and obtain a great deal of money from them.

Read this statement about another person.

Her entire wardrobe hung from a single rusty nail on the back of her hall-bedroom door, five flights up.

There are many inferences that can be formed from that statement. What kind of bedroom would have no place for clothing except a nail on the back of a door? How old or dingy would the room be if even the nail is allowed to become rusty? How poor is the woman if all her clothes can be hung from one nail? What do you think of the condition or appearance of her clothing? How expensive or how cheap is the rental of a room for which you have to climb up five flights?

Can you see that if you put together the facts in the story (even from a single sentence) and the facts from your own experience, you can discover many important inferences? That is exactly what the author of a story would expect you to do.

EXERCISE 4

The short paragraphs that follow will give you an opportunity to put facts together to see what they mean. Answer the questions on the next page and be ready to explain your answers.

A. The warplane came roaring down from the sky, flying low over the field and scattering the sheep in terror. Old Bardi shook his fist in violent anger, then set about patiently to recover his sheep.

1. What is Bardi's occupation?
2. Is this the first time he has seen a plane?
3. Is this the first time that his sheep have been scattered by a plane?
4. What is taking place, probably not far away, that brings planes across his pasture?
5. Is the pasture in America or in some other part of the world? Where do you think it might be?

     B. The sky was blood-red. Thick pulses of flame beat up from the darkness.

     "She's going to go fast," shouted Big Jim. "Brad, smash those windows. Tony, get that stream started." He was barking orders at everybody.

1. What is happening here?
2. Who or what is meant by "she"?
3. How many men are busy here? Three, or more?
4. Are they worried? About what?
5. Who do you think Big Jim is?

C. The teacher glanced at Randy, and she felt a glow of satisfaction. At last he was proving to her how attentive he could be. The big geography book was propped open on the desk before him, and he kept his eyes glued to the pages. Even when Jimmy's books dropped on the floor and were strewn all about, and the class laughed, Randy did not look up. The teacher was just about to tell the class about taking an example from Randy when her eye caught something new. A corner of some strange page, with a colored picture on it, was peeking out over the edge of the geography book. Miss Jasper's beaming face suddenly changed its expression.

1. What kind of boy was Randy usually?
2. Why was the teacher pleased to see him reading a textbook attentively?
3. What do you think he was reading?
4. Why did Randy continue reading when the rest of the class was laughing?
5. What made the teacher suspicious?
6. What was her name?
7. What change came into her face?

5. APPRECIATING A COMPLETE STORY

Inferences are the conclusions you draw as you read a story. They are really your judgments as to what is going on in the story. They are your interpretation of the meaning of what the author tells you. A story that tells everything, leaving nothing for the reader to figure out, is a poor story.

With all that you have learned about making inferences, you are now prepared to read a story with rich understanding and keen enjoyment. You will find pleasure in seeing what happens to, the people in the story and what they do. There will be greater pleasure in discovering *why* they act as they do and *how they feel* as each new event appears.

From the very beginning you should be on the alert to find out **who, what, where,** and **when** in the story. After you have made these discoveries and have them clearly in mind, the plot is bound to unfold easily for you.

The following story is a selection from the book, *Tom Sawyer*. Ordinarily you might read a story of this kind completely through the first time without stopping. However, this selection has been marked and numbered for you so that the class may read and discuss it step by step. You will discover all sorts of inferences, and you will extend your reading skills.

On pages 269–271 you will find a series of questions to guide the discussion. These questions may be asked by your teacher or by a student leader, and the class should read and discuss the story part by part as directed. You will begin by discussing the title of the story.

Tom Tests the Pain-Killer
By Mark Twain

1.   **A.** Tom Sawyer had found a new and weighty prob-
2. lem that was disturbing his mind. Becky Thatcher had
3. stopped coming to school. He had struggled with his pride
4. for a few days and tried to whistle her out of his thoughts,
5. but he had failed. He began to notice that he was hang-
6. ing around her father's house at night and feeling miser-
7. able. Becky was ill. What if she should die!
8.   **B.** That thought kept haunting him. He no longer
9. took an interest in war, not even in piracy. The charm of
10. life was gone; there was nothing left but dreariness. He
11. put his hoop away, and his bat; there was no joy left in
12. them any more.
13.   **C.** Aunt Polly became concerned about Tom. She
14. began to try all manner of remedies on him. She was one
15. of those people who are infatuated with patent medicines
16. and all newfangled cures. She was an enthusiastic experi-
17. menter in those things. When something fresh in this line
18. came out, she was in a fever, right away, to try it; not on
19. herself, for she was never ailing, but on anybody else that
20. came handy. All the "rot" about ventilation and how to
21. go to bed, and how to get up, and what to eat, and what
22. to drink, and how much exercise to take, and what sort of
23. clothing to wear, that was gospel to her. She never noticed
24. that her health magazines for one month upset every-
25. thing they had recommended the month before. She was
26. as simple-hearted and honest as the day was long, and so

27. she was an easy victim. She went about to the suffering
28. neighbors, never suspecting that she was not an angel of
29. healing.
30.   **D.** The water treatment was new now, and Tom's
31. low condition was an opportunity to her. She had Tom
32. out at daylight every morning, stood him up in the wood-
33. shed, and drowned him with a deluge of cold water; then
34. she scrubbed him down with a towel like a file, and then
35. brought him to; then she rolled him up in a sheet and
36. put him away under the blankets till she sweated his
37. soul clean.
38.   **E.** Yet notwithstanding all this, the boy grew more
39. and more melancholy and pale and dejected. She added
40. hot baths, salt baths, shower baths, and plunges. The boy
41. remained as dismal as a hearse. She began to assist the
42. water with a slim oatmeal diet and blister plasters. She
43. filled him up every day with quack cure-alls.
44.   **F.** Tom had become indifferent to all her persecu-
45. tion by this time. This fact filled the old lady's heart with
46. consternation. This indifference must be broken up at any
47. cost. Just then she heard of Pain-Killer for the first time.
48. She ordered a lot at once. She tasted it and was filled with
49. gratitude. It was simply fire in a liquid form! She dropped
50. everything else, and pinned her faith on Pain-Killer. She
51. gave Tom a teaspoonful and watched with the deepest
52. anxiety for the result. Her troubles were instantly at rest,
53. her soul at peace again, for the "indifference" was broken
54. up. The boy could not have shown a wilder, heartier in-
55. terest if she had built a fire under him.
56.   **G.** Tom felt that it was time to wake up. So he
57. thought over various plans for relief, and finally hit upon
58. that of pretending to be fond of the Pain-Killer. He asked
59. for it so often that he became a nuisance, and his aunt
60. ended by telling him to help himself and quit pestering
61. her. However, she watched the bottle clandestinely. She
62. found that the medicine did really diminish, but it did not
63. occur to her that the boy was curing a crack in the sitting-
64. room floor with it.
65.   **H.** One day Tom was in the act of giving the crack
66. a dose of the Pain-Killer when his aunt's yellow cat came
67. along, purring, eyeing the teaspoon avariciously, and beg-
68. ging for a taste.

69.   Tom said, "Don't ask for it unless you want it,
70. Peter."
71.   But Peter signified that he did want it.
72.   "You better make sure."
73.   Peter was sure.
74.   "Now you've asked for it, and I'll give it to you,
75. because there ain't anything mean about *me;* but if you
76. find you don't like it, you mustn't blame anybody but your
77. own self."
78.   **I.** Peter was agreeable. So Tom pried his mouth
79. open and poured down the Pain-Killer. Peter sprang a
80. couple of yards in the air, and then delivered a war whoop
81. and set off round and round the room, banging against
82. furniture, upsetting flowerpots, and making general havoc.
83. Next he rose on his hind feet and pranced around, in a
84. frenzy of enjoyment. Then he went tearing around the
85. house again, spreading chaos and destruction in his path.
86. Aunt Polly entered in time to see him throw a few double
87. somersaults and sail through the open window.
88.   **J.** The old lady stood petrified with astonishment,
89. peering over her glasses. Tom lay on the floor expiring
90. with laughter.
91.   "Tom, what on earth ails that cat?"
92.   "*I* don't know, Aunt," gasped the boy.
93.   "Why, I never see anything like it. What *did* make
94. him act so?"
95.   " 'Deed I don't know, Aunt Polly; cats always act so
96. when they're having a good time."
97.   "They do, do they?" There was something in the tone
98. that made Tom apprehensive.
99.   "Yes'm. That is, I believe they do."
100.   "You *do?*"
101.   "Yes'm."
102.   **K.** The old lady was bending down, Tom watching
103. with anxiety. Too late he divined her "drift." The handle
104. of the tell-tale teaspoon was visible under the bed. Aunt
105. Polly took it, held it up. Tom winced, and dropped his
106. eyes. Aunt Polly raised him by the usual handle—his ear—
107. and cracked his head soundly with her thimble.
108.   "Now, sir, what did you want to treat that poor dumb
109. beast so for?"
110.   "I done it out of pity—because he hadn't any aunt."

111.   "Hadn't any aunt!—you numskull. What has that got
112. to do with it?"
113.   "Heaps. Because if he'd 'a' had one, she'd 'a' burnt
114. him out herself 'thout any more feeling than if he was a
115. human!"
116.   **L.** Aunt Polly felt a sudden pang of remorse. This
117. was putting the thing in a new light. What was cruelty to a
118. cat *might* be cruelty to a boy, too. She began to soften;
119. she felt sorry. Her eyes watered a little, and she put her
120. hand on Tom's head and said gently, "I was meaning for
121. the best, Tom. And, Tom, it *did* do you good."
122.   **M.** Tom looked up in her face with just a perceptible
123. twinkle peeping through his gravity. "I know you was
124. meaning for the best, Auntie, and so was I with Peter. It
125. done *him* good, too. I never see him get around so since—"
126.   "Oh, go 'long with you, Tom, before you aggravate
127. me again. And try and see if you can't be a good boy, for
128. once, and you needn't take any more medicine."

For the Teacher or a Student Leader

The title: Tom is Tom Sawyer. Have you ever heard about Tom Sawyer before? What can be meant by *pain-killer?* Do you think this will be a sad story or a humorous one? What makes you think so? Is someone ill, needing medicine? Who? As you read on in this story, see how soon you can be sure whether your guesses were correct.

Before paragraphs A and B: Read these two paragraphs to find, if you can, who will take this medicine. Will it be Becky? Will it be Tom? Try a guess.

After A and B: We now know that Becky is ill. But Tom has a problem, too. What is it? Is there anything wrong or unusual with him? What? In what way is his condition due to Becky? Read the expressions that show how he feels. Why? What tells you that he himself was surprised that he should feel this way? Do you think, as Tom does, that Becky may die? Explain your answer.

Before C: See if this portion will tell who will get the medicine. Also read to find out what kind of person Aunt Polly is, and what you think of her.

After C: How would you criticize her? What is likable about her? What is her weakness? Read the parts that prove it. Have we found out yet who will get the medicine? Guess again.

Lines 15–16: Can you get the meaning of *infatuated* from the context? Of *newfangled?*

Line 18: What is meant by *she was in a fever?*

Line 23: What is meant by *that was gospel to her?*

Lines 27–29: What did she think of herself? What did her neighbors think?

Before D and E: What do you think Aunt Polly will do with all her knowledge about cures? Find out how Tom will be feeling. Will it be on account of Aunt Polly's treatment, or another cause? What other cause? Will we find out yet who will get the pain-killer?

After D and E: What do you think of the treatment Tom is getting? Would you like it? Would you keep taking it, like Tom? Did you expect Tom to take everything his aunt did to him? Is he really that kind of boy? Then why didn't he protest? Did he seem to get better or worse? What do you think is the real reason for his feelings shown in line 39? See if the context will help you get the meaning of *melancholy,* and of *dejected.* Has the pain-killer been given to anyone yet? Who do you think will receive it? What is the exaggeration in line 33?

Before F: Why haven't we heard about the pain-killer yet? Perhaps we will learn very soon. What new treatment do you think Aunt Polly is preparing for Tom? Tom has accepted everything patiently up to now. Will he continue? Let us find out in paragraph F.

After F: Have we learned about the new treatment? Now you know about the pain-killer. What do you think of Aunt Polly for giving it to Tom? How is Tom accepting it? Try to be sure about your answer. How does the medicine taste (note line 49)? How did Tom act when he took it? Which words tell you? But why was Aunt Polly satisfied? What change did she see that seemed like improvement to her? How do you feel for Tom now? Do you think he will continue this treatment? Read paragraph **G** to learn about it.

After G: Is Tom beginning to feel better now? Is the medicine doing him good? What was clever about Tom's method with his aunt? What is the meaning of *clandestinely,* in line 61? In what way did the aunt show that she was suspicious of Tom? How do you feel about Aunt Polly?

Before H and I: In the next two portions Tom will find a new way of getting rid of the pain-killer. Find out what it is.

After H and I: What do you think of Tom's method? Do you think he was fair to the cat in asking whether it wanted a taste? Does Tom feel that he was fair to the cat? Did the cat answer? Does the story say it answered? How do you explain that? How did the cat feel after taking the medicine? In lines 83–84, the cat was in a "frenzy of enjoyment." What does the author really mean? Was it really enjoyment? See if you can tell the meaning of *havoc* (line 82) and *chaos* (line 85).

Before J and K: Read these two portions quickly to find out how good a detective Aunt Polly is, and how Tom finds a clever excuse.

After J and K: Is Tom's excuse a good one? Why? See if you can find the meaning of *petrified* (line 88), *apprehensive* (line 98), and *divined her drift* (line 103). How do you feel about Tom now? If you were Aunt Polly, what would you do after hearing Tom's excuse? What do you think Aunt Polly will do? *Read to end.*

Do you like Aunt Polly now? Do you like Tom? If so, what is there about both that makes you like them? Do you forgive Tom for treating the cat with medicine?

Looking Ahead

Notice that the author has not said any more about Becky or about Tom's feeling sad about her. Has he been cured? Has he forgotten his misery? Did Aunt Polly's terrible treatment help him in any way? These questions can be answered only if you read the rest of the novel entitled *Tom Sawyer.* Your reading of this short story about the "Pain-Killer" will surely help you to find rich inferences in the novel.

Samuel Clemens (Mark Twain) was one of America's great humorists. In addition to writing novels, he also wrote short stories. You would enjoy reading "The Celebrated Jumping Frog of Calaveras County."

6. QUESTIONING AS YOU READ

Perhaps you felt impatient about the questions that interrupted the reading of "Tom Sawyer and the Pain-Killer." No one enjoys being interrupted in his reading by other people. But if he does the interrupting *himself,* his pleasure in reading is increased.

The purpose of the questions was to show you the kind of thinking you should do as you read any story. As you learn to read more and more effectively, these questions will flash by so fast that they won't really interrupt you. You can think many times faster than you can read. Your thoughts will not interrupt your reading; they will make it much richer and more enjoyable.

On the other hand, you should not hesitate to pause and to think as you read if you wish to do so. Feel free to think about questions and scenes that come to mind. One caution, however—don't let yourself dawdle as you read. Read with an alert mind and a sharp imagination. Read efficiently!

Now try the exciting dog story that follows, answering as you go the questions that will be given you.

WHITE FANG

By Jack London

(White Fang is one-quarter dog and three-quarters wolf. He was captured in the snowy north when he was a pup and brought up by masters who tried to train him as a sled-dog. But his wolf nature and the brutal beatings he received made him a ferocious beast, feared and hated by all the dogs about him. In turn, he hated them and all his masters. He is finally rescued from this cruel treatment when he is bought by Weedon Scott, a mining engineer in Alaska. Mr. Scott admired the courage and fighting skill of this animal, and he hoped to be able to tame him with kindness instead of cruelty.)

Jack London has written many stories about Alaska and several thrilling stories about the dogs of that part of the country. The story here is a small part of a novel about a wild dog. In this beginning you should try to form a mental picture of the characters, what they are doing or thinking, and where this is happening. Scott and the dog are not the only ones there. Who else? Also, see if Scott is beginning to have any success in his training program.

A. "It's hopeless," Weedon Scott confessed.

He sat on the step of his cabin and stared at the dog-musher, who responded with a shrug that was equally hopeless.

Together they looked at White Fang at the end of his stretched chain, bristling, snarling, ferocious, straining to get at the sled-dogs. Having received sundry lessons from Matt, said lessons being imparted by means of a club, the sled-dogs had learned to leave White Fang alone; and even when they were lying down at a distance, apparently oblivious of his existence.

"It's a wolf and there's no taming it," Weedon Scott announced.

> Are the men having any success? Who is the other man? Who received lessons with a club? Why? Why did Matt feel it was necessary to have the team dogs leave White Fang alone?
>
> Do you think the men will give up? Or will they find something to encourage them? Look for the answers in Section **B**.

B. "Oh, I don't know about that," Matt objected. "Might be a lot of dog in 'm for all you can tell. But there's one thing I know sure, an' that there's no gettin' away from."

The dog-musher paused and nodded his head confidently at Moosehide Mountain.

"Well, don't be a miser with what you know," Scott said sharply, after waiting a suitable length of time. "Spit it out. What is it?"

The dog-musher indicated White Fang with a backward thrust of his thumb.

"Wolf or dog, it's all the same—he's ben tamed a'ready."

"No!"

"I tell you yes, an' broke to harness. Look close there. D'ye see them marks across the chest?"

"You're right, Matt. He was a sled-dog before Beauty Smith got hold of him."

"An' there's not much reason against his bein' a sled-dog again."

Were they disappointed? What did they find that gave them hope? Read the part that says they are going to go on trying. Why did Scott call Matt a miser?

Find out what new method they are going to try. Will the men succeed? Read Sections **C** and **D** for your answer.

C. "What d'ye think?" Scott queried eagerly. Then the hope died down as he added, shaking his head, "We've had him two weeks now, and if anything, he's wilder than ever at the present moment."

"Give 'm a chance," Matt counselled. "Turn 'm loose for a spell."

The other looked at him incredulously.

"Yes," Matt went on, "I know you've tried to, but you didn't take a club."

"You try it then."

The dog-musher secured a club and went over to the chained animal. White Fang watched the club after the manner of a caged lion watching the whip of its trainer.

"See 'm keep his eye on that club," Matt said. "That's a good sign. He's no fool. Don't dast tackle me so long as I got that club handy. He's not clean crazy, sure."

Did you expect Matt to use the club on White Fang? Did he? Why was he holding it? What did he actually do? How did White Fang show that he knew more than a wolf could know? Can you infer how the dog was treated when Mr. Smith (Beauty Smith) had owned him? What is the meaning of *counselled*?

D. As the man's hand approached his neck, White Fang bristled and snarled and crouched down. But while he eyed the approaching hand, he at the same time contrived to keep track of the club in the other hand, suspended threateningly above him. Matt unsnapped the chain from the collar and stepped back.

White Fang could scarcely realize that he was free. Many months had gone by since he passed into the possession of Beauty Smith, and in all that period he had never known a moment of freedom except at the times he had been loosed to fight with other dogs. Immediately after such fights he had been imprisoned again.

What risk do you think Matt took when he unchained the dog? Will White Fang run away now? Read Section **E** to find out what he did, and why.

Do you think White Fang behaved like a wolf after he was unchained? What new thoughts is he beginning to have about his new master? What can be the meaning of *perpetrated*? *Unprecedented*? Who are the "two watching gods" and why does he think of them as *gods*? What did you think of the two men before this? How do you like them now? Why? Read on to find the answer.

E. He did not know what to make of it. Perhaps some new deviltry of the gods was about to be perpetrated on him. He walked slowly and cautiously, prepared to be assailed at any moment. He did not know what to do, it was all so unprecedented. He took the precaution to sheer off from the two watching gods, and walked carefully to the corner of the cabin. Nothing happened. He was plainly perplexed, and he came back again, pausing a dozen feet away and regarding the two men intently.

"Won't he run away?" his new owner asked.

Matt shrugged his shoulders. "Got to take a gamble. Only way to find out is to find out."

"Poor devil," Scott murmured pityingly. "What he needs is some show of human kindness," he added turning and going into the cabin.

He came out with a piece of meat, which he tossed to White Fang. He sprang away from it, and from a distance studied it suspiciously.

"Hi-yu, Major!" Matt shouted warningly, but too late. (Major was one of the dogs in the sled-team.)

Now that Scott has thrown White Fang a piece of meat, will the dog drop his suspicions? The other dog, Major, is probably going to go after the meat. What will White Fang do? Now read **F** to see if the men are making any progress with White Fang.

F. Major had made a spring for the meat. At the instant his jaws closed on it, White Fang struck him. He was overthrown. Matt rushed in, but quicker than he was White Fang. Major staggered to his feet, but the blood spouting from his throat reddened the snow in a widening path.

"It's too bad, but it served him right," Scott said hastily.

But Matt's foot had already started on its way to kick White Fang. There was a leap, a flash of teeth, a sharp exclamation. White Fang, snarling fiercely, scrambled backward for several yards, while Matt stooped and investigated his leg.

"He got me all right," he announced, pointing to the torn trousers and underclothes, and the growing stain of red.

"I told you it was hopeless, Matt," Scott said in a discouraged voice. "I've thought about it off and on, while not wanting to think of it. But we've come to it now. It's the only thing to do."

As he talked, with reluctant movements he drew his revolver, threw open the cylinder, and assured himself of its contents.

> Did you find any progress? Did you find anything discouraging? What do you think of White Fang for being so vicious and ungrateful? Why did Scott use *reluctant* movements in drawing his gun? What are the men going to do now? Read paragraphs **G** and **H**.

G. "Look here, Mr. Scott," Matt objected; "that dog's had a rough life. You can't expect 'm to come out a white an' shining angel. Give 'm time."

"Look at Major," the other rejoined.

The dog-musher surveyed the stricken dog. He had sunk down on the snow in the circle of his blood, and was plainly in the last gasp.

"Served 'm right. You said so yourself, Mr. Scott. He tried to take White Fang's meat, an' he's dead-O. That was to be expected. I wouldn't give two whoops for a dog that wouldn't fight for his own meat."

"But look at yourself, Matt. It's all right about the dogs, but we must draw the line somewhere."

"Serve me right," Matt argued stubbornly. "What'd I want to kick 'm for? You said yourself he'd done right. Then I had no right to kick 'm."

"It would be a mercy to kill him," Scott insisted. "He's untamable."

"Now look here, Mr. Scott, give the poor devil a fightin' chance. He ain't had no chance yet. He's just come through hell, an' this is the first time he's ben loose. Give 'm a fair chance, an' if he don't deliver the goods, I'll kill 'm myself. There!"

"I don't want to kill him or have him killed," Scott answered, putting away the revolver. "We'll let him run loose and see what kindness can do for him. And here's a try at it."

H. He walked over to White Fang and began talking to him gently and soothingly.

"Better have a club handy," Matt warned.

Scott shook his head and went on trying to win White Fang's confidence.

White Fang was suspicious. Something was impending. He had killed this god's dog, bitten his companion god, and what else was to be expected than some terrible punishment? But in the face of it he was indomitable. He bristled and showed his teeth, his eyes vigilant, his whole body wary and prepared for anything. The god had no club, so he suffered him to approach quite near. The god's hand had come out and was descending on his head. White Fang shrank together and grew tense as he crouched under it. Here was danger, some treachery or something. He knew the hands of the gods, their proved mastery, their cunning to hurt. Besides, there was his old antipathy to being touched. He snarled more menacingly, crouched still lower, and still the hand descended. He did not want to bite the hand, and he endured the peril of it until his instinct surged up in him, mastering him with its insatiable yearning for life.

> Why do you think Scott did not kill White Fang? How do you like Matt in this portion? Do you think he should have continued to forgive White Fang? What is Scott trying to do here? Isn't he taking too much risk? How does White Fang feel about having a hand come near his head? Will he finally accept a pat? What is meant by "antipathy to being touched"? Read paragraph **I** and see if you were correct.

I. Weedon Scott had believed that he was quick enough to avoid any snap or slash. But he had yet to learn the remarkable quickness of White Fang, who struck with the certainty and swiftness of a coiled snake.

Scott cried out sharply with surprise, catching his torn hand and holding it tightly in his other hand. Matt uttered a great oath and sprang to his side. White Fang crouched down and backed away, bristling, showing his fangs, his eyes malignant with menace. Now he could expect a beating as fearful as any he had received from Beauty Smith.

"Here! What are you doing?" Scott cried suddenly.

Matt had dashed into the cabin and came out with a rifle.

"Nothin'," he said slowly, with a calmness that was assumed; "only goin' to keep that promise I made. I reckon it's up to me to kill 'm as I said I'd do."

"No you don't!"

"Yes I do. Watch me."

Were you surprised to discover that White Fang actually bit Scott's hand? Try to put yourself in White Fang's place. Was this the right thing for this animal to do? Was it intelligent? Could he know that Scott was only trying to be friendly? *Now* what will the men finally do to the dog? Read **J** to get the answer.

J. As Matt had pleaded for White Fang when he had been bitten, it was now Weedon Scott's turn to plead.

"You said to give him a chance. Well, give it to him. We've only just started, and we can't quit at the beginning. It served me right, this time. And—look at him!"

White Fang, near the corner of the cabin and forty feet away, was snarling with blood-curdling viciousness, not at Scott, but at the dog-musher.

"Well, I'll be everlastin'ly gosh-swoggled!" was the dog-musher's expression of astonishment.

"Look at the intelligence of him," Scott went on hastily. "He knows the meaning of firearms as well as you do. He's got intelligence, and we've got to give that intelligence a chance. Put up that gun."

"All right, I'm willin'," Matt agreed, leaning the rifle against the woodpile.

"But will you look at that!" he exclaimed the next moment.

White Fang had quieted down and ceased snarling.

So they did not kill him. What surprises them about White Fang? Would you expect wolves to understand the purpose of

278

a rifle? Are dogs afraid of rifles? Then how do you explain White Fang's actions? How does all this explain why the men have not killed White Fang? Do you think they will now? What do you expect them to do? Now read to the end of the story for the answers.

K. "This is worth investigatin'. Watch."

Matt reached for the rifle, and at the same moment White Fang snarled. He stepped away from the rifle, and White Fang's lifted lips descended, covering his teeth.

Matt took the rifle and began slowly to raise it to his shoulder. White Fang's snarling began with the movement, and increased as the movement approached its culmination. But the moment before the rifle came to a level with him, he leaped sidewise behind the corner of the cabin. Matt stood staring along the sights at the empty space of snow which had been occupied by White Fang.

The dog-musher put the rifle down solemnly, then turned and looked at his employer.

"I agree with you, Mr. Scott. That dog's too intelligent to kill."

What has this part told you of White Fang's intelligence? Of his skill and speed? Is it any wonder that the men saved him and expect to go on trying to train him?

L. It was in the air. White Fang sensed the coming calamity, even before there was tangible evidence of it. In vague ways it was borne in upon him that a change was impending. He knew not how nor why, yet he got his feel of the oncoming event from the gods themselves. In ways subtler than they knew, they betrayed their intentions to the wolf-dog that haunted the cabin-stoop, and that, though he never came inside the cabin, knew what went on inside their brains.

"Listen to that, will you!" the dog-musher exclaimed at supper one night.

Section L, above, is from the last Part of the novel. What feeling do you get from reading it? What do you think the change may be?

The whole novel tells a great deal more about the dog. It begins with the story of his parents and his puppy days, and it ends with a truly surprising result for White Fang. It is a highly interesting novel, which you would enjoy reading.

7. THE THEME OF A STORY

If you were to recommend to a friend a story you have read, his first question would be, "Well, what is the story about?" Your answer should be a statement of the story in one sentence or two. Such a statement is called the **theme** of a story. It contains only the general idea and leaves out all the details.

Many students seem unable to condense a story into one or two sentences. They usually begin with some petty event, or with some small detail that cannot interest a listener. How can you pick the theme of a story without becoming confused by details?

Let us work out a theme together. You have just gone over *White Fang,* so that you remember it rather well. Which of the following statements do you consider to be the theme? Remember, it should give the *whole* idea, not just details.

1. White Fang is a vicious dog that was nearly killed by his master. (Wrong, because that describes only two incidents; there were many more.)
2. White Fang is part wolf and he was bought by Scott to be trained. (This is closer, but it omits some very important ideas; for instance, that he is naturally wild and vicious.)
3. Even though White Fang bites two men, they decide not to kill him. (This is important, too, but it leaves out *why* they decided to keep him and tame him.)

4. White Fang, though part wolf, understands the meaning of a club and a gun. (Wrong, because this describes only two incidents out of many.)
5. Though White Fang is mostly wolf, and therefore wild and vicious, two men try to tame him through kindness because of his intelligence, even after he has seriously bitten both of them. (This is somewhat long, but it *is* the theme. It contains the most important ideas in the whole story. Yet we should try to shorten it. We do not need all those details.)
6. Two men decide to tame by kindness a wolf-dog that is vicious but courageous and intelligent. (This is short, but it is the theme. It contains the important ideas of the story, though it omits all the details.)

EXERCISE 5

A. Which one of the following statements would you select as the theme of "Tom and the Pain-Killer"? Give the reason for your choice.

a. Tom loves Becky and feels miserable when she is ill, so Aunt Polly tries some rough treatment to cure him.
b. Tom endured all the difficult cures his aunt tried on him until he took revenge by giving some evil-tasting medicine to a cat.
c. Tom's aunt was a kind-hearted person who "fell" for every kind of medicine or cure that she saw advertised.
d. By giving his medicine to the cat, Tom makes his Aunt Polly realize that she has been mistreating him.
e. Tom enjoyed fooling his aunt by pouring the medicine down a crack and feeding it to the cat to see him jump around in Aunt Polly's sitting room.

B. Which of the following statements in each pair sounds more like a theme? Give the reason for your choice.

a. A king's clothes are stolen and he has to wear rags and then he is mistaken for a beggar, and everyone drives him away or beats him because he appears to be crazy.
b. A king who has no pity for poor people loses his royal clothes and is mistaken for a beggar. After much suffering he learns to understand their feelings and to have greater sympathy for them.

a. A boy who is a good tennis player loses all his match games because he is worried about losing. When he begins to think only of the pleasure of playing the game, he loses his fears and begins to win.

b. Henry is a good tennis player, yet when he played against Spike he felt he was not good enough for that match, so he began to hit too hard, and many of his returns went out of bounds.

a. A young drummer in the French army is seriously wounded while trying to deliver a message to Napoleon, and he loses his horse and is nearly drowned when crossing a river, but he goes on without resting even though he is bleeding badly.

b. A drummer boy, seriously wounded while attempting to deliver a message to Napoleon, struggles to keep alive until he reaches the general and then, his errand fulfilled, he falls dead.

STUDYING, ORGANIZING, REMEMBERING 16

Do you ever find it difficult to study an assignment? Many students do. Very likely it is only because they have not learned how to study. They do not have the reading skills that you need when you study.

Study is difficult if you do not clearly understand what you are reading. Here, for instance, is a list of nonsense syllables. There are only fifteen of them. Yet no matter how hard you try, it will still be a heavy task to memorize them even after fifteen minutes or half an hour. Try it for a few minutes.

plar	guj	bik	spep	clab
splod	krol	mim	tisk	falp
sark	blor	scrut	dref	skak

Do you think it will be easier with real words? Try these:

we	dinner	because
if	all	ink
together	forever	frame
there	dish	eleven
match	hang	certain

1. UNDERSTANDING IS THE FIRST NEED

You have discovered, of course, that it was very difficult to memorize either the nonsense syllables or the words. Perhaps you wonder why, since there were only fifteen short syllables to learn! Or fifteen words! *But they did not make any sense to you. You could not understand them.*

Now see how long it takes to memorize fifteen words *when they form a sentence.*

We asked Jerry to go to the supermarket to get some ice cream for us.

Did you notice that you could learn that sentence in an instant? Why? Because you could understand it easily. Those nonsense syllables and separate words were presented merely to show how difficult it is to learn anything if it has no meaning for you, if you do *not* understand it. The fifteen-word sentence shows that it is rather easy to learn what you *do* understand.

284

Understand What You Read

This is true of all study. Your first task is to make sure you understand. Understanding a whole selection or part of a chapter, however, is quite different from understanding the sentences in it. If you see the sentences as separate facts or separate details, they will be just as hard to understand as separate words in a list, like those you tried.

A chapter in a textbook is not just a jumble of facts. In order to understand their meaning you must see how those facts or details are related to each other. You must see the plan.

In your earlier study of paragraphs, you learned to see the plan of the paragraph. You learned how to recognize the main thought and to see how the details supported it. You also found out how to organize the paragraph in outline form so that you could see more easily how the details were related to the topic.

Here, for example, is a paragraph for study. It is on a serious topic such as you might meet in a textbook on science.

> *Light is not instantaneous. When a light is turned on, you do not see it at that instant.* You only think you do because light travels incredibly fast. Its speed is *186,000 miles per second.* Yet it takes time to travel from its source to your eyes. For example, the moon is 240,000 miles away. Therefore its light takes 1¼ seconds to reach us. The sun is 93 million miles from the earth. Therefore its light takes over 8 minutes to get to us. Stars are very, very far away. The star that is nearest to us is over 20 trillion miles distant. It takes an extremely long time for its light to get to us. If that star were to burn out suddenly and turn dark we would still continue to see it in the sky for nearly four years more!

This paragraph has made many different statements. But they all have a clear meaning for us if we can see what all of them are saying together. They tell us that *light is not instantaneous.* The supporting sentences help that thought. One explains how fast light is (but *not instantaneous*). Others give the time it takes for us to receive light from the moon, from the sun, or from one star.

The main thought, therefore, helps us to grasp the meaning of the paragraph. However, to understand the meaning we must see and understand the details.

Here they are in the form of an outline. Read over the outline and notice how much simpler the paragraph becomes.

Topic: Light not instantaneous [Second sentence only repeats this thought]

Details: 1. Speed, 186,000 miles per second
2. Time from moon, 1¼ seconds (distance 240,000 miles)
3. Time from sun, 8 minutes (distance 93 million miles)
4. Time from nearest star, nearly 4 years (distance 20 trillion miles)
5. If nearest star turned dark its light would still reach us for four years

Suddenly the paragraph does not appear so long or so difficult! Now it is easier to get the meaning. Now it is easier to see how the details carry out the main thought. Now it becomes easier to remember them.

This is what makes an outline so valuable for understanding and remembering. It **organizes** the ideas into a small package. It gives us the **plan** of the paragraph in one quick, easy view.

2. THE PURPOSE OF THIS CHAPTER

But how about an entire selection? How can we make a "small package" of a selection or an article if it contains many paragraphs?

True, a long selection will be more difficult, but we can simplify the problem a great deal if we can see its plan or organization. Just as the details of a paragraph belong together in the main thought, so the many paragraphs of a selection are related to the **general topic** of the entire article or story. When we can recognize that relationship, most of the difficulties can be solved.

The purpose of this section of the book is to help you develop the ability to see and understand the plan of a long selection—and then to learn how to study an assignment without hardship.

You will begin by reviewing five reading methods so as to have them uppermost in your mind as you proceed. You will learn to see and to make use of the author's plan. You will discover that the author's plan is actually some sort of outline.

3. REVIEW OF READING METHODS THAT HELP YOU TO STUDY

In order to study and remember an assignment, you must do more than read it in the ordinary way. There are several methods of reading that will make you a better reader. You have already met some of them in this book.

Following are five methods, or ways of reading, that are highly important:

1. You must make sure you understand the content. (You have discovered that it is extremely difficult to remember anything you do not understand.)
2. You should read with care and make a real effort to remember. (Naturally, if you are careless or indifferent in your reading, you will probably forget much of it.)
3. You should find the main thought of each paragraph as quickly as you can. It will tell you what to expect in the rest of the paragraph. (Understanding will be greatly improved when you know what to look for as you read the details.)
4. When you complete the reading of a section of the assignment, review each paragraph by making a brief outline of it. (Observing it in this short outline form is a further help to understanding.)
5. Now turn the paragraph thought into a question and try to answer it to yourself, without looking back at either the paragraph or its outline. (This is especially valuable in helping you remember the paragraph. You learned how to do this in the chapter, "The Plan Behind the Paragraph.")

These five steps may appear to be a lengthy task, but they are not as difficult as they may seem, especially after some practice. Steps 1, 2, and 3 are really done together, because you probably have learned to read in this way. Step 4 will take some time because it requires writing. After a while, however, you will be able to outline many paragraphs mentally. You will obtain a quick mental picture of the outline even while in the act of reading the paragraph.

Step 5 is probably the most important of all the study methods you have learned. When you change the main thought into the form of a question, you are doing just what your teacher does. Therefore you are really making good guesses about the very questions he will ask the class. No wonder you will seem so well prepared when you are called upon the next day!

We must now think about how to apply study methods to whole selections.

4. AN AUTHOR USES A PLAN

An architect always begins with a "skeleton" plan of a building before he fills in a single detail. He first makes sure of its general shape and structure.

A writer, too, begins with a plan for his book long before he begins to write a single sentence. First, of course, he decides on the subject or general topic of the book. Let us suppose that he is going to write on "Building Good Health." He may later change the wording of the title, perhaps to make it more interesting. He might call it "Keeping Healthy and Living Happily" or "Ensuring a Healthy Future," but all these titles would have the same general meaning. Then he has to decide on what it takes to build good health. What topics would deal with building a healthy person? Food? Yes, but serve foods for different purposes, such as growth, energy, repair, and prevention of disease. Each one of these would probably need a chapter.

Besides, the body needs water and vitamins. It also needs air and exercise. Finally, we cannot remain well unless we avoid accidents. We already have enough for the plan of the book by chapters. Still, we should also have a chapter to explain why all this is important to you.

This is about the way an author might work out his plan. His list of chapters would look like this:

Title: Building Good Health
    I. Importance of Building Good Health
   II. Parts of the Body
  III. Your Body Needs Water
  IV. Your Body Needs Food for Energy
   V. Your Body Needs Food for Growth
  VI. Your Body Needs Food for Repair
 VII. Your Body Needs Vitamins
VIII. Protecting Your Body Against Disease
  IX. Fresh Air and Proper Exercise
   X. Keeping Your Body Safe

You can usually see, just from the chapter titles in the Table of Contents, how all the headings belong together, and how they help to carry out the title of the whole book.

In the same way, each chapter must have its own plan. Let us take Chapter III above as an example and see how an author might divide that into its share of topics.

III. Your Body Needs Water
    A. Why the body needs water
    B. How it uses water
    C. How much water it requires
    D. Cautions in the selection of drinking water

Each of these topics will need many paragraphs to explain it, and each of the paragraphs will also have its own details.

Suppose that you are the author, and you are planning to develop the last chapter listed above. Study the outline plan for Chapter X. Would you drop any of these topics? Would you present the ones that are left in the order given?

X. Keeping your Body Safe
    A. Safety in Swimming
    B. Eating Green Vegetables
    C. Safety in the Home
    D. Safety on the Highways
    E. How to Prevent Fires
    F. Wearing Proper Clothing

5. WHAT YOU CAN LEARN FROM A PREVIEW

You found out that you could understand a paragraph more easily if you knew its main thought in advance. When you did, the main thought became the **preview** of the paragraph.

In a textbook, the table of contents forms the preview of the book. It provides you with a brief outline, actually an extremely brief outline, of the contents of the entire book. Try to keep the table of contents in your mind as you read the book.

Sometimes the complete table of contents covers too much ground to be helpful to us. However, we can still learn many things from it. Let us see how much information we can discover from the table of contents of *Building Good Health*. Try to answer the following questions by turning back to that table (page 289).

1. Does the book deal with the method of building good health (a) of the heart, (b) of the legs and arms, (c) of the whole body, or (d) of the muscles?
   (Consider Chapter II and Chapters III–VI.)
2. In what ways is food necessary to us?
3. Can food serve as medicine? In which chapter will you find the answer?
4. Even nourishing food is not enough for us. What other important element must we have?
5. What two things besides food and water does the body need to keep alive?
6. Chapter X means "keeping the body safe" from what?
7. Chapter VI refers to "repair." It might mean the repair of wounds or broken bones. What other kind of repair does it refer to?

Perhaps you were astonished at the amount of information and understanding you were able to get from this preview. The table of contents in most textbooks will give you even more information. Each chapter, or each section within a chapter, is likely to have subtitles, margin headings, and other heavy-type beginnings. If they were put together these would form a good outline.

Here is a portion of such a preview outline as it might appear in a textbook. For convenience, the actual text of the paragraphs will be indicated only by dots.

CHAPTER III. MINERS AND THEIR WORK

The preview outline you just read was composed of the headings and various subheadings of a whole chapter in a geography book. For each small-type heading the book contains a number of paragraphs. Sometimes there are only two, sometimes six or seven.

If you read this outline carefully and think over what each item might mean, you can obtain a great deal of information. That method is an excellent way to begin the study of a chapter. It is good preparation for the actual reading of a chapter in any textbook.

6. PREVIEW BY SKIMMING

There is another kind of preview that is very helpful in studying. This is the preview in which you skim rapidly over a whole chapter. This is worth doing even though your assignment covers only part of the chapter. In order to understand the part, you must have some idea of the whole so that you can see how the part fits in.

In previewing a chapter, you begin with the headings. If you think about them as you read, you will discover that they are related to one another. All together they are the outline or framework of the chapter. As you turn the pages, look at the pictures and the diagrams or maps. Read the captions under them. You will find that the captions tie in with the headings.

Now you are ready to go back to the beginning of the chapter. Read the first paragraph or two. They will usually present the author's statement of what the chapter is to cover. Finally, turn to the end of the chapter. Here you will usually find a summary. It will relate the ideas that you found in the chapter introduction.

By this time you will have a good idea of what the chapter is about. In this skimming process, you may meet ideas, names, or facts that you do not understand. These unknowns can be a real help to you. Turn them into questions and read to find the answers. You will then be ready for careful reading of the chapter.

That is how a preview can help you study. You have learned that reading demands the use of many skills, and study demands the use of the largest number of reading skills. However, study should not mean drudgery. It is indeed difficult and plodding work when you have not learned the reading skills, but it becomes a satisfying activity when your reading skills help you to learn your assignment with ease.

Summary of Preview Methods:

1. Watch for all the headings, subheadings, and margin headings in the assignment if there are any.
2. Go over them again as though they were a continuous outline. Think over what each one means and how it is related to the larger heading.

3. Look over the pictures, maps, and diagrams. Read the captions under these illustrations.
4. Read the introduction and summary to get an idea of what the *whole* chapter is about.
5. Now, with this advance information, you are prepared to read with normal care.
6. Use the outline of the text, which is really the headings, but fill in with some outline headings and details of your own.
7. If the text has no guiding headings and subheadings, make a preview by skimming. Then you can still make an outline of your own.
8. Here is one further hint for you. In the morning, just before you start for school, see how much you can remember of the outline. Take a last-minute look for any point you may have forgotten. You will be surprised to see how much this review will aid your memory.

7. USING THE STUDY METHODS ON A SELECTION

Thus far you have been seeing the plan of a whole book or whole chapter. We shall begin our actual outlining, however, with something much easier, a short article. You now know that a book has a plan, and that each chapter in a book has a plan. Even a single paragraph has a plan, too, if it is well written. Naturally, then, you would expect an article to have a plan also. When you see the plan as you read, you proceed with understanding. When you cannot recognize the plan, you will be reading blindly. Do not fail to look for the plan.

In the article that follows, you will meet the plan first. It is your preview of the selection. Look through it carefully till it makes sense to you. Then you will know what to expect or look for when you read the article itself.

THE MYSTERY OF THE FEATHERED TRAVELERS
   I. Every autumn birds suddenly begin to fly south.
  II. They fly in great swarms of over 100,000.
 III. The flights are very long.
 IV. The birds have various speeds, most of them very fast.
  V. The mystery remains: how do they know where to fly?

What should you expect to find in each paragraph?

    I. Some details to show how suddenly the birds' flight starts
    II. Some details about how the swarm becomes so large
    III. Some examples (or illustrations) of the length of their flights
    IV. Some examples of their speeds in flying
    V. Some details about what makes this a mystery

EXERCISE 1

You can see that the outline of topics is too general to satisfy you. It leaves you wondering, "What is so sudden about this migration?" "How do the birds collect in such enormous swarms?" and so on. An outline alone does not give enough information. You will read a selection for details that give meaning to the points in the outline.

It would be advisable to skim through the selection first. However, the selection is rather short. You may therefore omit the skimming and go immediately into a careful reading if you prefer.

The Mystery of the Feathered Travelers

Every year, during the fall season, the birds of our country start on a great journey that takes them far to the south. Each type of bird seems to know the exact day on which to begin. On the day before, they go about their usual activity of finding food while it is light and sleeping during the night. Then the next morning, as suddenly as though they had all heard the order over the radio, thousands of birds leave their favorite retreats.

They rise up in the air and begin to gather for a long flight. As the great swarm moves southward they are joined by thousands and thousands of other birds along the way who seemed to be waiting for their companions to get to them. There are so many of them, hundreds of thousands, that they darken the sky as they pass overhead.

All of these flights are very long. The smaller birds, such as the warblers, will cover about 500 miles in their journey. Even the tiny humming birds are able to fly across the Gulf of Mexico. That portion of their trip is more than 500 miles, and there is no place along that route to stop for a rest. Wild geese and ducks travel for distances of more than 1000 miles. And there are nighthawks that fly all the way from Alaska in the north to Argentina in South America. It is almost unbelievable that they should take such long flights just to avoid cold weather.

How fast do they fly? Many types of birds can make amazing speed and keep it up for many hours without rest. The blue jay is among the slowest, yet it can fly 30 miles an hour. The starling can do 50 miles an hour and the duck about 60. The humming bird is very small and delicate, but it can also move at a speed of 60 miles. But the bird called the *swift* can travel faster than most express trains. It shoots through the air at a speed of 100 miles an hour. No wonder it is called the *swift*.

We have learned a great many facts about these travels, but we have never discovered how the birds know where to go or how they find their way. That is still a great mystery. They cover exactly the same route every year, as though they were following a map. Yet they do not have a map or any guide that we know of. Do they follow landmarks that they see below them? Many groups travel only at night to escape their daylight enemies. How can they tell which way to fly? Neither the scientists nor the bird watchers have ever been able to solve this perpetual mystery.

You noticed, before you read this article on migration, that an outline of paragraph topics did not really tell enough. It left the details out. The article itself supplied the details.

However, for the purpose of remembering, or for study, you will want some short reminder. To prepare it you will not have to read the whole article again. That short reminder can be a better outline, one with the details filled in.

EXERCISE 2

You are now going to complete the outline on page 296. Some portions of it are filled in to show you how to use short expressions instead of whole sentences. Some sentences may contain *two* important thoughts, and you may find it advisable to enter them as two facts in your outline instead of one. Sometimes two sentences express the same thought, and one phrase will be enough for them.

This outline will take some time and some effort on your part, and it may not resemble the outlines made by your classmates. However, there are many good ways of wording the outline.

THE MYSTERY OF THE FEATHERED TRAVELERS

I. Birds fly south every fall
  A. Journey takes them far
  B. Each type of bird knows day to begin
  C. Usual activity occurs on the day before
  D. Next day all birds start as if ordered by radio

II. Birds gather into large groups
  A. Swarms are joined by many thousands along way
  B. They seem to be waiting for swarm to come
  C. Swarm grows in size to _____.
  D.

III. Flights are very long
  A. Smaller birds fly about 500 miles
  B. *(Complete B, C, D, E of your outline.)*
  C.
  D.
  E.

IV.
  A. *(Fill in main idea [IV] and complete A, B, C, D, E, F*
  B. *of your outline.)*
  C.
  D.
  E.
  F.

V. Mystery: how do they know the route?
  A. *(Complete A, B, C, D, E of your outline.)*
  B.
  C.
  D.
  E.

EXERCISE 3

Now that you have the outline completed, you should test it to see how much it helps you to remember the article. This is how you can make it work for you.

   1. Read the paragraph topics only. They should, by themselves, tell you the story in a very short yet sensible way. Their meaning should be clear.
   2. Look away from your paper and try to remember

those topics in the same order. The words may be your own. You might have to take a second look.

3. Then, if your teacher calls on a few students to repeat them from memory, repeat them also to yourself, silently.

4. Now read through the outline of paragraph I. Turn the main thought into a question. Look up and see how many details you can remember in answer to your question. Even if you do not recall all of them, can you recall enough to give meaning to the topic of the paragraph?

5. In paragraph II, first try to recall some of the details without looking at them at all. You may be surprised to find how much you are reminded of by the topic itself. Then read to catch what you have forgotten.

6. All the other paragraphs may be gone over in the same way.

As you complete your study of this outline, you will surely discover that the outlining has given you a great deal of help. You should feel encouraged to use this method with textbook assignments and then to note the gradual improvement in the results of your studies. When you can remember most of an outline, you can answer almost any question about the article immediately. As soon as you hear the question, you may see where it belongs in the outline, and the information at that point will pop into your mind.

8. WHAT FORM SHOULD YOU USE FOR AN OUTLINE?

It should not be necessary to write out the words *Title* or *General Topic* or *Paragraph Topics* or *Details*. The very form of the outline will make clear what is meant. Examine the form below.

I. _____

  A. ....

  B. ....

  C. ....

II. _____

  A. ....

  B. ....

III. _____

The *paragraph topic I* has three details, *paragraph topic II* has two details, *paragraph topic III* has not yet been completed. There may be additional paragraph topics and details for them.

Some paragraphs have subtopics that are explained by groups of details. Such a paragraph is shown in the form below, filled in to help you see the plan of the paragraph.

I. Icebergs are hills of floating ice
  A. Part above water towers up high
    1. Seen from afar
    2. Many four stories high
    3. Few more than 200 ft. high
  B. Part below water much larger
    1. Eight ninths beneath surface
    2. Twenty stories or more

Here you can see that subtopic A is explained by three details and subtopic B by two details.

You are now ready to outline a longer selection. You should have very little difficulty, for you will make an outline of each paragraph. Do each paragraph in turn.

This is the method you should use:

1. Read each paragraph until you understand what it is about.

2. Look for a sentence that expresses the idea of the paragraph. That is the key sentence, or main thought, or topic sentence.

3. If there is no key sentence in the paragraph, try to compose one mentally.

4. Shorten that sentence into as few words as possible.

5. Do the same for the details.

6. Sometimes several details may belong together under a subtopic.

EXERCISE 4

Directions: Following the steps given above, make a study outline of this article. You will find part of the outline at the end of the selection.

THE STRANGE LANGUAGE OF CHINA

I. Our own language is simple to learn. It has an alphabet of twenty six letters. Each letter represents one or more sounds.

Once we know the sounds we can read almost any word. When we see a word of three letters, such as *dog*, we can pronounce the word easily. We know the sound of each letter, and we put those sounds together.

II. The Chinese language, however, does not use letters and does not have an alphabet. Each of the characters in that language is a word, not a letter. On paper, each character is a kind of picture, made up of a number of strokes that seem to cross each other. American children need to learn the picture form of only twenty-six letters. The Chinese children, however, have to learn to recognize a different picture form for every word in their language. Instead of twenty-six different letters they must learn to recognize many thousands of word pictures or characters. That makes it extremely difficult to read the Chinese language.

BEAUTIFUL   MAN   RIVER

III. It takes a long time, therefore, for a Chinese pupil to learn to read. An American pupil can learn to do at least a little reading after a year or two. The Chinese pupil needs at least six years to learn to read simple books. Yet the children of China are as intelligent as our children. They take longer to learn reading only because their written language is so much harder.

IV. The Chinese pages are printed in a different way from ours, too. English words are printed in lines, reading from left to right. Chinese pages are printed in columns. They are read from top to bottom. The Chinese reader begins with the column at the right hand side of the page. When he gets to the bottom of the column, he goes on to the column to the left of it.

V. Even the direction of the paging in Chinese books is different. The Chinese begin with the page at the right-hand end of the book, and then they continue to turn the pages to the left. To us, it would seem like starting with the last page, and gradually reading back to the beginning.

VI. The strangest difference to be found in the Chinese language is the way words are sounded. In our language the meaning of a word does not depend upon the voice used by the speaker. In China the voice can produce several different meanings for the same word. In a high voice, it has one meaning. In a low voice, it has a second meaning. In a voice of middle pitch, it may have a third meaning. That is why Chinese has been called a sing-song language.

VII. To understand this, imagine how much trouble you would have with a word like *cat*, if we followed the Chinese rule. In a high voice it might have its usual meaning. In a middle voice it might mean *ice cream*. In a low voice it might mean *pencil*. That would be puzzling even if only one word in our language changed its meaning according to your voice. How confusing it would be if all the words in our language changed their meanings in the same way!

In completing this outline, fill in Parts II, III, and IV, and add V, VI, and VII.

The Strange Language of China

I. Our language simple to learn
    A. Alphabet of 26 letters
    B. Each letter has own sound
    C. With those sounds we can read any word
    D. For example, *dog* can be pronounced easily
    E. We know sounds and we put them together
II. Chinese does not have alphabet
    (Fill in rest of outline of this paragraph)
III. Chinese pupil takes long time to learn to read
    (Fill in rest of outline of this paragraph)
IV. Their pages look different from ours
    A. English words in lines, from left to right
    B. Chinese lines
    (Fill in rest of outline of this paragraph)

Now complete your outline with parts V, VI, and VII. Add details with letters as needed.

EXERCISE 5

After your outline is completed, put it to use. See how many details you can remember just from the outline. You will have an opportunity to test your memory in class if your teacher uses any one of the following tests:

a. He may call on one pupil at a time. Each one will answer by giving the topic of a paragraph and reciting the details. If some details are omitted, other pupils may be called on to supply them.

b. He may assign a different paragraph topic to each row, and the pupils within the row would then write out the details of that topic.

c. He may point out a certain topic to the whole class, and ask you to write not on that topic, but on the one *after* it, together with the details.

d. He may permit volunteers to select any topic. Each one would say it aloud, and then call on a classmate to supply the details.

EXERCISE 6

Now read and outline the following selection. Read each paragraph to the end before you decide on the topic. Remember that the key sentence is not always at the beginning. It may sometimes be the last sentence. In fact, some paragraphs may not have a key sentence and you will have to work out the paragraph idea yourself.

WHAT ARE CLOUDS?

I. There is always a great deal of water vapor in the air. You cannot see it, but it is there just the same. There is plenty of proof for that. The chalkboard at school gets dry soon after being washed. The wet streets become dry soon after a rain, especially if the sun is shining. Even if you forget to dry your hands after washing, they soon dry in the air. When these things get dry, what has happened to the water? Where did it go?

II. The water vapor was taken into the air, from the chalkboard, from the street, and from your hands. Water vapor is water that has evaporated. It can remain in the air because it is actually a dry gas which mixes readily with the other gases of the air. The amount of water vapor in the air differs in amount from time to time and from place to place, depending upon the temperature of the air. Water vapor itself is not wet, but rain, snow, fog, frost, and clouds are formed from it.

III. Water vapor cannot be seen, but we often see evidence of water vapor. Do you remember how your breath looks in cold weather? As you exhale, you see a little cloud in front of your mouth. Did you notice the word *cloud*? A cloud is simply water vapor that has become cooled and converted into minute droplets of water. This does not happen right at your mouth but near it. Another evidence of water vapor is seen when water is boiling in a tea kettle. Hot water vapor, called steam, comes out of the spout. As soon as it hits the cold air, it cools and becomes a cloud of minute water droplets that you can see. This does not happen at the very tip of the tea kettle spout, but near it. Fog, too, is just a cloud, but it is near the ground.

IV. Clouds in the sky are formed from water vapor that rises up high in the air. As the wind passes over lakes or rivers, it steals some of their water. If the air is warm it is pushed up by cooler air beneath it. It takes the water vapor with it. The higher the vapor travels, the colder it becomes. When the water vapor is cold enough, it becomes a cloud. From the earth, the clouds look like large wads of fluffy cotton, or like piles of snow floating in the sky. Some people say they look like big mounds of whipped cream. When an airplane passes into a cloud, the pilot is not reminded of whipped cream or cotton. To him, it is a nuisance because it blocks his vision.

Directions: 1. Complete the outline which is started for you below. Do not write in this book.

What Are Clouds?

I. Great deal of water vapor in air
  A. Can't always see it
  B. Proof it is there
    1.
    2.
    3.
  C. What happens to water when things dry?
II.
    (*Complete* A, B, C, *and* D)
III.
IV.

2. After you finish making your outline, close your book. Keep the outline before you and read it to yourself twice. Then turn your outline face down on the desk, and take five minutes to go over it in your mind. Can you remember the four main topics? Can you remember some of the subtopics and details for each main topic?

If your mind suddenly goes blank, turn your paper up again for a moment, for a little reminder. Turn it back again and give your memory another chance.

EXERCISE 7

Now test your memory to see how much you were able to learn by this method of outlining. Try this test without looking at your outline again. You may be surprised to find how many questions you can answer. Write the answers on your paper and number them to correspond with the questions.

1. Where does the water on a wet blackboard go when it dries?
2. What word is used to tell what happened to the water?
3. How much water does the air have?
4. Why can't you see it?
5. When something happens to water vapor can it be seen? What must happen to make it visible?
6. Give an example to show water vapor turning into a cloud.
7. Are the only clouds up in the sky? Where else can a cloud be found?
8. When a cloud is on the ground, what is it called?
9. What causes warm air to go upward?
10. Why does water vapor turn into a cloud when it rises very high up in the air?

If you answered six of the above questions correctly, you have a passing mark. Did you do better than that? If so, your outline helped you to learn your lesson quickly. Continue to use this out-line method. You will become more and more skillful in outlining as time goes on.

Keep in mind that your skill in outlining can be useful in two directions. First—when you read, you can make an outline to help you see the organization of what you are reading, and the ideas in it. Second—when you write, you can organize your own ideas and write them in outline form to guide you as you write.

EXERCISE 8

For practice in remembering, read the following selection for the purpose of making an outline of the main thoughts only. If you read carefully, an outline of just the main thoughts will remind you of many of the details.

The Great Eel Mystery

I. For a great many years there had been a mystery about where eels came from and how they got to our coast. Full-grown eels could be found in our rivers and in the ocean near the shores. But baby eels were rarely seen. The few that were caught were picked up hundreds of miles out in the ocean. How did they get there? If they were born there, why were the grown-up eels found at our shores and in our rivers?

II. The mystery of their long travels has finally been solved. We now know that eels begin their lives in the Atlantic Ocean several hundred miles east of our coast line. Some time during the month of November their eggs are laid in the cold and dark waters nearly 1000 feet below the surface. About 20,000 eggs are laid by each female. Several weeks after the eggs are hatched, the baby eels begin their long, long journey, swimming steadily toward the American shore.

III. The journey takes many months and it does not end at the coast. Millions of them die or are eaten by fish long before they complete their journey. Only a small portion reach their goal. They are almost a year old when they arrive at the many rivers that empty into the ocean. The females swim upstream in the fresh water of those rivers. The males generally stay just off the shore. For eight years or more they all remain in the waters they selected.

IV. Suddenly, on some day in October, as the water begins to get colder, they all seem to decide to start back to the place of their birth. The rivers almost become choked with the female eels rushing to get back into the ocean. There they join the males, and together they begin the 300 mile trip to the breeding grounds where they were born. Soon they lay their eggs, and within a week or two they die. They have fulfilled their purpose. By that time the new baby eels begin again the long travels of their parents.

V. We may know about their travels, but the reason for their travels still remains a mystery. What makes the baby eels swim toward America? What keeps them going for months in the same direction? Why do the females travel up the rivers? How is it possible for them to live in the fresh water of the rivers when they were born in the salt water of the ocean? What makes eels select the month of October for their return trip? How can they remember where they had been born? And how can they find their way back? These are mysteries that we may never solve.

Directions: **1.** Copy on your paper the form shown below, and fill in the blank spaces. Try to change the key sentences to phrases.

Title: The Great Eel Mystery

I. Mystery about where eels came from and how they got to our coast

II.

III.

IV. In October, all suddenly start back to birthplace

V.

2. Now read your outline slowly. Does it make sense? Do you understand it? Do the main thoughts seem to be in the right order as an explanation of the mystery of the eels? Do they tell the main parts of the story?

If they do all this, then your outline is easy to understand. Therefore it ought to be easy to remember. Now, without looking at the outline again, turn your eyes away and see if you can remember those five main thoughts, *not the exact words,* just the ideas.

If you are able to do this, you have made a good start. In addition, you will be able to remember many of the details, because each main thought is a reminder to you of the facts in the paragraph.

EXERCISE 9

Without turning back to the story, try to answer these questions about it.

1. Mention at least two things to show there had been a mystery about how eels got to our rivers and near our shores.
2. Mention at least three things we have discovered about their travels.
3. What is the distance of their journey?
4. To what separate places do the male and female eels go?

5. Mention at least three things about their return journey.
6. Mention at least three things about eels that still seem strange to us.

EXERCISE 10

Perhaps you were not able to remember everything in "The Great Eel Mystery." However, you were not given an opportunity to read over the whole selection for detail. The purpose of the exercise was to help you realize how much you can remember without studying for details. Did you surprise yourself? What do you suppose helped your memory? Surely it was the outline you made.

This was not a complete outline. If all the details had been included, your memory of the facts might have been much better. In this exercise you will practice outlining the details as well as the main thoughts of another selection.

Directions: First read over the entire article. Then prepare an outline, using the form on page 298. This will be a complete outline with the main idea and details for each paragraph.

THE RIVER IN THE OCEAN

I. We all know what a river is when it flows through land. However, there is a difference between an ocean river and a land river. We can see where the edge of the land meets the ocean. We can see where the water ends and where the shore begins. But how can there be a river in an ocean? How can there be an edge to this water if the "shore" is water also?

II. There is such a river. It is called the Gulf Stream. It flows through the Atlantic Ocean just as a river flows through land. Both the "river" and the ocean are composed of water, but the Gulf Stream's water is different from the water around it. The Gulf Stream is warm. The ocean is colder. You can actually see the edges of the Stream because its color is different from the ocean through which it flows.

III. This ocean river is much larger, much more mighty than any land river anywhere. When a land river is very wide, it is several miles across. The Gulf Stream is *thirty-two* miles wide. It often takes an ocean liner two hours or more just to cross it. Its length is hundreds of times as great as the Amazon, the largest real river in the world.

IV. It begins at the equator, continues up north into the Gulf of Mexico, and then travels up along the coast. It remains about one hundred miles from the shore. After reaching New-foundland, it starts east across the Atlantic. It becomes much wider when it reaches Europe. Its path brings it close to the lands of Norway, Great Britain, France, and Spain. Then it begins to spread out and disappear into the waters of the ocean. This is a very lengthy path for a river, even an ocean river.

V. The water of the Gulf Stream is warm. When a ship, on its voyage across the ocean, reaches the edge of the stream, or *current* as we shall now call it, the weather, too, suddenly becomes warm, even in the winter. The difference between the ocean water and the current water is very noticeable. Passengers on board can tell when the ship is straddling across the line between the current and the ocean. A bucket of water dipped from the current end of the boat would be twenty degrees warmer than the water dipped from the ocean end.

VI. The Gulf Stream is a blessing to many countries. Its warm waters give warmth to the breezes that blow over it. These breezes make the climate of Newfoundland much milder than it would be otherwise. The current also helps the climate of Norway, England, and France. England is as far north as Labrador. If it were not for the Gulf Stream, England would be as cold and bleak as Labrador.

VII. Like a land river, the Gulf Stream keeps flowing along in one direction. Its water has a speed of about four miles an hour. If a log is dropped into the current, an hour later it will be four miles farther north. If a ship is wrecked in this current somewhere near the southern part of the United States, some wood from the wreckage may be picked up on the shores of Ireland many months later. It does not need sails or engines to make this trip. The Gulf Stream supplies the power.

LIST OF EXERCISES

INDEX